Extraordinary Racial Politics

Extraordinary Racial Politics

Four Events in the Informal Constitution of the United States

FRED LEE

TEMPLE UNIVERSITY PRESS
Philadelphia • *Rome* • *Tokyo*

TEMPLE UNIVERSITY PRESS
Philadelphia, Pennsylvania 19122
www.temple.edu/tempress

Copyright © 2018 by Temple University—Of The Commonwealth System
   of Higher Education
All rights reserved
Published 2018

Library of Congress Cataloging-in-Publication Data

Names: Lee, Fred, 1979- author.
Title: Extraordinary racial politics : four events in the informal
   Constitution of the United States / Fred Lee.
Description: Philadelphia, Pennsylvania : Temple University Press, 2018. |
   Includes bibliographical references and index. |
Identifiers: LCCN 2018008771 (print) | LCCN 2018026358 (ebook) | ISBN
   9781439915776 (E-book) | ISBN 9781439915752 (cloth : alk. paper) | ISBN
   9781439915769 (pbk. : alk. paper)
Subjects: LCSH: United States—Race relations—Case studies. |
   Racism—Political aspects—United States—Case studies. | African
   Americans—Civil rights—United States—Case studies. | Indians, Treatment
   of—North America—History—Case studies. | Japanese Americans—Evacuation
   and relocation, 1942-1945—Case studies.
Classification: LCC E184.A1 (ebook) | LCC E184.A1 L414 2018 (print) | DDC
   305.80973—dc23
LC record available at https://lccn.loc.gov/2018008771

∞ The paper used in this publication meets the requirements of the
American National Standard for Information Sciences—Permanence
of Paper for Printed Library Materials, ANSI Z39.48-1992

Printed in the United States of America

092718P

Contents

	Acknowledgments	vii
1	An Introduction into Extraordinary Racial Politics	1
2	Racial Re-foundations and the Rise of the Nation-State	31
3	Racial Removal Contracts and the *Nomos* of the New World	71
4	Racial States of Exception and the Decision on Enmity	111
5	Racial Counter-Publics and the Power of Judgment	149
6	A Reaffirmation of Extraordinary Racial Politics	187
	Bibliography	203
	Index	221

Acknowledgments

Thanks to Kirstie McClure for introducing me to the literature on extraordinary politics and for working with me on multiple iterations of this project. Thanks to Cristina Beltrán and Cathy Schlund-Vials for workshopping the entire manuscript in the early stages of the book writing. Thanks to Claudia Van der Heuvel for copyediting in the later stages of the book writing. Thanks to Aaron Javsicas for editorial support throughout the publication process. Thanks to Kristin Burgess for emotional support and editorial comments. Thanks to Anne Kim for our partnership.

This book started as a dissertation project at the University of California, Los Angeles. Committee members Joshua Dienstag and Mark Sawyer guided the dissertation through its early stages. Faculty members Carole Pateman, Raymond Rocco, and Victor Wolfenstein all left their mark on this project. At UCLA, I had the pleasure of studying with Elizabeth Barringer, Natasha Behl, Theodore Christov, Arash Davari, Megan Gallagher, Cory Gooding, Mark Kaswan, Christopher Lee, Zachariah Mampilly, Helen McManus, Sybille Nyeck, Steven On, Gilda Rodríguez, Rebekah Sterling, Yongle Zhang, and Arely Zimmerman.

The book was written at the University of Connecticut, Storrs, where I have continued studying political theory with Zehra Arat, Jane Gordon, Lewis Gordon, Michael Morrell, and Cyrus Ernesto Zirakzadeh. I have continued learning about ethnic studies with Jason Chang, Debanuj Dasgupta,

Jeehyun Lim, Gladys Mitchell-Walthour, Shayla Nunnally, Cathy Schlund-Vials, Evelyn Simien, and Charles Venator-Santiago. I have enjoyed intellectual exchanges with Sam Best, Meina Cai, Jeff Dudas, Stephen Dyson, Tom Hayes, Prakash Kashwan, Jerry Phillips, Jeremy Pressman, Bhakti Shringarpure, Kathleen Tonry, and Chris Vials. At UConn, I have enjoyed working with Sebastián Chamorro, Steven Manicastri, and Katherine Pérez Quiñones on their research.

I workshopped parts of this project at the Western Political Science Association, Pacific Northeast (an Asian Americanist group), and the UConn Humanities Institute. I appreciate that Edwina Barvosa, Natasha Behl, Kevin Bruyneel, Jason Chang, Joshua Dienstag, Jane Gordon, Lewis Gordon, Jeehyun Lim, Brendan Kane, Ju Yon Kim, Helen McManus, Melanie Meizner, Philip Michelbach, Dana Miranda, Michael Morrell, Naomi Murakawa, Gregg Santori, Mark Sawyer, Rebekah Sterling, and Arely Zimmerman commented on various chapters. Luann Liang proofread various chapters. Liz Jennerwein proofread all chapters.

The University of California Office of the President, the UCLA Graduate Division, the UConn Department of Political Science, and the UConn Asian/Asian American Studies Institute financially supported this research. The Humanities Institute, Provost's Office, Research Foundation, College of Liberal Arts and Sciences Dean's Office, and the Office of the Vice President for Research at UConn financially supported its publication.

Extraordinary Racial Politics

1

An Introduction into Extraordinary Racial Politics

> Our work begins with an engagement with the past, out of which we imagine, create, and dare to secure a future.
> —LISA LOWE, *Immigrant Acts*

> These single instances, deeds or events, interrupt the circular movement of daily life in the same sense that the rectilinear *bios* of the mortals interrupts the circular movement of biological life. The subject matter of history is these interruptions—the extraordinary, in other words.
> —HANNAH ARENDT, *Between Past and Future*

Trumpism may well be both a last and a first gasp. What might be passing away and what might be coming about, however, is precisely the question for the opposition. According to many liberal democrats, Donald Trump's presidency is an unprecedented threat to U.S. constitutional government. Their broader proposal is that transatlantic democracies recommit to liberal values and make recourse to legal measures to contain authoritarian populisms. For many progressives, by contrast, Trumpism is rooted in North Atlantic "traditions" of white nationalism. In their view, the Trumpist movement is continuous with prior reactions to civil rights reforms, transnational migrations, and economic globalization; likewise, anti-Trumpist struggles are continuous with histories of antifascist and anticolonial struggles.

We should not exaggerate differences among the opposition, though. The diagnoses of authoritarian populism and white nationalism are compatible if the nation of Trumpist populism is authoritatively white. Furthermore, the reactions of outraged liberals and unfazed leftists are complementary if the Trump presidency is an episode in ongoing dramas of race and nation. Trump is a break from the post–civil-rights-era mainstream politicians who conformed to color-blind—including "color-blind racist"[1]—norms. Yet Trumpism is an intensification of the 1970s and 1980s new right, which blamed the 1960s and 1970s new left for wreaking disorder on the United States. How Trump marks the end of the post–civil rights era from which Trumpism emerged is suggestive of a general dynamic: what I call the relationship between extraordinary racial politics and everyday racial politics.

In my usages, extraordinary racial politics are unusual, episodic, intensive, decisive, and transformative, while ordinary racial politics are quotidian, ongoing, extended, negotiated, and reproductive. The thesis of this book is that extraordinary racial politics rupture out of and reset everyday racial politics. Exceptional racial crises are partly continuous with normalized racial conflict, yet the resolution of these crises reconstitutes the terrain of those conflicts. Extraordinary racial events are, in part, extensions of ordinary racial processes; ordinary racial trajectories are, in turn, redirected by extraordinary racial turns. I examine four moments of this kind in U.S. history: southeastern Indian removals in the 1830s and 1840s, the Japanese internment of World War II, the postwar civil rights movement, and racial empowerment movements during the 1960s and 1970s. In so doing, I recover the extraordinary dimension of U.S. racial politics from the combined standpoints of ethnic studies and political theory.

Radical political theorists have traditionally imagined the relationship between the extraordinary and the ordinary as the relationship between the revolutionary and the pre- and postrevolutionary. While I share this orientation toward transformative crises,[2] I think that revolutionary struggle far from exhausts the field of extraordinary politics, which also encompasses state-declared emergencies and mass-mobilized movements. Similarly, I agree with Andreas Kalyvas that radical political theorists need to recuperate "the politics of the extraordinary" from a Jacobin-Leninist tradition whose emancipatory potential is likely exhausted.[3] As a political theorist, I argue that extraordinary politics is best revitalized in the register of the

---

1. Eduardo Bonilla-Silva, *Racism without Racists: Color-Blind Racism and the Persistence of Racial Inequality in the United States*, 2nd ed. (Lanham, MD: Rowman and Littlefield, 2006), chap. 2.

2. See, e.g., Alfonso Gonzales, *Reform without Justice: Latino Migrant Politics and the Homeland Security State* (Oxford, UK: Oxford University Press, 2014); Ruth Gilmore, *Golden Gulag: Prisons, Surplus, Crisis, and Opposition in Globalizing California* (Berkeley: University of California Press, 2007).

3. Andreas Kalyvas, *Democracy and the Politics of the Extraordinary: Max Weber, Carl Schmitt, and Hannah Arendt* (Cambridge: Cambridge University Press, 2008), 2–4.

political, constitutive politics, or what I call "public constitution."[4] All these terms gesture toward the moment that generates and transforms the public world of selves and groups, relations and structures. This moment, though, only emerges against the backdrop of the routinized functioning and reproduction of the constituted public.

Ethnic studies scholars have long theorized something analogous to the relationship between public constitution and constituted publics under the heading of "racial formation." Racial formation, in Michael Omi and Howard Winant's classic formulation, is "the sociohistorical process by which racial identities are created, lived out, transformed, and destroyed."[5] This definition in principle encompasses both the everyday and the extraordinary, but contemporary ethnic studies in fact has an abiding concern with quotidian life and *longue durée* processes—often for good reasons. I want to shift our center of attention to *courte durée* events and extraordinary experiences in order to restore the other half of the racial formation story, as it were. For the normal politics of negotiation, reworking, and subversion are prefigurations and fulfillments of the crisis politics of extremes, creation, and confrontation. I am particularly attentive to how the fall and rise of racial orders disrupt and reconstitute the extended processes of racial formation.[6]

Let us say, in synthesizing the concepts of racial formation and public constitution, that particular black, indigenous, and Asian formations can acquire the general significance of reconstituting the entire U.S. public. This idea is already familiar to ethnic studies, which—after all—has taken my four events as paradigmatic turning points. The historiographical convention of attaching "pre-" and "post-" to events, for instance, informs many accounts of the "post–civil rights era" of African American and U.S. politics. Asian American studies and indigenous studies have made homologous periodizations with regard to wartime Japanese incarceration and nineteenth-century Indian removals, although scholars outside those fields still underappreciate the implications of these events for U.S. politics overall. An

---

4. Cf. Chantal Mouffe, *On the Political* (London: Routledge, 2005); Jason Frank, *Constituent Moments: Enacting the People in Postrevolutionary America* (Durham, NC: Duke University Press, 2010).

5. Michael Omi and Howard Winant, *Racial Formation in the United States*, 3rd ed. (New York: Routledge, 2015), 109, italics removed.

6. See, e.g., Desmond King and Rogers Smith, "Racial Orders in American Political Development," *American Political Science Review* 99, no. 1 (2005): 75–92.

extraordinary racial politics that seems to affect only one group can "touch all"—that is, reidentify who "all" are and reimagine how all are "touched." What political theory contributes to ethnic studies here is "the public" as a constitutional rather than a sociological category, "the people" as a symbolically articulated rather than a positively existing entity.

I seek, then, to racially inflect the intuitive linkage between U.S. peoples and U.S. constitutions. What is too often narrowly understood as "the U.S. constitution" is the symbolically constituted product of an ongoing project of U.S. racial formation. For the U.S. constitution, especially in its nonlegal aspects, *is* the articulation of racial identifications and institutions ("racial formation") at the level of generative powers and conflict ("extraordinary politics"). Upon this expanded account of constitutionalism, the United States has been informally constituted multiple times for all its citizens, denizens, and subjects. Here ethnic studies must help political theory overcome prejudiced views of race as merely social, purely illusory, or otherwise unworthy of serious theorization. Race as public identity belongs in a series with other modern political concepts, such as citizenship as social standing and the body politic as body politics.[7]

This book was written out of the conviction that the concepts of racial formation and public constitution refer to interlocked, if not identical, phenomena in the U.S. context. This is the case, however, for reasons neither concept as it is currently articulated can provide. My own explanation is articulated in terms of questions common to political theory and ethnic studies—questions of generative conflicts, historical transformations, and social crises. To use Jane Gordon's terms, it seeks to "creolize" closely related concepts in a transdisciplinary fashion and warns us against approaching our disciplines as "discrete."[8] Furthermore, it reminds us of the perils and promises of extraordinary racial politics in times and places of stasis for critical theory with emancipatory interests. We need neither rehabilitate revolutionary Marxism nor resign ourselves to liberal reformism if we can recuperate the genuinely radical experiences at the roots of both traditions.

---

7. Joel Olson, *The Abolition of White Democracy* (Minneapolis: University of Minnesota Press, 2004); David Theo Goldberg, *Racist Culture: Philosophy and the Politics of Meaning* (Oxford, UK: Blackwell, 1993).

8. Jane Gordon, *Creolizing Political Theory: Reading Rousseau through Fanon* (New York: Fordham University Press, 2014), 14–15.

The remainder of this introductory chapter is divided into four sections, the first two of which offer critical reconstructions of previous scholarly work and the second two of which construct the theoretical framework of this study. Section I brings forward the tacit distinctions of extraordinary politics and everyday politics in Michael Omi and Howard Winant's account and Charles Mills's account of racial formation. Section II examines the explicit distinctions of extraordinary politics and everyday politics in Carl Schmitt's and Hannah Arendt's accounts of public constitution. Turning from interpretive to original claims, Section III unpacks the three powers of extraordinary racial politics: disrupting ordinary politics, opening extraordinary possibilities, and reinstituting ordinary politics. Finally, Section IV situates my selected historical cases within the framework of extraordinary racial politics established in the previous sections.

Section I: Racial Formation as Extraordinary Politics

Political theorists of color (and our white allies) must be credited for insisting on the importance of race for investigations of solidarity politics,[9] democratic citizenship,[10] and progressive discourse.[11] Political theorists have even begun to ask what "race" itself means,[12] a question historically raised within the disciplines of anthropology and sociology or within the paradigms of natural sciences. These studies hold that race is not only socially constructed as opposed to naturally given; race is also, as ethnic studies scholars have long contended, deployed by states, saturated with power, and—in short—politically constituted. This insight about the inherently political character of race has come attached to a largely quotidian notion of politics, however.[13]

---

9. See, e.g., Danielle Allen, *Talking to Strangers: Anxieties of Citizenship since* Brown v. Board of Education (Chicago: University of Chicago Press, 2004); Juliet Hooker, *Race and the Politics of Solidarity* (Oxford, UK: Oxford University Press, 2009).

10. See, e.g., Cristina Beltrán, *The Trouble with Unity: Latino Politics and the Creation of Identity* (Oxford, UK: Oxford University Press, 2010); Jack Turner, *Awakening to Race: Individualism and Social Consciousness in America* (Chicago: University of Chicago Press, 2012).

11. See, e.g., Vanita Seth, *Europe's Indians: Producing Racial Difference, 1500–1900* (Durham, NC: Duke University Press, 2010); Thomas McCarthy, *Race, Empire, and the Idea of Human Development* (Cambridge: Cambridge University Press, 2009).

12. See, e.g., Olson, *The Abolition of White Democracy*; Falguni Sheth, *Toward a Political Philosophy of Race* (Albany: State University of New York Press, 2009).

13. Two exceptions are Michael Hanchard, *Party/Politics: Horizons in Black Political Thought* (Oxford, UK: Oxford University Press, 2006) and Cristina Beltrán, "Going Public: Hannah

This focus on the everyday signals the choice of the theorist as much as it sketches a dimension of racialization.

To explore the extraordinary dimension of racialization, we return to two classics of critical race theory, broadly construed. In this section, I examine (the third edition of) Michael Omi and Howard Winant's *Racial Formation in the United States*, a historical sociology of U.S. racial formation, and Charles Mills's *The Racial Contract*, a philosophical model of global white supremacy. Both Omi and Winant's work and Mills's work raise racial questions that have direct, albeit racially unspecified, analogues in political theories of extraordinary politics. Neither, though, fully appreciates the qualitative difference between extraordinary and ordinary racial politics. In response, I amplify this conceptual distinction that ethnic studies articulates in a somewhat muted fashion.

My interpretation of Omi and Winant's theory of racial formation accordingly focuses on questions of process and rupture. To reiterate, Omi and Winant define "racial formation" as that sociohistorical process through which racial orders are created, maintained, changed, and destroyed. The early-modern European colonization of the Americas and of Amerindian peoples, for instance, was a racial formation with a theological cast. The building of Western nation-states was a different kind of racial formation, one dependent on racial pseudo-sciences—initially natural historical, later biological developmental.[14] It is not until after World War II that the process of racial formation acquires predominantly sociopolitical meanings in the United States: "race is now a preeminently political phenomenon" in that race is understood to signify "social conflicts and interests" more than natural divisions and hierarchies.[15]

Omi and Winant expand their time horizons to capture extended racial trajectories.[16] They conceive of the *longue durée* of racial formation as "*a constantly reiterated outcome . . . of the interaction of racial projects.*" A racial project, the basic unit of organized racial politics, consists in "an interpreta-

---

Arendt, Immigrant Action, and the Space of Appearance," *Political Theory* 37, no. 5 (2009): 595–622.

14. See Howard Winant, *The World Is a Ghetto: Race and Democracy since World War II* (New York: Basic, 2001), pt. 1.

15. Omi and Winant, *Racial Formation in the United States*, 120, 110. Omi and Winant correctly note that scientific and other naturalistic concepts of race are making a troubling resurgence.

16. The notion of "racial trajectory," while present in the second edition, comes to the fore only in the third edition. Cf. the "race cycles" approach of Mark Sawyer, *Racial Politics in Post-Revolutionary Cuba* (Cambridge: Cambridge University Press, 2006), chap. 1.

tion, representation, or explanation of racial identities" conjoined to "an effort to organize and distribute resources . . . along racial lines."[17] Periods like "the 17 years of the Civil War/Reconstruction (1860–1877) and roughly 22 years (1948–1970) of the post–World War II racial 'break'" are "exceptional,"[18] the rising phase of a racial trajectory. The falling phase of a racial trajectory begins when the state re-contains popular forces and partially satisfies popular demands. Conversely, an extraordinary event will contract the time horizon of U.S. racial formation to the *courte durée* once the *longue durée* of institutionalized politics can no longer contain popular insurgencies.

The rise and fall of a racial trajectory consist in the confrontational, rapid reformulation of U.S. racial order followed by the creeping, measured effort to restore the *status quo ante*. For instance, the redistributive and participatory trajectory of the civil rights and allied movements peaked in the late 1960s and began a decades-long decline in the 1970s.[19] A rising phase reconstituted a U.S. racial order of domination (wherein racial oppositions are violently crushed) as a U.S. racial order of hegemony (wherein racial oppositions are nonviolently incorporated). This "Great Transformation" expanded normal politics to accommodate the interests of racial oppositions, but the new normal re-contained the very black, Amerindian, Latino/a, and Asian American movements responsible for it. In this falling phase, the new right and neoconservative movements appropriated new left and liberal keywords such as "equality" and "freedom" in order to push the U.S. racial mainstream rightward.[20]

The norm of racial formation is the extension of sociohistorical trajectories, while the exception of racial formation is the establishment of new terrains (on which sociohistorical trajectories travel). Omi and Winant's distinction is, in sociological terms, the social reproduction/transformation distinction or, in my terms, the ordinary/extraordinary politics distinction. The primary difference is that Omi and Winant are oriented to extended processes, while I am oriented to episodic crises. If anything, the extended subsumes, historicizes, and explains the episodic within their theory of racial formation "process." An additional complication is that Omi and Winant analyze only one "Great Transformation" and—despite numerous references to Asian, Amerindian, and Latina/o formations—center their exceptional

---

17. Omi and Winant, *Racial Formation in the United States*, 127, 125, italics original.
18. Ibid., 148; see also Howard Winant, *New Politics of Race: Globalism, Difference, Justice* (Minneapolis: University of Minnesota Press, 2004), 15–18.
19. Omi and Winant, *Racial Formation in the United States*, 253–56.
20. Ibid., 192.

periods (1860–1877 and 1948–1970) on black Americans.²¹ My point is not that the civil war and civil rights movement did not change the entire United States, but that nonblack racial formations have done the same.

Omi and Winant offer a historical sociology of the racial formation process in the United States. Mills, for his part, offers a philosophical modeling of what Omi and Winant might call an epoch- and globe-shaping racial formation. As a contribution to the social contract tradition,²² Mills's theory of the racial contract is more attuned to foundational moments than Omi and Winant's theory of racial formation. The racial contract is the "original" structure through which whites and nonwhites come into existence as such. The term "contract" marks the establishment of "global white supremacy" as "a political system" of formal and informal rule; social privileges and disadvantages; moral, aesthetic, and epistemic normativity: "the Racial Contract is that set of formal or informal agreements or meta-agreements" between "one subset of humans, henceforth designated by (shifting) 'racial' (phenotypical/genealogical/cultural) criteria $C_1, C_2, C_3 \ldots$ as 'white'" so as to "categorize the remaining subset of humans as 'nonwhite.'"²³

Mills makes the existential claim that white supremacy exists and the ontological claim that it is grounded in convention rather than nature.²⁴ The contract, Mills claims, is "clearly locatable" in "the creation of the modern world by European colonialism," where white/nonwhite *gradually* became the formal marker of [the] differentiated status" between European/non-European, civilized/uncivilized, and Christian/non-Christian.²⁵ Mills, of course, cannot point to a document stipulating the unequal moral, civil, and political status of whites and nonwhites. It is rather as if "clearly locatable" European colonizers had signed such a contract.²⁶ It is "in the beginning"

---

21. To be clear, the black/white binary has legitimate usages—e.g., keeping specifically black problems front and center. Ronald Sundstrom, *The Browning of America and the Evasion of Social Justice* (Albany: State University of New York Press, 2008), 82–88.

22. Mills was partially inspired by Carole Pateman, whom he locates in the Rousseauvian tradition of uncovering injustices. Charles Mills, "The Domination Contract," in Carole Pateman and Charles Mills, *Contract and Domination* (Cambridge: Polity, 2007), 81; cf. Carole Pateman, *The Sexual Contract* (Cambridge: Polity, 1994), chap. 4.

23. Charles Mills, *The Racial Contract* (Ithaca, NY: Cornell University Press, 1997), 3, 11.

24. Ibid., 127.

25. Ibid., 21, 23, italics added.

26. I leave aside various controversies surrounding this claim, including whether racialist ideologies infused the original colonization of the Americas and whether the origins of any states—racial or otherwise—can be contractually modeled. On the former controversy, see Seth, *Europe's Indians*, 175–76; on the latter, see David Theo Goldberg, *The Racial State* (Oxford, UK: Blackwell, 2002), 36–37.

that Mills's variant of the social contract is closest to my understanding of an informal constitutional moment. Mills, however, is quick to clarify that the racial contract is *"continually being rewritten"* by new signatories, who have materially reproduced white supremacy for some five centuries.[27]

Even more than Omi and Winant, Mills imagines racial trajectories on expansive time scales. Omi and Winant's account of the transformation of racial domination into racial hegemony in some ways parallels Mills's account of the transformation of violently enforced racial contracts into ideologically enforced racial contracts.[28] For Mills, the ideology that white supremacy is the "exception" rather than the "rule" of European modernity is "an artifact of the Racial Contract in the second, *de facto* phase," an ideology that would have been inconceivable in the first, *de jure* period.[29] Yet the second period is only a modest rewriting of the racial contract that continues to underwrite the social contract. While Omi and Winant think that the U.S. racial order underwent a "Great Transformation," Mills thinks that the global racial polity is steeped in social reproduction. The power of extraordinary politics to push white supremacy far into the contemporary world is founded on deep consensus.

The racial contract as the extraordinary foundation of the *Herrenvolk* polity establishes norms of equality and freedom for whites over and against norms of exclusion and subordination for nonwhites. The racial contract as the everyday operation of white privilege, by contrast, enforces this two-tiered system of normativity. Both Mills's "the racial contract" and my "racial constitution" account for the determination and institution of racial rules. My idea differs from Mills's insofar as I argue that the U.S. polity has undergone several re-constitutions, all of which exceed the rewriting of *de jure* clauses of the racial contract as *de facto* ones and most of which fall short of the qualitative transformation of the racial formation process (as in Omi and Winant's Great Transformation). This question of multiple racialized constitutions raises the related question of multiple racialized trajectories.[30] Any racial constitution by definition affects the whole polity or the entire public, but its consequences are disproportionately borne by groupings too crudely identified as not-white. My claim is not incompatible with, yet also not in the spirit of, Mills's assertion of a Manichean split between white and nonwhite.

---

27. Mills, *The Racial Contract*, 72, italics original.
28. Ibid., 72–73, 83–87.
29. Ibid., 122.
30. The question of multiple racial trajectories is also the question of multiple racial positions. See Claire Kim, "The Racial Triangulation of Asian Americans," *Politics and Society* 27, no. 1 (1999): 105–38.

This section has analyzed analogous elements from Omi and Winant's and Mills's theories of racial construction: the original moment of Mills's racial contract is an analogue to the initiatory moment of Omi and Winant's racial formation (extraordinary politics), while the rewriting process of Mills's racial contract is an analogue to the reiterative process of Omi and Winant's racial formation (ordinary politics). What I would maintain, *pace* Mills as well as Omi and Winant, is that a multiplicity of heightened conflicts has initiated a multiplicity of intertwined, group-differentiated trajectories. What I would warn is that both theories threaten to reduce eventlike ruptures to quasi-causal moments of historical processes, especially in those times and places I would highlight as strange and creative.

One reason that ethnic studies scholars like Mills or Omi and Winant turn sharply to everyday politics is that standard histories downplay the agency, viewpoints, and vernaculars of everyday people. For instance, W.E.B. Du Bois took white and other nonblack Americans behind "the Veil" surrounding black American lifeworlds, just as Ronald Takaki offered Americans a multicultural "mirror" consisting of the life stories of ordinary "strangers" from other shores.[31] I acknowledge that many groups are constantly renegotiating their engagements with the informal U.S. constitution (e.g., peoples indigenous in a settler colonial society, peoples descended from slaves in a society founded on slave labor, peoples migrating under an exclusionary immigration regime). The point to emphasize is that ordinarily, extraordinary racial politics is embedded within everyday life as the potential transformation of the public world. Only at "critical junctures," as American Political Development scholars put it,[32] does extraordinary racial politics emerge from everyday life to actually transform lived experiences for better and for worse.

Section II: Extraordinary Politics as Public Constitution

My articulation of informal constitution taps into the ambivalence of the modern term "constitution," which describes both the action and the prod-

---

31. W.E.B. Du Bois, *The Souls of Black Folk* (New York: Dover, 1994); Ronald Takaki, *A Different Mirror: A History of Multicultural America*, rev. ed. (Boston: Little, Brown, 2008).

32. See the notion of "critical juncture" in Paul Pierson, *Politics in Time: History, Institutions, and Social Analysis* (Princeton, NJ: Princeton University Press, 2004); see the parallel notion of the "structural event" in Karen Orren and Stephen Skowronek, *The Search for American Political Development* (Cambridge: Cambridge University Press, 2004).

uct of creating a public.³³ It is partially inspired by early modern notions of Original Compact, Republican Foundation, or Constituent Power.³⁴ However, I resituate the constitution-making power of early modern revolutionaries inside the broadly modern problematic of racial formation. What constituent power (the power to create constitutional order) is to constituted power (authorized powers within that order) for juridical constitutionalism, extraordinary racial politics (the power to create racial order) is to ordinary racial politics (legitimized powers within that order) for informal constitutionalism. Postjuridical constitutionalism, in addition, harkens back to ancient notions of constitution obscured by modern legal discourse: constitution (*politeia*) is connected to offices of the city (*polis*), but also connected to arrangements of the citizens (*polítes*).³⁵

This section discusses how Carl Schmitt and Hannah Arendt connect public constitution to the very existence of political communities and actors. The books in Arendt's and Schmitt's *oeuvres* are interpreted here as directly concerned with constitutive moments. Schmitt, in *The Concept of the Political*, argues that the official decision that identifies enemies creates public order; Arendt, in *The Human Condition*, makes an analogous claim that the collective action that discloses selves enacts public freedom. Unlike our race theorists, who subsume the extraordinary into the ordinary, our political theorists have the opposite tendency—they go too far in treating the extraordinary as a break from or bracketing of the ordinary. In moderating both tendencies, I venture that ordinary politics constitutes extraordinary politics as much as extraordinary politics constitutes ordinary politics.

Carl Schmitt sharply differentiates the political—his term for extraordinary politics—from the aesthetic, the moral, and the economic. But the sharp distinction between the political and the nonpolitical is softened by the fact that the political is always and never purely itself. The political is the friend/enemy distinction on which European international law authorizes

---

33. Hannah Arendt, *On Revolution* (New York. Penguin, 1990), 136.

34. See, e.g., John Locke, *Two Treatises of Government* (Cambridge: Cambridge University Press, 1988); Niccolò Machiavelli, *Discourses on Livy*, trans. Harvey Mansfield and Nathan Tarcov (Chicago: University of Chicago Press, 1996); Emmanuel Sieyès, *What Is the Third Estate?* trans. M. Blondel (London: Pall Mall, 1963).

35. Aristotle. *Aristotle: "The Politics" and "The Constitution of Athens,"* ed. Stephen Everson (Cambridge: Cambridge University Press, 1996). It should also be noted that Plato's *Republic* was originally entitled *Politea*. Plato, *The Republic*, trans. Tom Griffith (Cambridge: Cambridge University Press, 2000).

the sovereign state to decide.[36] The friend/enemy distinction is "independent, not in the sense of a distinct new domain," but in that it is irreducible to ugly/beautiful, good/evil, and profitable/unprofitable distinctions.[37] The political is dependent, however, in that it "does not describe its own substance, but only the intensity of an association or dissociation of human beings whose motives can be religious, national . . . , economic, or of another kind."[38] As a form of (dis)association, the friend/enemy relationship presupposes actually nonpolitical, yet potentially political forms of association. Politics is parasitic on substantial differences that, as of yet, lack the intensity of friend/enemy antagonism.

The political for Schmitt is to the prepolitical (which, following Arendt, I call "the social") what the extraordinary break is to ordinary fault lines. A "concrete" rupture from everyday forms of tension,[39] the political is the point at which an entire people—and, less circularly, the sovereign authorized to represent it—decides on the boundaries of membership, law, and territory (e.g., a decision to handle enemies in "our" midst extra-legally). More concisely, the state's articulation of the friend/enemy distinction closes the inside of "a whole nation" against the outside of a concrete enemy.[40] For Schmitt, the closure of the public in the face of existential conflict makes the legal operations of administration and regulation possible.

Consistent across Schmitt's *oeuvre* is the notion that politics is the creation, protection, and destruction of public order. His pre–World War II work is clearly marked by a concern with maintaining constitutional order in the legal state.[41] This commitment to the nation-state carries into Schmitt's wartime and postwar work as a concern with maintaining Eurocentric glob-

---

36. Carl Schmitt, *The Nomos of the Earth in the International Law of the Jus Publicum Europaeum*, trans. G. L. Ulmen (New York: Telos, 2003), pt. 3.

37. Carl Schmitt, *The Concept of the Political: Expanded Edition*, trans. George Schwab (Chicago: University of Chicago Press, 2007), 26. An account of Schmitt's Weberian understanding of value spheres can be found in William Rasch, *Sovereignty and Its Discontents: On the Primacy of Conflict and the Structure of the Political* (London: Birkbeck Law, 2004), 26–31.

38. Schmitt, *The Concept of the Political*, 38.

39. An account of Schmitt's usage of "concrete" can be found in Mika Ojakangas, *A Philosophy of Concrete Life: Carl Schmitt and the Political Thought of Late Modernity*, 2nd ed. (Bern, CH: Peter Lang, 2006), 32–34.

40. Schmitt, *The Concept of the Political*, 28.

41. See, e.g., Carl Schmitt, *Political Theology: Four Chapters on the Concept of Sovereignty*, trans. George Schwab (Chicago: University of Chicago Press, 2005), chap. 4; Carl Schmitt, *The Crisis of Parliamentary Democracy*, trans. Ellen Kennedy (Cambridge, MA: MIT Press, 1985), chap. 4.

al order.[42] Public order, whether national or international, is not "law and order" for its own sake; the defensive posture toward public order is taken for the sake of a particular way of life. The political presupposes that a collectivity is willing and able to stake the physical existence of its members to preserve a way of life consisting of more than physical existence.[43] For Schmitt, the political way of life—this standing for friendship and standing against enemies—is the properly human way of facing up to death.

Schmitt, in this vein, stands against liberal hopes that economics and morality will one day eliminate war and politics. Liberal theorists, in turn, criticize the friend/enemy distinction for partaking of amoral, if not belligerent formalism.[44] Formalism is potentially both a weakness and a strength, however. It is a strength if Schmittian friendship and enmity are universal structures of experience, but it is a weakness if they are peculiar to the European nation-state system. It will suffice for my purposes if friend versus enemy conflict is a—and not the only—structure of racial constitution in the United States. When it racially constitutes the U.S. public, the friend/enemy distinction typically divides white against nonwhite, two categories whose criteria of membership are historically rather than logically determined.[45] The crucial point is that at least one of, and perhaps both of, the antagonistic racial groupings is willing to utilize violence against a perceived existential threat.

Hannah Arendt, like Schmitt, draws a stark distinction to the effect of underscoring the distinctiveness of political life.[46] Arendt holds that politics for moderns is no longer what it was for ancients—the speech of the public actor who stands out against the background of private labor.[47] Arendt's story of "the rise of the social" is that the emergence of once-private labor into the

---

42. These latter works temper Schmitt's earlier "decisionism" through their turn toward "concrete order thinking." See, e.g., Schmitt, *Nomos of the Earth*, pt. 4; Carl Schmitt, *Writings on War*, trans. Timothy Nunan (Cambridge: Polity, 2011), 125–97.

43. Schmitt, *The Concept of the Political*, 27, 34.

44. See, e.g., John McCormick, *Carl Schmitt's Critique of Liberalism: Against Politics as Technology* (Cambridge: Cambridge University Press, 1997), 111–12.

45. The shifting criteria of whiteness allow for groups once treated as "not-white" to become "white" over time. Noel Ignatiev, *How the Irish Became White* (New York: Routledge, 1995); Karen Brodkin, *How Jews Became White Folks and What That Says about Race in America* (New Brunswick, NJ: Rutgers University Press, 1998).

46. Action is to Arendt's "public" what decision is to Schmitt's "the political"; Arendt would call Schmitt's faculty of decision "the will." Hannah Arendt, *The Life of the Mind* (New York: Harcourt Brace Jovanovich, 1978), pt. 2.

47. Hannah Arendt, *The Human Condition*, 2nd ed. (Chicago: University of Chicago Press, 1998), 72–73.

public realm has blurred the once-bright public/private distinction.[48] Hence modern polities lack the common sense of (Arendt's) Greeks that certain phenomena are essentially public, while others are essentially private. Indeed, in "socialized" polities, the lines between public and private, action and labor, are slippery because essentially contestable. Here Arendt's activities of action and speech appear to be as formal as Schmitt's identities of friend and enemy; these concepts refer to intersubjective forms of grappling with substances, not to substances themselves. In its independence from others, speech-as-action can pertain to "private" matters (e.g., domestic violence) or "social" matters (e.g., welfare provision). In its dependence on others, speech-as-action must take something other than itself as its concrete content.[49]

While both Schmitt and Arendt relate the political as form to the social as content, Arendt more than Schmitt stresses that the political as extraordinary event breaks from the social as ordinary process. We need not read Arendt against Arendt—as we have to read Schmitt against Schmitt—to assert that the political is the disruption of the existent and the irruption of the emergent. Extraordinary politics for Schmitt is a conservative closing against enemies, while extraordinary politics for Arendt is a creative opening between citizens. In contrast to Schmitt's decision, which bounds a public identity and a constitutional order, Arendt's action establishes relationships between distinctive selves that "force open all limitations and cut across all boundaries" (legal, physical, or otherwise).[50] This informal constitution, as I call it, "predates and precedes all formal constitution of the public realm and the various forms of government."[51]

Across her corpus, Arendt holds that politics is the enactment, maintenance, and augmentation of public freedom. We can, at the risk of anachronism, trace a distinction between political action and social behavior back to Arendt's early work on European Jewish assimilation.[52] With more respect for chronology, we can see a turn toward less "heroic," more ordinary spaces of freedom in Arendt's later publications on mental experience and consti-

---

48. Benhabib rightly observes that for Arendt "each type of human activity has a proper 'place.'" Seyla Benhabib, *The Reluctant Modernism of Hannah Arendt*, new ed. (Lanham, MD: Rowman and Littlefield, 2003), 124.

49. Arendt, *The Human Condition*, 182.

50. Ibid., 190.

51. Ibid., 199.

52. See, e.g., Hannah Arendt, *The Origins of Totalitarianism*, rev. ed. (San Diego, CA: Harvest, 1973), pt. 1, chap. 3; Hannah Arendt, *Rahel Varnhagen: The Life of a Jewish Woman*, rev. ed. (New York: Harcourt Brace Jovanovich, 1974).

tutional endurance.⁵³ The public actor or the free self is the existential achievement that Arendt worries is withering under the social pressures of modernity. The political for both Arendt and Schmitt is a problem of being, existing as potential "beginners" for Arendt and as potential combatants for Schmitt. Both hold that political existence presupposes that physical existence might be at risk, as Arendt no less than Schmitt holds that politics is oriented toward death and life. Then again, Arendt differentiates political life (*bios*) from physical life (*zoe*) in terms of the courage to die rather than the commitment to kill.⁵⁴

Speech-as-action, with its emphasis on persuasion and plurality, is assuredly friendlier to liberal commitments than the friend/enemy distinction, with its emphasis on violence and identity. Even so, liberal theorists also charge Arendt with excessive formalism, asking what exactly the substance of speech-as-action might be.⁵⁵ Like Schmitt's, Arendt's formalism can be a hindrance or a help: hers is a hindrance if action is peculiar to Greek *poleis* (or Hellenophile imaginations), yet hers is a help if action is a human faculty that makes certain kinds of politics possible. It will suffice for my purposes if Arendtian public freedom, like Schmittian public order, is a structure of racial constitution in the United States. Friend/enemy distinction, as we have seen, has the tendency to divide the U.S. public into white versus nonwhite identifications. Speech-as-action, by contrast, has the tendency to distinguish selves from one another, deny that existent social formations are incontestable, and affirm that humans "are not born in order to die but in order to begin."⁵⁶

On the question of how the extraordinary constitutes the ordinary, we see that decision for Schmitt sets identitarian limits for a legally ordered public, while action for Arendt initiates new processes within socially articulated publics. On the question of how the ordinary conditions the extraordinary, we see that the political for Schmitt ratchets social tensions up into friend/enemy conflicts, whereas the public for Arendt has been overrun by labor and other social preoccupations. This mutually constitutive rela-

---

53. See, e.g., Hannah Arendt, *Lectures on Kant's Political Philosophy*, ed. Ronald Beiner (Chicago: University of Chicago Press, 1982), 33–51; Hannah Arendt, *Crises of the Republic* (New York: Harcourt Brace Jovanovich, 1972), 51–102.

54. Arendt, *The Human Condition*, 36–37.

55. See, e.g., George Kateb, *Hannah Arendt: Politics, Conscience, Evil* (Oxford, UK: Martin Robinson, 1984), 18.

56. Arendt, *The Human Condition*, 246.

tionship between the political and the social, to which the next section returns, is perhaps *the* problem for thinking public constitution and racial formation together.⁵⁷

Part of the problem is that where race theorists subsume the punctuated moment of the political into the epochal processes of the social, political theorists posit the "miraculous" break of political actions from social structures.⁵⁸ That is, Arendt and Schmitt tend to exaggerate how far the political overrides the social as compared to how far the social underpins the political, while Mills as well as Omi and Winant have the opposite tendency. If extraordinary politics have indeed declined under the vicissitudes of modernity, Arendt's polemics against the social and Schmitt's attacks on liberalism may be warranted. If the political has instead been resituated in racial and other formations of the social, however, my appraisal of the *relatively* miraculous power of the extraordinary is the more appropriate response.⁵⁹ Hence I differ from scholars who seek to loosen whatever hold Arendt's and Schmitt's extramundane politics have on our theoretical visions.⁶⁰ I want, if anything, to cultivate a fascination with extraordinary politics in the expectation that neither a constitutionalized liberalism nor a revolutionary Marxism will be the final word for critical theory.

Section III: Extraordinary Racial Politics in Relation to Ordinary Racial Politics

Political theorists and ethnic studies scholars largely talk past one another not only because the former are relatively uninterested in critical race theory and the latter are relatively uninterested in Western political philosophy. They also talk past each other because each takes their preferred mode of politics—extraordinary or everyday—as the whole of politics, or because each assumes their favored mode is particularly "good" and their disfavored

---

57. Cf. Bonnie Honig, *Political Theory and the Displacement of Politics* (Ithaca, NY: Cornell University Press, 1993), 120–21.

58. Schmitt, *Political Theology*, 36–37; Arendt, *The Human Condition*, 246–47.

59. By contrast, Arendt's view is that action has relocated to scientific interventions into natural processes. Hannah Arendt, *Between Past and Future: Eight Exercises in Political Thought*, rev. ed. (New York: Penguin, 2006), 57–63; Arendt, *The Human Condition*, 231–32.

60. See, e.g., Frank, *Constituent Moments*, chap. 1; Bonnie Honig, *Emergency Politics: Paradox, Law, Democracy* (Princeton, NJ: Princeton University Press, 2009), chap. 3. The hold is not that tight, in my view.

mode is especially "bad." Overcoming one-sided conceptions of politics is as crucial as uncovering shared theoretical interests for creolizing political theory and ethnic studies. Each field enjoys a vantage point that corrects for the blind spot of the other: the concept of public constitution, once rearticulated in racialized terms, will appear more ordinary, just as the concept of racial formation, once rearticulated in constitutional terms, will appear more extraordinary.

My concept of extraordinary racial politics, then, remixes elements from Arendt's and Schmitt's theories of public constitution with elements from Omi and Winant's and Mills's theories of racial formation. Extraordinary racial politics is (1) the power to disrupt the processes of racial ordering, (2) the power of enacting transformative possibilities, and (3) the power to reinstitute the terms of racial ordering. Extraordinary racial politics remains tethered to ordinary racial politics in all three moments: extraordinary racial politics (1) emerges out of, (2) achieves relative autonomy from, and (3) submerges back into ordinary racial politics. My key claim—expressed in the second item of both lists—is that "the event" of extraordinary racial politics is the worldly appearance of our capacity to achieve "the new." This claim acquires generality in the turn toward philosophical anthropology, while it acquires specificity in the turn toward critical race studies.

It would be prudent to remark at the outset that I do not aspire to provide a "free-standing" theory of either politics or race. To play on Frantz Fanon, I only propose to indicate how Schmittian and Arendtian concepts of public constitution must be "stretched" to address events in U.S. racial formation.[61] Furthermore, while the inconsistency of racial typologies[62] suggests that "race" itself is an empty signifier,[63] usages of racial signifiers can only be explained at the explicitly political—that is, power-centered and conflict-oriented—register. Politics is not necessarily racial (e.g., the premodern politics of Mediterranean or Asian empires), but race is necessarily political (e.g., the varied purposes of indigenous classifications throughout

---

61. Fanon says that "a Marxist analysis should always be slightly stretched when it comes to addressing the colonial issue." Frantz Fanon, *The Wretched of the Earth*, trans. Richard Philcox (New York: Grove, 2004), 5.

62. Ian Haney López, *White by Law: The Legal Construction of Race*, rev. ed. (New York: New York University Press, 2006); Claudette Bennett, "Racial Categories Used in the Decennial Censuses, 1790 to the Present," *Government Information Quarterly* 17, no. 2 (2000): 161–80.

63. Stuart Hall, *Race: The Floating Signifier*, DVD dir. by Sut Jally (Northampton, MA: Media Education Foundation, 1997); Kandice Chuh, *Imagine Otherwise: On Asian Americanist Critique* (Durham, NC: Duke University Press, 2003).

the modern Americas).⁶⁴ Consequently, I can treat extraordinary/ordinary racial politics as a special case of the extraordinary/ordinary politics distinction. This subsumption of race to politics cannot explain everything about race, but it can explain how extraordinary and ordinary racial politics differ.

It would also be prudent to remark that I bracket several controversies that comprehensive theorists of race and politics would have to resolve. To take one such conflict, either race is a logic of subordinating nonwhite to white, as Mills says, or race is a logic of conflict in the absence of determinate criteria, as Omi and Winant say. To consider another, either politics occurs between friends and enemies, as Schmitt affirms, or politics occurs between friends who are equals, as Arendt avows. My tack will be to render my usages of "politics" and "race" consistent with a minimum of intervention into what W. B. Gallie might call "endless debates about their proper uses."⁶⁵ As I focus on specific conflicts and conjunctures, I leave open the question of how far my usages can travel outside the ever-shifting boundaries of the United States. Let this caveat also remind us that extraordinary racial politics is defined by three powers in the situation of conflict.

My first thesis is that extraordinary racial politics is the power to disrupt everyday racial politics. Such disruptions are not necessarily large scale—they can be as small scale as selves resisting an assigned role, withdrawing from a popular consensus, or acting as if extant authorities did not exist.⁶⁶ The extraordinary does not erupt out of no time or nowhere; rather, the political moment emerges at the limits of and from the inconsistencies of the social order.⁶⁷ That friend/enemy distinction striates a smoothed-over public is an implication of Schmitt's location of the political at the point of peak intensity for a social cleavage. That speech-as-action contradicts "good behavior" is an implication of Arendt's rendition of the modern public as ex-

---

64. This asymmetry allows for the actuality of nonracial politics prior to modernity or even within modernity, e.g., Ivan Hannaford, *Race: The History of an Idea in the West* (Baltimore, MD: Johns Hopkins University Press, 1996). It also allows for the possibility of nonracial politics during or after modernity, e.g., Paul Gilroy, *Against Race: Imagining Political Culture beyond the Color Line* (Cambridge, MA: Harvard University Press, 2000).

65. W. B. Gallie, "Essentially Contested Concepts," *Proceedings of the Aristotelian Society* 56 (1955–1956): 169.

66. Fred Lee, "Fantasies of Asian American Kinship Disrupted: Identification and Disidentification in Michael Kang's *The Motel*," *Critical Philosophy of Race* 4, no. 1 (2016): 6–29.

67. The decision, for example, only *appears* to explode out of nowhere from the standpoint of legally constituted order. Schmitt, *Political Theology*, 31–32.

traordinarily political, yet ordinarily social.⁶⁸ The trick is to see that the extraordinary and the ordinary inhabit the same modern public, albeit with opposed valences (e.g., rule-setting versus rule-bound, unusual versus commonplace).

Extraordinary politics brackets patterns of public interaction in a manner that anticipates their reworking. Many racially specific examples of this dynamic come from new social movements. As Chapter 2 shows, the civil rights movement suspended the norms of white supremacy, creating the very public spaces needed to delegitimize them. Contemporaneously, the Supreme Court suspended southern "states' rights" under U.S. federalism, opening the very juridical space required to de-authorize them. To use Kaylvas's metaphors, the civil rights movement occurred both "beside" (mass mobilization) and "inside" (legal strategy) the state apparatus. Yet the movement also pushed "below" the existing U.S. constitution, where it became a renewed source of constitutional authority.⁶⁹ Black and allied movements of the period, as seen in our analysis of Omi and Winant, expanded normal politics to more explicitly address racial issues.

My second thesis is that extraordinary racial politics is the power of enacting historical events. The event at the level of racial structures is social transformation, which makes the difference between regimes of social reproduction. The event at the level of human capacities is collaborative creativity, a moment of what existential philosophers call the joy and anguish of freedom.⁷⁰ Whether ordinary or extraordinary, freedom is a tangible, visible, and audible reality within an embodied, historical, and intersubjective world. Worldly freedom is an externalized experience very different from inward experiences of freedom (e.g., free thought); as such, it is excluded from philosophical equations of freedom with the will.⁷¹ Freedom arises outside of the psychic realm, where "free will" can appear to be a metaphysical absurdity, and inside the public realm, where events are generative of new possibilities.

We cannot disclose the meaning of extraordinary politics without considering existential freedom. Events demand to be interpreted in terms of

---

68. This is my charitable reading of "the rise of the social"; a less charitable reading is Hannah Pitkin, *The Attack of the Blob: Hannah Arendt's Concept of the Social* (Chicago: University of Chicago Press, 1998), chap. 9.

69. Kalyvas, however, puts social movements in the "beside" category. Kalyvas, *Democracy and the Politics of the Extraordinary*, 12–13.

70. Lewis Gordon, *Fanon and the Crisis of European Man: An Essay on Philosophy and the Human Sciences* (New York: Routledge, 1995), 45.

71. Arendt, *Between Past and Future*, 145.

lived experience, even as these phenomena "underdetermine" our conceptual, affective, and evaluative responses to them.[72] For the very intelligibility of events depends on understanding them as spontaneous enactments—neither as predictable effects of causes nor as tokens of universal types, as social scientists might analyze them. Political concepts like freedom and event take "humanity" as their ultimate interpretive horizon or point of reference,[73] at least according to the existential-phenomenological tradition, which has had a formative influence on the critical philosophy of race.[74] To affirm our capacities to make the extraordinary happen is to defend what Lewis Gordon calls "the place for the human being in misanthropic times."[75]

The extraordinary means freedom—its relations and its negations, its experience and its effects. This I say in the spirit of Schmitt's and Arendt's associations of public constitution with human faculties. The position that decision is a constituent of human nature is not available to Schmitt, who thinks that all political concepts—including the concept of "humanity"—are polemical concepts. All Schmitt can offer is an "anthropological presupposition" that the human being has the potential for intersubjective violence and that human existence is "dangerous and dynamic."[76] Arendt, for her part, poetically associates action with the alterity of our selves and the newness of our births, the human conditions of plurality and natality. More prosaically, action can achieve relative freedom because all "conditions of human existence ... never condition us absolutely."[77] Each person, Arendt thinks, must enact historical and political life against the backdrop of social and biological life.

One might object that "political existentialism" of this sort made Arendt and Schmitt enamored of normatively groundless, dangerously arbitrary politics. Kalyvas, who rejects this classification of Schmitt and Arendt, dem-

---

72. Linda Martín Alcoff, *The Future of Whiteness* (Cambridge: Polity, 2015), 58.

73. While I take seriously suspicions that the very concept of "humanity" is historically specific, I worry that these skeptics have their own transhistorical presuppositions about human being. Poststructuralists, for instance, imply human beings are signifying beings. Saba Mahmood, *Politics of Piety: The Islamic Revival and the Feminist Subject* (Princeton, NJ: Princeton University Press, 2004), 164.

74. See, e.g., Frantz Fanon, *Black Skins, White Masks*, trans. Richard Philcox (New York: Grove, 2008); Linda Martín Alcoff, *Visible Identities: Race, Gender and the Self* (Oxford, UK: Oxford University Press, 2006); George Yancey, *Black Bodies, White Gazes: The Continuing Significance of Race* (Lanham, MD: Rowman and Littlefield, 2008).

75. Gordon, *Fanon and the Crisis of European Man*, x.

76. Schmitt, *The Concept of the Political*, 61.

77. Arendt, *The Human Condition*, 11.

onstrates that both were intent on finding democratic sources of legitimacy for extraordinary politics.[78] I, by contrast, am more concerned with the normative valence of events than with the normative promise of "existentialism," which I use to describe how human capacities are constitutive of both emancipatory and dominative politics. To take an emancipatory moment, Chapter 5 concerns how red power, black power, and Asian American activists rendered judgments in the enactment of social movement freedoms. Chapter 4, to take up a dominative moment, considers how U.S. state officials decided which populations qualified as security threats and which qualified as worth protecting during World War II.

In sum, the second power of extraordinary racial politics is the capacity to make events happen or, if you prefer, to allow events to transpire.[79] The event opens a gap between surrounding conditions and their probable consequences, within which an alternative set of possibilities is produced and from which another series of effects follows. What closes these gaps within historical processes, generating the semblance of uneventful continuity, is the third power of extraordinary racial politics—namely, that of reconstituting racial order. This power rearticulates an informal constitution of institutional dynamics, everyday habits, and collective representations.[80] Everyday politics will resist, negotiate, and reproduce this constitutional order until an extraordinary politics emerges to suspend it (first power), open it to historical alternatives (second power), and reconstitute it yet again (third power). At this point, we can imagine a U.S. racial politics traveling from the extraordinary creating the ordinary to the ordinary conditioning of the extraordinary over an extended period. This is a dynamic representation of a structural problem raised earlier, where we found Schmitt and Arendt insufficiently attentive to how the extraordinary and the everyday work on one another.

Fortunately, I am not the first political theorist or ethnic studies scholar to work on this problem. Schmitt scholars in both fields have already envisaged a reciprocal relationship between extraordinary and ordinary politics. Chantal Mouffe, for instance, claims that any order of "sedimented prac-

---

78. Kalyvas, *Democracy and the Politics of the Extraordinary*, 196.
79. While I am most interested in events of public constitution, I am open to the possibility that there are many kinds of events. Others are keener on philosophical events, e.g., Slavoj Žižek, *Event: A Philosophical Journey through a Concept* (New York: Melville House, 2014); Alain Badiou, *Being and Event*, trans. Oliver Feltham (London: Continuum, 2005).
80. Cf. Omi and Winant, *Racial Formation in the United States*, 137.

tices" coheres around the "constitutive exclusion" of enemies, who represent certain possibilities denied by a hegemonic order.[81] I would keep going in this direction: constitutive friend/enemy distinctions remain latent within social cleavages (e.g., white over not-white hierarchy); this latency, in turn, makes future friend/enemy conflicts more likely to fall along those lines (e.g., white friendship versus nonwhite enmity). This formulation is resonant with Falguni Sheth's claim that sovereignty, as Schmitt and others theorize it, is conditioned by extended trajectories of racialization. State power is more patterned than "random" in that law "consistently" cuts in favor of certain populations (e.g., white non-Muslim Americans) and against others (e.g., nonwhite Muslim Americans).[82] Even as they arise from habitual "otherings," extraordinary decisions rework daily racial formations (e.g., the heightened salience of Muslim identifications for the post-9/11 national-security state).

Extraordinary and ordinary politics have also been co-articulated by political theorists and ethnic studies scholars in the Arendt literature. Working against Arendt's tendency to oppose the two,[83] Claude Lefort intertwines the political and the social, as "the latter is given sense [*mise en sens*], is set up, and is staged [*mise en scène*] by means of the former."[84] We can speak again of the political latent within the social: speech-as-action is submerged within the sociohistorical trajectory it initiates (e.g., 1960s to 1970s Chicana/o movements); this submergence, in turn, makes subsequent actions more likely to emerge along those lines (e.g., 2006 mega-*marchas*).[85] The social and the political define one another in the modern public, where social groupings are always potentially political and where political conflicts are never without social connotations. Cristina Beltrán argues, for example, that the sociopolitical realm that devalues Latino/a laborers is the same place in which Latina/o protestors carried out 2006 mega-*marchas*.[86]

---

81. Mouffe, *On the Political*, 17–18. Imagine a liberal democratic hegemony that closes itself against antiliberal fascisms or antiliberal communisms.

82. Sheth, *Toward a Political Philosophy of Race*, 54.

83. Claude Lefort, *Democracy and Political Theory*, trans. David Macey (Cambridge: Polity, 1988), 54–55.

84. This Lefortian formulation is from Pierre Rosanvallon, *Democracy Past and Future*, ed. Samuel Moyn (New York: Columbia University Press, 2006), 60.

85. I have oversimplified greatly in the parentheses of this sentence: the "genealogy of struggle" behind the 2006 mega-march also included the 1980s Central American peace movement and the 1990s campaign against California Proposition 187. Gonzales, *Reform without Justice*, chap. 3.

86. Beltrán, *The Trouble with Unity*, 149–54.

For peoples struggling to live ordinary lives under extraordinary conditions of racial domination and dehumanization, Lewis Gordon argues, the aims of extraordinary politics are the transformation of everyday life and the reclamation of their humanity.[87] A renewal of society and species, in short, actualizes the extraordinary potential of ordinary people. While both agree that extraordinary politics necessarily involves our humanity, Schmitt and Arendt deny that extraordinary politics has a necessary relation to social justice. Theirs is a useful reminder that extraordinary politics can be tragic, farcical, and disastrous. To take the injustice considered in Chapter 3, nineteenth-century federal-Indian treaties undermined southeastern Amerindian autonomy; these signs of indigenous "consent" led to massive U.S. appropriations of native land and, yet more ironically, enhanced U.S. domination over native peoples. Mills's racial contract in this case is an "expropriation contract" and a "colonial contract" constitutive of asymmetrical power relations.[88] Extraordinary politics equally admits of unexpected promise and unprecedented perils—but it can offer no guarantees, normative or otherwise.

Section IV: Four Events in the Informal Constitution of the United States

My study is in the good company of political theory books that double for ethnic studies books. However, even as political theorists have strengthened connections especially with Africana studies, we have missed opportunities to engage with comparative ethnic studies, that is, the comparative study of distinctive racializations on local,[89] (trans)national,[90] and global scales.[91] My study contributes to comparative ethnic studies, albeit in a somewhat idio-

---

87. Gordon, *Fanon and the Crisis of European Man*, 41–42; cf. Frantz Fanon, *A Dying Colonialism*, trans. Haakon Chevalier (New York: Grove, 1965), chap. 3.

88. Mills, *The Racial Contract*, 24.

89. See, e.g., Leland Saito, *Race and Politics: Asian Americans, Latinos, and Whites in a Los Angeles Suburb* (Urbana: University of Illinois Press, 1998); Claire Kim, *Bitter Fruit: The Politics of Black-Korean Conflict in New York City* (New Haven, CT: Yale University Press, 2000).

90. See, e.g., Evelyn Nakano Glenn, *Unequal Freedom: How Race and Gender Shaped American Citizenship and Labor* (Cambridge, MA: Harvard University Press, 2002); Nicolas De Genova, *Working the Boundaries: Race, Space, and "Illegality" in Mexican Chicago* (Durham, NC: Duke University Press, 2005).

91. See, e.g., Lisa Lowe, *The Intimacies of Four Continents* (Durham, NC: Duke University Press, 2015).

syncratic way. It compares not intertwined histories of racial formations (e.g., ties between maroon and indigenous communities in North America, "coolie" Asians mixing with emancipated Africans in the Caribbean). It rather compares extraordinary modes of racial formation, which—in principle, although not in fact—can pertain to groups located anywhere on the U.S. "field of racial positions."[92] Comparisons of this kind show that groups sharing few other ties have endured similar crises, as I argue with respect to nineteenth-century southeastern Indian removal and twentieth-century Japanese American relocation.

This section is an introduction to my preferred cases of black, Amerindian, and Asian American racial formation, my selected events in the informal constitution of the United States: the civil rights movement, 1830s to 1840s southeastern Amerindian removals, the incarceration of Japanese Americans, and 1960s to 1970s racial empowerment movements. I explain why the next four chapters—one for each case—will take the shape of narratives, exploring the affinities of existential political theory with historically inflected political theory. I classify each event in terms of a certain kind of racial formation and a certain mode of public constitution before outlining the distinctive story of each chapter. The basic idea is that narration is the central activity of my manner of political thinking.

The storyteller and the actor meet at the crossroads of historical narrative and political existence. For Arendt, the actor still caught in the consequences of their action cannot grasp its full meaning; fuller comprehension falls to the storyteller who might, say, work from the "source material" of the actor's own account of themselves.[93] Story is very close to action, the direct experience of which is proto-narrative in structure.[94] Conceptualization, though, is a step removed from the lived experiences out of which storytelling also arises. "No matter how abstract our theories may sound or how consistent our arguments may appear," Arendt claims, "there are incidents and stories behind them which, at least for ourselves, contain in a nutshell the full meaning of whatever we have to say."[95] Theory that decenters lived

---

92. Kim, "The Racial Triangulation of Asian Americans," 106–7.
93. Storytelling, in Arendt's terms, "works" on this material. Arendt, *The Human Condition*, 192.
94. Cf. Paul Ricoeur, *Time and Narrative*, vol. I, trans. Kathleen McLaughlin and David Pellauer (Chicago: University of Chicago Press, 1984), chap. 3.
95. Hannah Arendt, "Action and the Pursuit of Happiness," *Hannah Arendt Papers*, Library of Congress, accessed April 18, 2017, https://memory.loc.gov/cgi-bin/ampage?collId=mharendt&fileName=05/051010/051010page.db&recNum=0, 1–2. See also Arendt, *Between Past and Future*, 14.

experience is not so much overextended as it is disoriented; theory that focuses on an appropriately selected incident, in contrast, can illuminate an entire realm of experience.

This introductory chapter has labored to conceptualize the distinction and relationship between extraordinary and ordinary racial politics. When I describe actual incidents here, I use them as illustrations for points already or also theoretically established. The following chapters do not belabor the construction of abstract theory. They instead push "behind" the concept of extraordinary racial politics into those "incidents" of living experience to which my thought remains bound. When I deal with actual incidents there, I do not primarily use them to exemplify theoretical claims. I instead theorize an event in its immediate situation and its trans-contextual implications.[96] Put otherwise, I bring together existentially inflected and historically inflected political theory for the following reasons.

Historically inflected political theory reminds analytic philosophers of race that history is more than a "grab bag" of examples; history for me is the logic of inquiry into how events have repeatedly constituted the U.S. polity. There is little room for event-driven transformation, which Omi and Winant's concept of racial formation explains (perhaps too well), in Mills's concept of the racial contract, for instance. Mills by no means lacks evidence for his claims, which he supports with an abundance of examples.[97] The problem is that Mills flattens many varieties of evidentiary support into epochal, global generalizations ("theses"). His story, while more fluid than stories told by analytic philosophers, is far more fixed than most histories—for Mills's moral is that nothing has really changed in racial modernity. The illumination of concrete events, I claim, quickly dispels this impression that everything is the same.

Existentially inflected political theory, for its part, reminds historical sociologists of race that lived experience is irreducible to the everyday. The extraordinary moment, which Mills models as an original contract, appears to Omi and Winant as the "big bang" of the racial universe, a naturalistic metaphor for the initial colonization of the Americas.[98] By contrast, racial

---

96. My understanding of the differences between illustration and storytelling is indebted to Lisa Disch, "More Truth Than Fact: Storytelling as Critical Understanding in the Writings of Hannah Arendt," *Political Theory* 21, no. 4 (1993): 687–89.

97. See the paragraph-long sentence within Mills, *The Racial Contract*, 111–13. Other philosophies of race read more like narratives, but still tend to be illustrative, e.g., Sheth, *Toward a Political Philosophy of Race*, 59–61.

98. Omi and Winant, *Racial Formation in the United States*, 115.

subjectivity is explained in terms of the American pragmatist, largely quotidian notion of action.[99] Like critical race theorists in the legal academy, Omi and Winant seek to understand how people of color make sense of everyday realities of race.[100] Popular subjectivities, on their theory, long nourish and support Great Transformations that only emerge and become visible during exceptional periods. My impression is somewhat different: because the political and the social inhabit the same public realm, the ever-present potential for extraordinary events can appear nowhere else but amid ordinary processes.

As one can see in the remarks here, I consider myself to be first and foremost a political theorist. Yet I do not take myself to be applying "universal" theories (coded European or white) to "particular" experiences (marked black, indigenous, or Asian). Political theory concepts are as particularistic as ethnic studies concepts. Twentieth-century European theorists coined "the political," for example, to critique liberalism and totalitarianism, and U.S. political theorists later took up the neologism to critique social scientific notions of "politics."[101] So I plan to resituate Arendt's and Schmitt's concepts of the political within U.S. contexts overlooked by Schmitt and Arendt themselves;[102] these situations, in turn, will expose Schmitt's and Arendt's powers and limits.[103] If we can discern where Arendt and Schmitt are most powerful as interlocutors, and what kinds of "stretching" (to use Fanon's term) are required to overcome their limitations, we will in effect make suggestions as to what is general in and what is particular to their Europe-centered theories.

I propose that public constitution and racial formation are practically indistinguishable in at least four—and likely more—U.S. contexts. All four

---

99. Ibid., 146.

100. See, e.g., Richard Delgado and Jean Stefancic, *Critical Race Theory: An Introduction* (New York: New York University Press, 2001), chap. 3; Robert Chang, "Toward an Asian American Legal Scholarship: Critical Race Theory, Post-Structuralism, and Narrative Space," *California Law Review* 81, no. 5 (1993): 1278–86.

101. Emily Hauptmann, "A Local History of 'the Political,'" *Political Theory* 32, no. 1 (2009): 38.

102. Arendt and Schmitt themselves dealt with racial politics, often in problematic ways. See Kathryn Gines, *Hannah Arendt and the Negro Question* (Bloomington: Indiana University Press, 2014); see also Joseph Bendersky, *Carl Schmitt: Theorist for the Reich* (Princeton, NJ: Princeton University Press, 1983).

103. My methodological problem is similar to the one faced by psychoanalytic Marxists working on U.S. racialization, e.g., Michael Rogin, *Fathers and Children: Andrew Jackson and the Subjugation of the American Indian* (New York: Alfred A. Knopf, 1975); Victor Wolfenstein, *The Victims of Democracy: Malcolm X and the Black Revolution*, rev. ed. (New York: Guilford, 1993).

will test and stretch Arendtian public freedom and Schmittian public order, two categories under which two events can be largely subsumed: the civil rights movement provides paradigmatic instances of Arendt's notion of action, whereas the Japanese internment offers paradigmatic instances of Schmitt's notion of decision. The subsumption of the two remaining events, though, leaves behind substantial remainders: 1960s to 1970s racial empowerment movements approached Arendt's notion of freedom, yet moved away from her critique of enmity; 1830s to 1840s southeastern Amerindian removals fell in line with Schmitt's notion of order, but fell short of friend/enemy intensity.

This selection of events reflects my interests in both citizen-driven, Arendtian and official-driven, Schmittian politics. The chapters on the civil rights movement and racial power movements account for mass movements as the extraordinary politics of racialized civil societies, while the chapters on Japanese American relocations and southeastern Indian removals account for state emergencies as the extraordinary politics of the racial state. Furthermore, I have constellated black, Amerindian, and Asian racial formations because I am interested in pluralizing political theorists' views of U.S. racial politics. Doing so complicates bipolar continuums of black-to-white racial positions that "whiten," "blacken," or just plain overlook Amerindians and especially Asian Americans.[104]

Finally, I contend that these events, while widely accepted as foundational for ethnic studies, have not yet been fully appreciated for their political theoretical significance.[105] In the four subsequent chapters, I make the case for how a "racial formation," a locus of racial conflict in U.S. history, should be understood in terms of "public constitution," an arrangement of power familiar to transatlantic modernity. Introduced under these headings in table 1.1 are additional terms of art, which the chapter outline that follows will unpack.

Chapter 2 interprets the U.S. civil rights movement as an Arendtian moment of re-foundation. If the American Revolution is *the* U.S. constitutional foundation, then the civil rights movement is *the* U.S. constitutional refoundation. Both events put the U.S. citizenry and U.S. racial order on new

---

104. A more comprehensive study of U.S. racial formation would engage more seriously with white, Latina/o, Jewish, and Muslim racializations. This book does not aspire to that level of comprehensiveness.

105. Cf. Patchen Markell, "The Rule of the People: Arendt, *Archê*, and Democracy," *American Political Science Review* 100, no. 1 (2006): 13.

TABLE 1.1 EVENTS OF RACIAL FORMATION AND PUBLIC CONSTITUTION

Chapter	Event	Racial formation	Public constitution
2	Civil rights movement	Black citizenship	Re-foundation
3	Southeast Indian removal	Amerindian placement	Land appropriation
4	Japanese internment	Asian enmity	State of exception
5	Racial power movements	Nonwhite common senses	Judgment

normative foundations. However, citizenship in the first case excludes black identity on the basis of U.S. federalism, whereas citizenship in the second internalizes black difference on the grounds of U.S. nationalism. This is why I assert that the civil rights movement was a revolutionary movement and an extraordinary politics, refuting claims that it was reformist in orientation and normal in character. The movement, albeit ambiguously, authorized black citizenship as a practice of political contestation and a claim of social rights; with equal ambiguity, it de-authorized the southern segregationist order and the white monopolization of U.S. citizenship.

Chapter 3 turns to Schmittian moments of land appropriation—namely, the 1830s to 1840s removals of southeastern Amerindians from their territories east of the Mississippi and their relocations to lands in present-day Oklahoma. Federal-Indian treaties effected a racial and spatial re-placement of southeastern Indians within the U.S. federal system: the United States would racially substitute "civilized" (white) for "savage" (Indian) habits, while the United States would spatially resituate Amerindian polities on bureaucratically governed territories. I center the federal question to challenge contractual and Marxist accounts of these and similar land appropriations. Indigenous consent in the formation of federal-Indian treaties is obscured by Mills-like models that center on consensus among white settler colonists. Furthermore, the logic of territorial ordering evident here is distinct from the logic of land commodification outlined by Marxist theorists.

Chapter 4 continues in the register of state-driven politics, interpreting the Japanese internment in light of the Schmittian state of exception. The national-security state set up two emergency projects to manage purported wartime dangers: Japanese exclusion from the West Coast and their incarceration in camps, as well as Japanese resettlements outside the West Coast and their assimilation into U.S. society. I argue that the first project worked from biologically racist understandings of Japanese enemies, while the second adopted cultural-racial assumptions about Japanese American friends. My account of contradictory wartime policies enacted by multiple officials points to the limits of Schmitt's imagination of unified sovereign power. My account of the state's obsession with "the American way of life," in turn, challenges claims to the effect that sovereign power is constitutively linked to biological life.

Chapter 5 explores 1960s to 1970s black power, red power, and Asian American movements as moments of Arendtian judgment.[106] Strong stances against the *status quo* made it impossible for racial power activists to make recourse to given names and ideologies; they instead decided on their identities and demands along the Arendtian lines of appealing to community sensibilities and common sense. Yet Arendt's understanding of a sense of community common to *the* public, I argue, obscures how various movements judged that (nonwhite) "minority" publics were at odds with the (white) "majority" public. That is not to say, as some scholars of new social movements would, that racial power activists focused on selected issues on behalf of particular constituencies. State appropriations of these movements—including projects of official U.S. multiculturalism—indicate the general, even global scope of their original aspirations.

As a final preliminary, I would admit that I prioritize both race and politics over their potential others. I lack an intersectional theory of race, gender, and class,[107] even where I discuss women and men, wealth and poverty. Likewise, I lack an integrated theory of polity, society, and culture, even where I discuss behavior and norms, values and practices. This is to say that my extraordinary/everyday distinction is internal to racial politics, which is not to say that extraordinary racial politics cannot be either conditioned by everyday gender stratification (e.g., wage differentials) or constitutive of extraordinary class culture (e.g., cultural revolution). Having said that, I would contend that its irreducibly political character makes race especially avail-

---

106. Because the larger project compares black, Amerindian, and Asian racial formations, this chapter excludes Chicano and Puerto Rican movements. See Carlos Muñoz, *Youth, Identity, Power: The Chicano Movement*, rev. ed. (London: Verso, 2007); see also Miguel Melendez, *We Took to the Streets: Fighting for Latino Rights with the Young Lords* (New Brunswick, NJ: Rutgers University Press, 2003).

107. See, e.g., Ange-Marie Hancock, *Solidarity Politics for Millennials: A Guide to Ending the Oppression Olympics* (New York: Palgrave Macmillan, 2011).

able for public constitution throughout the Americas.[108] This availability is especially apparent whenever U.S. racialization rearticulates the U.S. "constitution" as the "life of the city,"[109] as it did in the aftermaths of the Civil War, the Mexican-American War, the Spanish-American War, and September 11, 2001. With these and other events, the interpretation of extraordinary racial politics is the *via regia* into the informal constitution of the United States.[110]

---

108. See Diego Von Vacano, *The Color of Citizenship: Race, Modernity and Latin American/Hispanic Political Thought* (Oxford, UK: Oxford University Press, 2012); see also Charles Mills, *From Race to Class: Essays in White Marxism and Black Radicalism* (Lanham, MD: Rowman and Littlefield, 2003), chap. 6.

109. Aristotle, *"The Politics" and "The Constitutione of Athens,* 107.

110. The "royal road" metaphor is from Sigmund Freud, *The Interpretation of Dreams*, trans. James Strachey (New York: Avon, 1998), 647.

2

Racial Re-foundations and the Rise of the Nation-State

> For if it is true that all thought begins with remembrance, it is also true that no remembrance remains secure unless it is condensed and distilled into a framework of conceptual notions within which it can further exercise itself.
> —HANNAH ARENDT, *On Revolution*

> So it was that, to the Negro, going to jail was no longer a disgrace but a badge of honor. The Revolution of the Negro not only attacked the external cause of his misery, but revealed him to himself. He was *somebody*. He had a sense of *somebodiness*. He was *impatient* to be free.
> —MARTIN LUTHER KING JR., *Why We Can't Wait*

For Derrick Bell, the usual practices of white interest-group politics betrayed the promise of the civil rights movement. Civil rights reform only occurred, Bell argues, when black Americans' interests coincided with Cold War liberals' interests; such reforms were abrogated precisely at the moment black equality threatened entrenched white advantages. *Brown v. Board of Education* and the rollback of school desegregation is the very paradigm of "interest convergence" followed by "racial sacrifice."[1] Bell recalls how, on a day in the 1960s, a Mississippi judge delayed hearing a desegregation case in order to administer a naturalization oath to European immigrants. An attorney for the National Association for the Advancement of Colored People (NAACP) Legal Defense Fund, Bell recognized that the whiteness of these new citizens "made them more acceptable to this country, more a part of it, than [his] black clients would probably ever be."[2]

While Bell rightly reminds us of the limits of legal reform, I would caution that we should not forget the extraordinary achievements of the civil rights

---

1. Derrick Bell, *Silent Covenants: "Brown v. Board of Education" and the Unfulfilled Hopes of Racial Reform* (Oxford, UK: Oxford University Press, 2004), chaps. 5–7.
2. Ibid., 104–5.

movement. I argue that political theorists who accept something like Hannah Arendt's account of revolution must acknowledge this achievement—even if Arendt herself did not. The civil rights movement reset the constitutional foundations of racial conflict: it legitimized contests between racially differentiated citizens (specifically blacks and whites, generally all "races"), whereas the U.S. founding de-legitimized conflicts between racially identified slaves and citizens. Yet more radically, the civil rights movement re-founded U.S. citizenship as a whole: it replaced a federal U.S. citizenship divided by state and monopolized by whiteness with a national U.S. citizenship undivided by state and divided into black and white.

In short, the civil rights movement transformed the U.S. constitutional regime of racial conflict and national citizenship. More generally, I argue that revolutions condition how racial claims will be heard—for instance, either as the claims of legitimate contestants or as the claims of illegitimate "complainers"—in postrevolutionary publics. As stated in Chapter 1, I theorize particular moments of racial formation as paradigmatic modes of public constitution. Our first of four events concerns how the civil rights movement as a new trajectory for black citizenship acquires the general significance of constitutional re-foundation. This event raises an Arendtian set of concerns with revolution.

For Arendt, constitutional foundation aims to create a lasting republic for the sake of public freedom. Like their eighteenth-century French counterparts, American revolutionaries never questioned the need for "a constitution to lay down the boundaries of the new political realm and define the rules within it . . . so that their own 'revolutionary' spirit could survive the actual end of the revolution."[3] Arendt faults French revolutionaries for abandoning their original aim of popular government to pursue a sentimental, not to mention bloody, solution to "the social question" of poverty. By contrast, Arendt praises American revolutionaries for remaining faithful to the aim of establishing a new order of the ages. She does not blame them for ignoring their own social question of slavery, the "hypocrisy of the United States" in "its very foundations," as Kathryn Gines puts it.[4] What is more, Arendt implies—idiosyncratically, to say the least—that race did not enter into the U.S. constitution.

---

3. Arendt, *On Revolution*, 117.
4. Gines, *Hannah Arendt and the Negro Question*, 66. As discussed in Chapter 5, Arendt dismisses charges of hypocrisy as inappropriate to political life.

Given this line of critique, it might seem counterintuitive to use Arendt to think black social conditions and black practices of freedom together. The primary reason for doing so is that the revolutionary aspects of the civil rights movement appear starkly in light of Arendt's own criteria for revolutionary action. To avoid Arendt's own framing of the civil rights movement as an instance of civil disobedience, however, we must blur Arendt's bright-line distinctions between social behavior and political action, social interest and political freedom.[5] We must work against Arendt's tendency to claim that the United States was founded "once and for all," her imagination of an unrepeatable act that legally constituted a citizenry. A corrective here is Danielle Allen's reminder that the U.S. constitution encompasses unspoken norms and informal habits of citizenship. "If one takes 'constitution' in this broad sense," says Allen, "the United States has had several foundings"—including the women's suffrage movement and the civil rights movement.[6]

I claim, on basically Arendtian grounds, that if the American Revolution is *the* constitutional foundation, the civil rights movement is *the* constitutional re-foundation. Re-founders re-cast white/black division as an open conflict over segregated conditions—a racial division that "original" founders cast as a barely disguised "state of war." Re-founders did so by authorizing conflicts between social divisions differently. The founding legitimated conflicts between northern and southern states, while it de-legitimated conflicts between black slaves and white citizens. U.S. founders, at a minimum, allowed southern masters to rule over "their" slaves and, at a maximum, authorized state governments to police enslaved populations. As a result, black American challenges to enslavement often took the form of violent assaults against the repressive state apparatus.

While in some ways only the consummation of post–World War II trajectories of racial reform, the civil rights movement also constituted a new U.S. racial foundation. Re-foundation legitimated conflicts initiated by black citizens who, in many ways, had to self-authorize acts of enfranchisement; concomitantly, it de-legitimated conflicts between federal and state governments over conditions of racial segregation. U.S. re-founders, at a minimum, confronted the state government policing of nonviolent black protest and, at

---

5. See Danielle Allen, "Invisible Citizens: Political Exclusion and Domination in Arendt and Ellison," in *Nomos XLVI: Political Exclusion and Domination*, ed. Stephen Macedo and Melissa Williams (New York: New York University Press, 2005), 32.

6. Allen, *Talking to Strangers*, 6–7.

a maximum, integrated subaltern participation in the official process of racial formation. Omi and Winant's "Great Transformation" expanded the terrain of civil contestation, on which racially organized movements could make demands to a somewhat less-repressive state.[7]

This broadening of what counts as a legitimate racial claim has extended from the formal institutions of the state into quotidian, emotional, and cultural life. It is in this respect the "politicization of the social,"[8] the obverse of what Arendt might call "the socialization of the political." As we will see, Arendt considers "the rise of the social" to be the illegitimate entrance of economic processes and social interests into public life.[9] What Arendt misses, though, is that the black American articulation of civil rights *as* social rights has been an existential achievement or, as the King epigraph puts it, a revolutionary experience of "somebodiness." An entrance of black identifications into the official public (a socialization of the political) was an extension of political contest into everyday lifeworlds (a politicization of the social): the re-founding confronted "the social question" of blackness and whiteness disavowed by the founding. Re-foundation de-authorized a federal compromise on slavery/segregation and newly authorized a national conception of citizenship in the same gesture.

Section I of this chapter positions slaves in the revolutionary period as racial enemies of southern state governments. I account for how this state-level relationship made its way into the federal constitution, which represented slavery in terms of regional interests. Section II shows that civil rights movement activism created spaces of contest where dominative relationships had prevailed in segregated states. Next I turn to movement activity at the federal level, where the Supreme Court conjoined civil rights to racial conditions. Both on the ground and in the courts, the civil rights movement intervened into a trajectory of black membership—a long-running trajectory connecting the three-fifths compromise to postbellum reconstruction amendments to "Jim Crow" segregation. A consequence of this event is that the re-founding of black citizenship is now distinguishable from the anti-black enmity of the founding.

---

7. Omi and Winant, *Racial Formation in the United States*, 140–44; cf. Antonio Gramsci, *Selections from the Prison Notebooks*, trans. Quintin Hoare and Geoffrey Nowell Smith (New York: International, 1971), 229–39.

8. Omi and Winant, *Racial Formation in the United States*, 150–54.

9. Arendt, *The Human Condition*, 38–49, 28.

Section I: The Racial and Federal Foundations of Slavery

This section examines the constitutional founding of the United States primarily to establish a point of contrast to the civil rights movement. My thesis, to reiterate, is that the civil rights movement "internalized" racial division and legitimized racial conflict in a revolutionary manner; building toward that conclusion, I contend in this section that U.S. founders "externalized" racial division and legitimized regional conflict in a no less revolutionary fashion. Like Arendt's, my concept of foundation concerns the informal and formal constitution of authority. That said, my understanding of the U.S. founding is more attuned than Arendt's to the conflicts surrounding slavery at both state and federal levels. My Arendtian account of the U.S. revolution therefore centers on the problem of legitimating some forms of conflict, while delegitimizing others—all in the name of order and stability.

Racial Enmity in Slave States

A "social question" for Arendt is why American revolutionaries were underwhelmed by the suffering of slaves, even as their counterparts in France were overwhelmed by the suffering of poor people. In contrast to *les malheureux* in France, the (free) poor in America were not miserable on account of their social condition. Social condition, however, did ensure that the American poor played little part in public affairs. That John Adams seemed more concerned with the poor's nonparticipation than with the slave's suffering strikes Arendt as "very strange indeed," for "the absence of the social question from the American scene was, after all, quite deceptive.... [A]bject and degrading misery was present everywhere in the form of slavery." Arendt infers that "slavery carries an obscurity even blacker than the obscurity of poverty; the slave, not the poor man, was 'wholly overlooked.'"[10]

Arendt claims that slavery, insofar as it concerned American revolutionaries at all, was a problem of freedom. "For if Jefferson, and others to a lesser degree, were aware of the primordial crime upon which the fabric of American society rested," she writes, "they did so because they were convinced of the incompatibility of the institution of slavery with the foundation of freedom."[11]

---

10. Arendt, *On Revolution*, 60–61. The choice of "blacker" speaks to the racial character of slavery.
11. Ibid., 61.

What Arendt overlooks, with decisive consequences for her understanding of the social question, is that the slave is an enemy, as in Jefferson's *Notes on the State of Virginia*.[12] My introduction of Schmittian dynamics into Arendtian constitutionalism suggests that U.S. founders viewed slavery as a peculiar kind of social problem—one of controlling racial violence and policing racial order.

Thomas Jefferson, a slaveholder who never argued for the justice of slavery, denies that (what he took to be) the white and black races had equal capacities. He confesses, on the one hand, "I tremble for my country when I reflect that God is just: that his natural justice cannot sleep for ever [*sic*]."[13] On the other hand, he obsessively searches out the signs of racial difference in black "colour, figure, and hair," in their "[requiring] less sleep," "more ardent [desire] after their female," and transient grief. As for mental and moral capacities, Jefferson could not "find that a black had uttered a thought above the level of plain narration" and had "never seen even an elementary trait of painting or sculpture" fashioned by black hands.[14]

Maybe Jefferson's equal hostility toward slavery and blacks is not all that paradoxical. For one thing, Jefferson is less sure that blacks are "naturally inferior" than he is sure that blacks are "natural enemies."[15] To the objection that Virginia should incorporate emancipated blacks, Jefferson answers that "deep rooted prejudices entertained by whites; ten thousand recollections, by the blacks, of the injuries they have sustained; new provocations; the real distinctions that nature has made; and many other circumstances, will divide us into parties, and produce convulsions which will probably never end but in the extermination of the one or the other race."[16] Blending natural historical discourses of "morphology" with English historical discourses of "race war,"[17] Jefferson recommends that the emancipation of Virginian slaves be followed by their colonization abroad.

---

12. As we now know, Jefferson was intimately involved with his slave Sally Hemings. Fred Lee, "Reconsidering the Jefferson-Hemings Relationship: Nationalist Historiography without Nationalist Heroes, Racial Sexuality without Racial Significance," *Political Research Quarterly* 66, no. 3 (2013): 500–515.

13. Thomas Jefferson, *Notes on the State of Virginia* (Chapel Hill: University of North Carolina Press, 1955), 163.

14. Ibid., 138–40.

15. Peter Onuf, "'To Declare Them a Free and Independent People': Race, Slavery, and National Identity in Jefferson's Thought," *Journal of the Early Republic* 18, no. 1 (1998): 35.

16. Jefferson, *Notes on the State of Virginia*, 138.

17. Ladelle McWhorter, *Racism and Sexual Oppression in Anglo-America: A Genealogy* (Bloomington: Indiana University Press, 2009), 87–95.

Jefferson cannot imagine a civil relationship of former slaves and masters because he can only envision black agency as a capacity for collective violence. The fantasized "black body" fixed before the white gaze is both below capacity and dangerously violent. In the grip of such fantasies, Jefferson worries that freed blacks could not achieve the self-control required of whites in a republican government.[18] His foreclosure of the possibility of black political membership and his perception of black mental and physical difference (beauty, smell, sexual desire, sensation, imagination, reflection, etc.) mutually reinforce, but do not necessitate, one another. Indeed, in Jefferson's time and place, claims of black inferiority played a relatively minor role for white defenses of slavery.[19] Natural enmity predominates over natural difference.

The enslaved as a natural enemy is an enemy excluded contrary to natural rights to liberty and equality. Slavery is an unnatural and uncivil institution, if not already a racial and civil war. Jefferson imagines "with what execrations should the statesman be loaded, who permitting one half of the citizens thus to trample on the rights of the other, transforms these into despots, and these into enemies, destroys the morals of the one part, and the amor patriae of the other."[20] Whether or not Jefferson intends "citizens" to be ironical, his re-counting of citizenship ("one half") encodes the racialized division that dirempts the public.[21] The violent uprising of the paradoxical enemy-citizen would be legitimate if God's justice cannot authorize the free/slave division of the Virginian people.

An enemy need be neither subhuman nor unjust—as Carl Schmitt might say, the otherness of the enemy is existential, not normative. The enemy is whom the friend sees as "something different and alien" in the sense that "one fighting collectivity of people confronts a similar collectivity."[22] For Jefferson, blacks are outside of even the potential sphere of friendship, but do

---

18. Ronald Takaki, *Iron Cages: Race and Culture in 19th-Century America*, rev. ed. (Oxford, UK: Oxford University Press, 2000), 42–55.

19. Winthrop Jordan, *White over Black: American Attitudes toward the Negro, 1550–1812* (Chapel Hill: University of North Carolina Press, 1968), 454–56.

20. Jefferson, *Notes on the State of Virginia*, 162–63.

21. It would be most ironic if Jefferson meant "citizen" to be unironic: Virginian citizenship in his time was hierarchically differentiated. In Loudon County, Virginia, between the revolutionary and civil wars, free blacks could not vote, and white men who did not own property could not vote until 1852. Brenda Stevenson, *Life in Black and White: Family and Community in the Slave South* (Oxford, UK: Oxford University Press, 1996), 34, 297.

22. Schmitt, *The Concept of the Political*, 27–28.

not fall under one of Schmitt's several specifications of enmity, all of which are rooted in European history and international law.[23]

As my chapter on the Japanese internment will most clearly show, the "racial enemy" appears through the markers of race as the antagonist to the friend. The racial friend/enemy relationship is suffused with the perceived threat of violence between racially identified groupings. The exploitation of slave labor—whether household or plantation in scale—demonstrates that friends and enemies can be economically associated, even as they are necessarily politically disassociated. A racial enmity premised on economic integration is a case of internal enmity or inclusive-exclusion. As Falguni Sheth puts it, the conjuring of "internal enemies" is used to "regulate potentially 'unruly' or threatening populations by re-orienting other subpopulations to understand them as a threat to 'themselves.'"[24]

The decision on racial enmity, in other words, is constitutive of the very problems of social order and public peace to which it purports to be merely responding. Events like Bacon's Rebellion—a 1676 event in which both blacks and whites participated—convinced Virginian planters that "the danger from slaves" was "less than that which the colony had faced from its restive and armed freedmen."[25] Thereafter, planters attempted to bring the European "rabble" within the purview of whiteness, which became a "cross-class alliance" between yeoman farmers and large plantation owners.[26] An increase in the importation of slaves correlated to a decrease in the importation of servants, while the tightening of slave restrictions corresponded to the loosening of restrictions placed on servants.[27] Such policies displaced potentially violent class conflict into a newly fortified divide of free white and black slave.

The irony of a white friendship that depends on the constitutive outside of black enemies is that the slave is a perpetual, internalized danger for a southern way of life. Anxieties over slave rebellions would be ongoing in

---

23. For a discussion of perpetual enemies, just enemies, and the enemies of humanity in Schmitt's work, see Julia Lupton, "Shylock between Exception and Emancipation: Shakespeare, Schmitt, Arendt," *Journal for Cultural and Religious Theory* 8, no. 3 (2007): 45–46.

24. Sheth, *Toward a Political Philosophy of Race*, 116.

25. Edmund Morgan, "Slavery and Freedom: The American Paradox," *Journal of American History* 59, no. 1 (1972): 26. An extended version of this argument is Edmund Morgan, *American Slavery, American Freedom: The Ordeal of Colonial Virginia* (New York: Norton, 1975), chap. 15.

26. Olson, *The Abolition of White Democracy*, 36–37.

27. Morgan, "Slavery and Freedom," 28.

antebellum Virginia. The southern reaction to the Haitian Revolution is encapsulated in the 1801–1805 spate of state legislation that aimed at greater surveillance and control of slaves; free and educated blacks, who had played leading roles in the Haitian Revolution, were seen as particularly dangerous.[28] The southern states policed and crushed violent slave rebellions just as masters in small households or large plantations disciplined and punished rebellious slaves. Across the public/private divide, or—in a word—socially, southern elites maintained a racial order of inclusive-exclusion.

The racial enemy fell inside the slave states' realm of sovereignty, which the constitutional founding attenuated more than abolished. It is true that James Madison, in the debates on constitutional ratification, insists that the peace and safety of the union cannot be sacrificed so that the states might "be arrayed with certain dignities and attributes of sovereignty" (the sovereignty of Westphalian nation-states). Yet, assuaging fears of centralized authority "under the proposed Constitution," Madison guarantees that states will retain "a very extensive portion of active sovereignty."[29] States would continue to maintain "the ordinary course of affairs" for the sake of "the internal order, improvement, and prosperity of the state."[30] This implied authority to distinguish "ordinary" affairs from extraordinary situations means state governments will have certain powers of the nation-state.

Our Schmittian look at the southern racial order complicates Arendt's account of the nonrevolutionary impact of slavery on the American Revolution. The social question did not divide revolutionaries into violent factions in the United States, as it may have in France.[31] What it did, rather, was divide state populations into potentially violent groupings of blacks and whites. The U.S. social question was the constitutional authorization of states to decide on what counted as public (dis)order. Black slaves would be sources of existential threat and identitarian dependence for white southerners. This figuration of the internal enemy draws out the antagonism of Arendt's metaphor of the "overlooked" slave.

---

28. Tim Matthewson, "Jefferson and the Non-Recognition of Haiti," *Proceedings of the American Philosophical Society* 140, no. 1 (1996): 25. It should be noted, however, that Toussaint L'Ouverture had little formal education. See C.L.R. James, *The Black Jacobins: Toussaint L'Ouverture and the San Domingo Revolution*, rev. ed. (New York: Vintage, 1989), 91.

29. Alexander Hamilton, John Jay, and James Madison, "No. 45," in *The Federalist Papers*, ed. Clinton Rossiter (New York: Signet, 1999), 289–90.

30. Ibid., 293. A slave-holding society, for example, might declare that a slave rebellion is an exceptional situation to maintain a normal situation of slave subordination.

31. Arendt, *On Revolution*, 88–90.

Arendt privatizes U.S. slavery, while I have been "socializing" it. As Arendt observes, the Greek slave was without the status of citizen, yet within the walls of the *polis*, that is, inside of the private realm of violence and outside of the public realm of persuasion.[32] The American slave was more ambiguously situated because the United States has never admitted of a clear public/private divide. U.S. slavery had a public meaning insofar as slaves fell inside of the social realm of domination, yet outside of the political realm of equality or, put equivalently, insofar as the southern racial order was a part of the overall U.S. public. It is untenable to hold, then, that American revolutionaries "founded a completely new body politic without violence and with the help of a constitution."[33] Arendt can only hold that the polity was founded "without violence" if she refers to the "within" of the political rather than the "within" of the public. The federal constitution institutionalized the violence of southern slavery.

Regional Division in the Federal Constitution

The federal division of power for Arendt made the U.S. republic "utterly unlike the European nation-states," a polity not beholden to "the idea that when the chips were down diversity must be sacrificed to the 'union sacrée' of the nation."[34] Following Montesquieu, the constitutional framers designed a system of checks and balances to ensure that "the power neither of the union nor of its parts, the duly constituted states, would decrease or destroy one another."[35] Much of Arendt's claim of the United States' uniqueness turns on this arrangement of federal power and state power—a pluralistic arrangement whose popular acceptance Arendt tends to overstate.[36] Moreover, as our first look at slavery has shown, the founding preserved state-level constitutions of whiteness as citizenship over and against blackness as danger.

The federal level of this inclusive-exclusion concerns how the founding institutionalized slave-state interests as an object of congressional representation. This constitutional arrangement consisted in a complex constellation of republican and federal principles. Reading James Madison's contributions

---

32. Ibid., 104.
33. Arendt, *Between Past and Future*, 140.
34. Hannah Arendt, *Responsibility and Judgment*, ed. Jerome Kohn (New York: Schocken, 2003), 4.
35. Arendt, *On Revolution*, 142; see also 162.
36. For instance, anti-federalists resisted, sometimes violently, the authority claimed by the federalists in the postrevolutionary era. Frank, *Constituent Moments*, 93–95.

to the Federalist Papers, I claim that the deadlock over the representation of slave-state interests was resolved precisely by institutionalizing sectional contests over slavery. The constitutionalizing of this conflict is a characteristically liberal democratic process of (de)legitimizing certain kinds of social contestation.

Slavery became a constitutional controversy in the debate over representation in the House of Representatives. The House, according to Madison, was a republican rather than a democratic institution in that "the people" would be represented rather than assemble "in person" there.[37] The promise of republicanism is contrasted to the powerlessness of democracies "to break and control the violence of faction . . . under which popular governments everywhere have perished."[38] Republicanism of the Madisonian variety resides in Article I, whose enumeration of offices can be understood to contain factional conflict within the legislative arena. Article I also has an affinity with the more robust republicanism of Machiavelli's argument that Rome owed its stability to the institutionalized conflict between patrician and plebian. Counterintuitively, Machiavelli taught that Rome in fact endured because of, not in spite of, class divisions.[39]

Like Machiavelli, Madison sought to legitimate intractable conflicts between representatives of enduring social divisions. On the other hand, Madison's usage of "faction" called into question the United States' division into fixed status orders of the Roman variety. "Faction" more flexibly designates a group of citizens "united and actuated by some common impulse of passion, or of interest, *adverse to* the rights of other citizens, or to the permanent and aggregate interests of the community."[40] Factions defined by adversarial relations are by definition related by potential conflicts. Madison opines that conflict, which arises most commonly from "the various and unequal distribution of property," cannot be eliminated without destroying freedom and diversity.[41] Hence the plan is to control rather than eradicate conflicts endemic to popular governments. The legitimation of adversarial conflict is the alternative to the diremptions of friend/enemy antagonism that haunted Madison, Jefferson, and other founders' visions of the United States as an extended republic.

---

37. Hamilton et al., "No. 14," in Rossiter, *Federalist Papers*, 95.
38. Hamilton et al., "No. 10," in ibid., 71–72.
39. Machiavelli, *Discourses on Livy*, bk. I, chaps. 4–6; cf. Arendt, *On Revolution*, 180.
40. Madison "No. 10," 72, italics added.
41. Ibid., 74.

Adversarial conflict abounded under conditions of federalist hegemony at the Philadelphia Convention. There the issue of representing large and small states weighed heavily, as did questions of protecting property against confiscation and shielding creditors against debt suspension.[42] Yet Madison realized that the division most inundated with conflict was between southern and northern states, two regions primarily differentiated in terms of slavery.[43] A balance of federal and national principles could manage this conflict without resorting to a unitary national government. "National" meant power in the federal government unmediated by membership in a state; "federal," by contrast, meant power in the federal government as a member of a state.[44] To use Madison's terms, the House of Representatives was both republican and national. Even in the national legislature, though, House rules of apportionment would institutionalize federal conflicts over slavery.

The Philadelphia Convention debate over House apportionment turned on the question of what exactly the new government would represent. One side contended that only the free population should count in the distribution of seats because government existed to represent rights-bearing persons. So William Patterson of New Jersey wanted to know "if Negroes are not represented in the States to which they belong, why [they should] be represented in the Genl. Gov."[45] The other side claimed that the enslaved population should also count because government existed to preserve property, and property owners had the highest stake in government. For John Rutledge of South Carolina, the point was not to represent slaves, but to represent the free man's wealth in the same proportion as it would be taxed.[46] This disagreement between Madisonian factions—roughly, northern and southern states—structured the three-fifths compromise, according to which one slave would be equivalent to three-fifths of a free person for purposes of federal apportionment and direct taxation.

---

42. Class conflict in the revolutionary period—e.g., populist financial policies of state legislatures—disconcerted the founders. Gordon Wood, *Creation of the American Republic, 1776–1787* (Chapel Hill: University of North Carolina Press, 1969), 403–9.

43. James Madison, "June 30, 1787," in *Records of the Federal Convention of 1787*, vol. I, ed. Max Farrand, rev. ed. (New Haven, CT: Yale University Press, 1966), 486.

44. Hamilton et al., "No. 46," in Rossiter, *Federalist Papers*, 240.

45. James Madison, "July 9, 1787," in Farrand, *Records of the Federal Convention of 1787*, vol. I, 561.

46. James Madison, "August 8, 1787," in *Records of the Federal Convention of 1787*, vol. II, ed. Max Farrand, rev. ed. (New Haven, CT: Yale University Press, 1966), 223.

Madison himself casts the three-fifths ratio as a compromise of the positions that government exists to protect personal rights and that it exists to protect private property. Asking his northern audience to adopt the standpoint of "our Southern brethren," he reassures them that "the reasoning which an advocate for the Southern interests might employ... fully reconciles me to the scale of representation which the convention has established."[47] Madison's hypothetical southerner avers that if one accepts that the object of taxation is wealth and that the object of representation is rights, the same ratio should apply to taxation and representation. The slave, on this reasoning, is both property and person. In his forced labor for the master, the slave (like any other "irrational animal") is regarded as property, yet in being protected from violence (in rare cases, even against the master) and held accountable for crimes, the slave is "regarded by the law as a member of society."[48] A spirit of reciprocity infuses the southerner's explanation of why disenfranchised slaves should be represented: every state has inhabitants who are legally denied the right to vote but who will be included in the apportionment of House seats.

Although differences of constitutional interpretation spurred regional conflict in the years to come—especially over the westward expansion of slavery—the founders did not *politically* question the existence of slavery.[49] For his part, Madison avers that southern and northern states are parties to a reasonable disagreement: "Could it be reasonable to expect that the Southern States would concur in a system which considered their slaves in some degree as men when burdens were to be imposed [in taxation], but refused to consider them in the same when advantages were to be conferred [in representation]"?[50] His interest-based reasoning disavowed the racial enmity that could be represented in neither monetary value nor congressional seats. What could be represented within Congress, as well as other channels of bargaining and compromise, was the southern interest in slavery.

As the three-fifths compromise involves no rational calculation, Madison can only offer the fundamental "miscount" of political exclusion via

---

47. Hamilton et al., "No. 54," in Rossiter, *Federalist Papers*, 337–38.
48. Ibid., 334.
49. Most objections to slavery were ethical-humanitarian. Governor Morris's attack on slavery as "the most prominent feature of the aristocratic countenance of the proposed Constitution" is an exception. James Madison, "August 8, 1787," in Farrand, *Records of the Federal Convention of 1787*, vol. II, 222. See also Donald Robinson, *Slavery in the Structure of American Politics, 1765–1820* (New York: Harcourt Brace Jovanovich, 1970), 245.
50. Madison, "No. 54," 335.

social inclusion.⁵¹ Exceptions to the rule that others without the vote would count as full inhabitants, slaves were subjected to the exceptional rule of the three-fifths ratio: no other "others" (e.g., women) counted as a fraction of a person and no other forms of "property" (e.g., land) counted for the apportionment. (With rights enjoyed differentially from state to state, free blacks were an exception to this exception; they occupied an interstitial position created by the legal slippage of free/slave into white/black that happened in most colonies around the late seventeenth century.)⁵² Slaves, in section 2 of Article I, would be nationally represented as "all other Persons." This circumlocution, in part expressing the founders' preference for the terms "people" and "persons" to "citizens" and "races," bore the traces of a social domination not stated within the constitutional text, but which for this reason was no less lodged in U.S. foundations.

We are beginning to discern the federal-republican articulation of the social question as the southern interest of maintaining racial order. American slavery, in its narrowly economic aspect, may have been "above all a labor system."⁵³ At a deeper level, though, slaves have been utilized across global-historical contexts—as laborers, retainers, concubines, soldiers, tutors, and so on—only on the condition of their natal alienation. A "genealogical isolate," the slave in Orlando Patterson's formulation is "denied all claims on, and obligations to, his parents and living blood relations" and, "by extension, all such claims and obligations on his more remote ancestors and descendants."⁵⁴ The American configuration of social integration into white households (fictive kinships) amounts to the political exclusion of "the permanent enemy on the inside."⁵⁵ Such internal enemies appear at the margins of the political realm in the guise of violent threats in the states and the preeminent population of the nation.

---

51. Cf. Jacques Rancière, *Disagreement: Politics and Philosophy*, trans. Julie Rose (Minneapolis: University of Minnesota Press, 1999), 6.

52. Slavery was a racial institution at the time of the founding because, first, while not all blacks were slaves, all slaves were black, and, second, while not all whites were free, all whites were not slaves. See Cheryl Harris, "Whiteness as Property," in *Critical Race Theory: The Key Writings That Formed the Movement*, ed. Kimberlé Crenshaw, Neil Gotanda, Gary Peller, and Kendall Thomas (New York: New Press, 1995), 278.

53. Kenneth Stampp, *The Peculiar Institution: Slavery in the Ante-Bellum South* (New York: Alfred A. Knopf, 1956), 34.

54. Orlando Patterson, *Slavery and Social Death: A Comparative Study* (Cambridge, MA: Harvard University Press, 1982), 5.

55. Ibid., 39.

While they were the inclusively excluded population par excellence, the enslaved were not the only population of the U.S. founding. "The people" themselves were treated like a population to be managed in the one representative per 30,000 inhabitants ratio of House apportionment. This normal norm, along with the exceptional three-fifths norm, prompted the constitutional provision for the decennial census. Early censuses tellingly included race questions, yet excluded occupational questions; in fact, every U.S. census has asked questions about racial identity. Congress rejected proposals—including that of James Madison—to introduce categories like agriculture, manufacture, and commerce into the 1790 and 1800 censuses. Technical issues aside (e.g., some farmers were also traders), critics charged that such changes would encourage competition among an artificially divided population.[56] This extension of the Madisonian legitimation of factionalization, they were saying in so many words, would disrupt the supposed harmony of a white republican society.[57]

Counting occupational divisions would have legitimated class conflict in the same way that counting federal divisions actually legitimated state conflict. Racial divisions of the national population, by contrast, authorized states to compete for House seats on a regional basis and, bluntly put, rewarded plantation owners for "growing" their enslaved populations. Counting state populations and counting racial populations had these contrary effects, for racial divisions de-legitimated conflict between the politically included and excluded, whereas state divisions legitimated conflict between only the politically included (whites). U.S. federalism authorized states to manage their racial conflicts and, in the same gesture, institutionalized racial divisions as population categories ("others" and slaves).[58]

By now, Madison's definition of "national" as unmediated power in the federal government looks more complicated than it did at first glance. The Madisonian nation, as Arendt would point out, carries few of its nineteenth-century connotations of common descent, culture, and history. However, the founding of "the people" as variously represented populations brings the

---

56. Melissa Nobles, *Shades of Citizenship: Race and the Census in Modern Politics* (Stanford, CA: Stanford University Press, 2000), 29–30.

57. Kenneth Prewitt, "Immigrants and the Changing Categories of Race," in *Transforming Politics, Transforming America*, ed. Taeku Lee, S. Karthick Ramakrishnan, and Ricardo Ramirez (Charlottesville: University of Virginia Press, 2006), 20.

58. The first national census of 1790 categorized the U.S. population in these ways: 1. Free White Males over sixteen, 2. Free White Males under sixteen, 3. Free White Females, 4. All Other [read: not white] Free Persons (~1%), and 5. Slaves (~10%). See Nobles, *Shades of Citizenship*, 28.

social and the nation together in Arendt's senses of the terms. The social is synonymous with the nation when Arendt writes that the social's "political form of organization is called 'nation.'"[59] The nation purports to run the national economy on behalf of its members, whom the social stratifies according to the opinions of "polite society."[60] Whether inflected as economy or ranking, the social is the place of discriminating valuations. The social hierarchizes identities along a variety of consistent or contradictory measures (e.g., race, class, gender, sexuality) and (pre)occupies the public realm with the production, exchange, and consumption of goods.

Arendt presents the problem of poverty in the French Revolution as an episode in "the rise of the social," which—as Kirstie McClure reads it—is an "account of the emergence of 'the modern age' as a distinctive historical epoch."[61] I have presented the problem of slavery in the American Revolution as another. Surely, as Arendt argues, the social question turned postrevolutionary U.S. politics away from participatory citizenship and toward private interests.[62] It is even more the case that the founders established an adversarial system for the legitimation of certain kinds of social conflict (state based, but not race or class based). It is a short step from eighteenth-century Madisonian republicanism to twentieth-century American interest-group liberalism. Madison himself admitted that rule of a few nationally minded representatives—one of the primary methods of controlling and checking factions—necessitated the "total exclusion of the people in their collective capacity from any share" of governance.[63]

Section II: The Racial and National Re-foundation of Citizenship

The constitutional re-founding, then, perforce organized the many outside of the representational apparatus instituted by the constitutional founding. This section demonstrates how the re-founding not only authorized black contestations of southern segregation, but also legitimized racial conflict

---

59. Arendt, *The Human Condition*, 29.
60. Ibid., 41. Critics have argued that Arendt's account of the social as the public provision of bodily needs and the social as the discriminations of polite society is not well put together; see, e.g., Pitkin, *The Attack of the Blob*, chap. 1. My simple point is that these are the two faces of the phenomenon for Arendt, not two entailments of a logically consistent concept.
61. Kirstie McClure, "The Social Question, Again," *Graduate Faculty Philosophy Journal* 28, no. 1 (2007): 90.
62. Arendt, *On Revolution*, 128–29, 134.
63. Hamilton et al., "No. 63," in Rossiter, *Federalist Papers*, 385.

throughout the U.S. polity. Put another way, the civil rights movement rearticulated black citizenship and, in this manner, re-founded U.S. citizenship. I claim that these achievements were revolutionary in the Arendtian sense of establishing constitutional authority as well as national in the Arendtian sense of socially inflected membership, contesting Arendt's own account of the movement as a case of interest-group and insufficiently federal politics. In this section, I exploit the gap between Arendt's concepts, which I mostly rework, and Arendt's judgments, which I largely reject.

Racial Contest in Segregated States

Arendt appreciated, although only partially, the movement's "civil disobedience": "We are dealing here with organized minorities that are too important, not merely in numbers, but in *quality of opinion*, to be safely disregarded."[64] As a republican thinker, Arendt is more concerned with the durability of the public realm than with normative or legal justifications of so-called disobedience. For she conceives of the law as a stabilizing element for modern republics rather than, say, a sovereign command that citizen-subjects ought to obey. Her real concern is that constitutional authority is undergoing a crisis of endurance. It is as if an undercurrent of anxiety draws Arendt toward the comforting conclusion that civil disobedience is "the latest form of voluntary association" in the United States and "thus quite in tune with the oldest traditions of the country."[65]

Arendt was not alone in worrying that antisegregation protests, like their antiwar counterparts, followed traditional authority and eroded legal authority at the same time. Martin Luther King Jr. in his "Letter from Birmingham Jail" also expressed a republican concern with preserving the authority of the U.S. founding. Yet King triangulates "the new" of the civil rights movement with constitutional authority and direct action in ways that might have exacerbated Arendt's anxieties.[66] Following King, I claim that the civil rights movement was far more than an example of what Arendt calls "voluntary association," but rather an instance of revolutionary politics. Our turn

---

64. Arendt, *Crises of the Republic*, 76, italics original.
65. Ibid., 96.
66. "Direct action" refers to mass-mobilization techniques such as boycotts, sit-ins, and demonstrations. These contrasted with NAACP efforts to win court cases like *Brown v. Board*. Aldon Morris, *The Origins of the Civil Rights Movement: Black Communities Organizing for Change* (New York: Free Press, 1984), 35–37.

to King will disclose a mass mobilization against antiblack racism that sets into motion the re-foundation of the entire U.S. public.

To isolate one moment of this movement: in April 1963, Birmingham police arrested King for violating a state-level court injunction against sit-ins and demonstrations led by the Southern Christian Leadership Conference. Eight white Alabama clergymen had recently published an open letter in a local paper accusing recent movement protests of being unwise, untimely, and partially directed by outside agitators. King responded with his letter, published first as a pamphlet and reprinted later in several national periodicals. Though disappointed in the lack of solidarity shown by white moderates, King saves his harshest criticisms for the southern clergy. He warns that "if the church of today does not recapture the sacrificial spirit of the early church, it will . . . be dismissed as an irrelevant social club with no meaning for the twentieth century." So he commends those "noble souls from the ranks of organized religion [who] have broken loose from the paralyzing chains of conformity and joined us as active partners in the struggle for freedom."[67]

Resonating with Arendt and other critics of mass society, King opposes the "innumerable and various rules" regulating the social conformist to the "spontaneous action" of the political agonist.[68] Politics for King, however, transpires on the very social terrain that encompasses both public and private life. King thereby blurs the line between household and polity in a manner familiar to all new social movements. For instance, much like the sinners and saints of a traditional black sermon,[69] the familial members of the letter—fathers and mothers, sons and daughters, brothers and sisters, husbands and wives—signify public relationships:

> When you have seen vicious mobs lynch your mothers and fathers at will and drown your sisters and brothers at whim; when you have seen hate filled policemen curse, kick, brutalize and even kill your black brothers and sisters with impunity; when you see the vast majority of

---

67. Martin Luther King Jr., "Letter from Birmingham Jail," in *Why We Can't Wait* (New York: Penguin, 1964), 92.

68. Arendt, *The Human Condition*, 40. Many nineteenth- and twentieth-century thinkers could be mentioned here: De Tocqueville, John Stuart Mill, Nietzsche, Ortega y Gasset, David Riesman, to name a few.

69. For a precise analogy between the "Letter" and the traditional black sermon, see Wesley Mott, "The Rhetoric of Martin Luther King Jr.: Letter from Birmingham Jail," *Pylon* 36, no. 4 (1975): 413.

your twenty million Negro brothers smothering in an airtight cage of poverty in the midst of an affluent society; when you . . . see the depressing clouds of inferiority begin to form in [your daughter's] little mental sky, and see her begin to distort her little personality by unconsciously developing a bitterness toward white people; when you have to concoct an answer for a five-year-old son asking in agonizing pathos: "Daddy, why do white people treat colored people so mean?"; when you take a cross-country drive and find it necessary to sleep night after night in the uncomfortable corners of your automobile because no motel will accept you; when you are humiliated day in and day out by nagging signs reading "white" and "colored"; when your first name becomes "nigger," your middle name becomes "boy" (however old you are) and your last name becomes "John," and your wife and mother are never given the respected title "Mrs."; when you are harried by day and haunted by night by the fact that you are a Negro, living constantly at tip-toe stance never quite knowing what to expect next, and plagued with inner fears and outer resentments; when you are forever fighting a degenerating sense of "nobodiness"; then you will understand why we find it difficult to wait.[70]

Reading about social dominance at such great length represents the "agonizing pathos" of "your" experience of it. Agonism that interrupts social reproduction is as straightforward as "our" judgment that it is "difficult to wait." These grammatical shifters request that white readers counseling moderation adopt the standpoint of blacks with intimate experiences of segregation, eliciting reciprocity in the vein of Madison's dialogue of northerners and southerners on slavery. If you were us, King asks, would you deem it appropriate to wait?

Movement struggles for social justice prefigure a world beyond the symbolic and literal violence of the segregationist order. Invoking the Indian struggle for decolonization, King calls nonviolence a "*way of life* in a world where the wildly accelerated development of nuclear power has brought into being weapons that can annihilate all humanity."[71] Here King, like Arendt, separates power from violence: the direct action of the political confronts the legal regulation of the police.[72] He co-articulates power and justice, not

---

70. King, "Letter from Birmingham Jail," 81–82.
71. King, *Why We Can't Wait*, 152, italics added.
72. This formulation is broadly informed by Rancière, *Disagreement*, chap. 2.

justice and law—for political struggle against "Jim Crow" law almost completely coincides with the moral struggle against antiblack racism.[73] Turning the accusation of animalistic violence against law enforcement, King doubts one could praise the police "for keeping 'order'" once they had seen "angry violent dogs literally biting six unarmed, nonviolent Negroes."[74]

Civil disobedience actualized power in confronting state violence on the streets of Birmingham, where Arendt might have said that violence threatened to overwhelm power.[75] While en route to City Hall on May 5, 1963, a black congregation led by Reverend Charles Billups encountered Birmingham Public Safety Commissioner "Bull" Connor and his fire-hose-wielding men. Connor ordered protestors to turn around. As King recounts the incident, the protestors fell to their knees before they "stood up and began to advance. Connor's men, as though hypnotized, fell back, their hoses sagging uselessly in their hands while several hundred Negroes marched past them."[76] The sagging hoses made the "impotence" of law-preserving violence plain for all to see; the protestors, by contrast, enacted a mode of visibility rooted in the capability to begin something new. It was not only national and international spectators that restrained the hand of the segregationist.[77] It was also fleeting moments of equality in which "standing before [the segregationist] were hundreds, sometimes thousands of Negroes who for the first time dared to look back at a white man, eye to eye."[78] To be clear, segregationists and antisegregationists did not come to a substantive agreement. Rather, the exchange of "eye-to-eye" looks transformed a space of enmity into a space of contestation for all parties. Connor and his forces entered, however briefly, into a shared space of legitimated disagreement to confront Billups and his congregation.

In addition to its normative commitment to nonviolence, direct action demands the existential commitment to struggle. King claims that "we who engage in nonviolent direct action are not the creators of tension," which is

---

73. More precisely, King distinguishes just from unjust laws. King, "Letter from Birmingham Jail," 82.
74. Ibid., 93.
75. Hannah Arendt, *On Violence* (New York: Harcourt Brace, 1970), 82.
76. King, *Why We Can't Wait*, 101.
77. The Kennedy administration feared that negative publicity regarding Birmingham would look bad to nonaligned third world nations. Manning Marable, *Race, Reform, and Rebellion: The Second Reconstruction and Beyond in Black America, 1945–2006*, 3rd ed. (Jackson: University of Mississippi Press, 2007), 71.
78. King, *Why We Can't Wait*, 39.

obscured by the image of a harmoniously segregated society. "We merely bring to the surface the hidden tension that is already alive," King continues; we "bring it out in the open where it can be seen and dealt with."[79] To render visible the "tense" character of segregation is to confront and move forward rather than to fall back or strike back in the face of the repressive state apparatus. This form of nonviolent confrontation is agonistic rather than antagonistic, to use Chantal Mouffe's distinction: "While antagonism is a we/they relation in which the two sides are enemies who do not share any common ground, agonism is a we/they relation where the conflicting parties . . . are 'adversaries,' not enemies."[80] Although the civil rights movement responded to racial antagonisms, its agonistic orientation undermined the formation of racial friend/enemy relationships. Rather, movement activists invited their adversaries to participate in a common space of contestation.

A contrast of agonistic contestations of segregation with antagonistic struggles against slavery about a century earlier is illuminating. As W.E.B. Du Bois points out, enslaved masses sometimes acted on "[feelings] of revolt and revenge," but their violent uprisings met with little success in the antebellum United States.[81] As fugitive slaves began fleeing en masse to the North throughout the U.S. Civil War, however, the existential revolt of the slave took on an emancipatory valence. This "general strike against the slave system," as Du Bois calls it,[82] rearticulated the racial enmity of slavery along a regional axis, as the strike (political protest) against conditions of slave labor was a strike (wartime blow) against the region of the slave master.[83] Du Bois offers a rejoinder to Jefferson's lack of imagination regarding the agency of the slave as well as a counterimage to King's imagination of black political mobilization. While King was a well-known articulator of an open struggle with segregation, Du Bois was an idiosyncratic narrator of a half-hidden strike against slavery.

It is outside of the purview of my investigation to ask what authorizes Du Bois's general strike, but it is entirely within the purview of King's purposes to ask what authorizes direct action. Civil disobedience returns the

---

79. King, "Letter from Birmingham Jail," 85.
80. Mouffe, *On the Political*, 20.
81. Du Bois, *The Souls of Black Folk*, 28–29.
82. W.E.B. Du Bois, *Black Reconstruction in America* (New York: Atheneum, 1992), 64.
83. "This slow, stubborn mutiny of the Negro slave was not merely a matter of 200,000 black soldiers and perhaps 300,000 other black laborers, servants, spies, and helpers. Back of this half million stood 3½ million more. Without their labor the South would starve." Du Bois, *Black Reconstruction in America*, 80.

United States to its political and religious foundations: "One day the South will know that when these disinherited children of God sat down at lunch counters they were in reality standing up for the best in the American dream and the most sacred values in our Judaeo-Christian heritage, and thusly, carrying our whole nation back to those great wells of democracy which were dug deep by the founding fathers."[84] The King "Letter" cites freely from various theologians (Augustine, Aquinas, and Martin Buber) and references sundry examples of "extremists" for justice (Jesus, Lincoln, and Jefferson). Elsewhere, channeling Du Bois, King roots the movement freedom songs in a tradition of black protest as "old as the history of the Negro in America."[85] The citation of these multiple authorities covers over "tensions" such as Christian justifications of slavery and Jefferson's colonization schemes. Authorizing the present conflict with the most profane, King foretells that the fullness of the future will be the culmination of the "most sacred" of the past.[86]

On the less prophetic question of juridical authority, King contends that the state court order that landed him in jail violates constitutional and federal law. After all, segregationists often abused legal injunctions to prevent black citizens and their white allies from exercising their right to assembly.[87] Yet, as the sacred and secular times of King's notion of re-foundation indicates, direct action cannot be evaluated in purely legal terms (e.g., is it sanctioned by federal law or protected by the Bill of Rights?). The difficulty of directly authorizing direct action lies in its becoming authority, as re-foundation can only obtain partial authorization from existent foundations or traditions ridden with inconsistencies.[88] The "constituent moment" of direct action, as opposed to civil disobedience proper, draws on the self-grounding "authority of the people themselves" rather than the authority of the legal state.[89] The surest vindication of any action taken in the name of the people is retrospective, as when future actions along the same lines treat it as a source of constitutional authority.[90]

---

84. King, "Letter from Birmingham Jail," 94.
85. King, *Why We Can't Wait*, 61; cf. Du Bois, *Souls of Black Folk*, chap. 14.
86. Cf. Mott, "The Rhetoric of Martin Luther King Jr.," 416.
87. King, *Why We Can't Wait*, 70.
88. If civil disobedience wants to change the world, it cannot fully accept the authorities that be. Arendt, *Crises of the Republic*, 77.
89. Frank, *Constituent Moments*, 8.
90. New social movements at least partially modeled on the civil rights movement are a testament to its authority. Omi and Winant, *Racial Formation in the United States*, 126.

Both Arendt and King realized that one crisis of the republic is the aforementioned tension between action and authority as the two intersect in time. King seeks to intensify this crisis in the name of justice, whereas Arendt wants to diminish it in the name of endurance. Arendt proposes a constitutional amendment that would grant "the same recognition for civil-disobedience minorities that is accorded to numerous special-interest groups,"[91] one that would "augment and increase the original foundations of the American republic."[92] Counterintuitively, Arendt looks like a legal-institutionalist in her desire to bring "the latest form of voluntary association" into the daily affairs of government, while King looks like a proponent of agonistic conflict. He might reply to Arendt that only the intensification of crisis can bring about its resolution: "nonviolent direct action seeks to create such a crisis and establish such a tension that a community which has constantly refused to negotiate is forced to confront the issue."[93]

Such statements cast doubt on the misappropriation of King as a "new founding father" who allows Americans to celebrate their racial progress.[94] If King is a founder, as the Martin Luther King Jr. Memorial in Washington, DC, would suggest, he is one in virtue of his re-foundational approach to the social question. The civil rights movement could not have functioned as what Arendt calls a "special-interest" group, and an augmentation of "original foundations" could not have resolved the racial crisis surrounding the movement. For one thing, the proposal to augment foundations takes for granted what it is meant to establish—namely, the legitimacy of black claims to citizenship. Imagine that the public is "a table . . . located between those who sit around it; the world, like every in-between, relates and separates men at the same time."[95] The proposal to integrate direct actors into a pressure-group system, in turn, presupposes that all parties already have a seat at the negotiating table. The revolutionary aim of direct action, by contrast, is to reconstitute the table/the world so that it includes more and different kinds of seats/positions.

---

91. Arendt, *Crises of the Republic*, 101.
92. Arendt, *On Revolution*, 194.
93. King, "Letter from Birmingham Jail," 79. Direct action can also be read in purely strategic terms, e.g., Doug McAdam, *Political Process and the Development of Black Insurgency, 1930–1970* (Chicago: University of Chicago Press, 1982), 178.
94. Nikhil Pal Singh, *Black Is a Country: Race and the Unfinished Struggle for Democracy* (Cambridge, MA: Harvard University Press, 2004), 4.
95. Arendt, *The Human Condition*, 52.

My contention that the civil rights movement is a case of extraordinary politics is based on an extended analogy between European and American instantiations of the social question. What qualifies any politics as revolutionary, Arendt argues, is its aim of founding authority rather than its aim of changing society. (Agricultural, industrial, and digital revolutions are only loosely revolutionary on this criterion.) Arendt recognizes that European labor organized itself to improve labor conditions; "however, one of the most important side effects of the actual emancipation of laborers was that a whole new segment of the population" appeared in public "without at the same time being admitted to society." Much like blacks in the United States, laborers in Europe found themselves within the social, but outside of "polite society"; also like black Americans, European laborers entered the public realm with the objective of changing social conditions. Thusly positioned, the early labor movement struggled "against society as a whole" in "[fighting] a full fledged political battle."[96]

Similarly, the civil rights movement is revolutionary not in virtue of its social objectives, but in virtue of the achievement of political selfhood. King declares that "the Revolution of the Negro not only attacked the external cause of his misery, but revealed him to himself. He was *somebody*."[97] Arendt says "this revelatory quality of speech and action comes to the fore where people are *with* others," as the Arendtian political collapses when collectivities utilize force "to achieve certain objectives for their own side and against an enemy."[98] The civil rights movement disclosed selves who "were with" those whose laws they contested; to anticipate the contrast case of the fifth chapter, the racial power movements identified selves who "were against" those whose ways of life they opposed. In the case at hand, the self makes a nonviolent "attack" against the public order, that is, King's "external cause of his misery" or Arendt's "society as a whole." The target of attack is not other human beings.

The fleeting movement of contestation, to repeat an important caveat, only attains the status of a foundational moment if it retroactively acquires authority. In this light, the Civil Rights Act of 1964 and the Voting Rights Act of 1965 both continued and constrained radical democratic struggle within the parameters of liberal democratic citizenship. The Kennedy ad-

---

96. Ibid., 218–19.
97. King, *Why We Can't Wait*, 30, italics original.
98. Arendt, *The Human Condition*, 180, italics original.

ministration's desire to channel the energies of direct action into voter-registration drives likewise tried to contain existential conflict within electoral strictures.[99] In this same light, however, the state's canalization of citizens' action is already indicative of the re-institutionalization of racial division. As Claude Lefort argues, "The erection of a political stage on which competition can take place shows that division is . . . constitutive of the very unity of society." Elections are the privileged site of competition for Lefort, but this "legitimation of purely political conflict contains within it the principle of a legitimation of social conflict in all its forms."[100] In this vein of expanding the scope of legitimate conflict, King positions direct action as the revolutionary supplement to legal reforms.[101]

The critical alternative to both violence and pacification, direct action in the civil rights movement pushes forward on two fronts. Its radical democratic aim is the revolutionary response to the social question of racial domination, while its liberal democratic aim is the reformist extension of existing rights to black Americans. The official U.S. public has resolved the tension between the radical and liberal dimensions of the civil rights struggle largely in favor of liberal-legalism. From the very start, the institutionalization of black civil rights incorporated African Americans into "the system" as yet another pressure-group and yet another interest-bearing constituency.[102] The terms of this incorporation has limited the legibility of specifically black claims on the terrain of legitimated racial conflict, an ever-narrowing space kept open by Black Lives Matter and prison abolition movements in the Trump-era United States. But the rise of Trumpism (or the new right before it) is not wholly responsible for blunting the revolutionary edge of the civil rights movement. We turn now to track how a legalistic color-blindness of the civil rights era came to eclipse the racialized experience of the movement itself.

Racial Division in the National Constitution

My interest in the essay "Reflections on Little Rock" is not with the validity of Arendt's controversial judgment that school desegregation is tantamount to depriving parents of "the private right over their children and the social

---

99. Morris, *Origins of the Civil Rights Movement*, 234.
100. Lefort, *Democracy and Political Theory*, 18.
101. King, *Why We Can't Wait*, 42.
102. A parallel analysis of the European labor movement is Arendt, *The Human Condition*, 219.

right to free association."¹⁰³ While a more robust discussion of Arendt's model of judgment occurs in Chapter 5, suffice it to say at present that Arendt's particular judgment cannot be deduced from her general distinction between the political realm of equality, the social realm of discrimination, and the private realm of intimacy.¹⁰⁴ What interests me is Arendt's account of how the social appears in the school desegregation crisis in 1950s Arkansas. I claim that what Arendt sees as the social rights of white parents and, yet more problematically, the social climbing of black parents is a politics far more extraordinary.¹⁰⁵ The Little Rock crisis is part and parcel of rearticulating civil equality as social equality and, ultimately, re-founding the United States as a nation-state.

The racial division of national unity had been authorized years before Dwight Eisenhower dispatched federal troops to quell the Arkansas rebellion against desegregation. In declaring segregated public education unconstitutional, the Supreme Court reauthorized U.S. citizenship on national rather than federal grounds. If the constitutional founding de-legitimated racial conflict and legitimated the (limited) sovereign power of the states, the civil rights re-founding legitimated racial conflict and de-legitimated state-mediated exclusions from citizenship. Re-foundation culminated in a nationalized polity in which a classically liberal form of difference-blindness sits uneasily next to a radically democratic form of social recognition.

The way that Arendt disassociates school desegregation from the political and aligns it with the social only makes sense if U.S. racial foundations have not been nationalized. We have come across one version of Arendt's claim about the distinctiveness of the United States in the context of the founding; in the context of the Little Rock crisis, Arendt provides two qualifications for her claim that "the United States is not a nation-state in the European sense and never was." The first is a regional exception: although changing under pressures of industrialization, the South is "more homogeneous and more rooted in the past than . . . any other part of the

---

103. Hannah Arendt, "Reflections on Little Rock," in *Responsibility and Judgment*, 212.

104. The judgment on Little Rock is, in Kant's language, a reflective judgment. Kirstie McClure, "The Odor of Judgment: Exemplarity, Propriety, and Politics in the Company of Hannah Arendt," in *Hannah Arendt and the Meaning of Politics*, ed. Craig Calhoun and John McGowan (Minneapolis: University of Minnesota Press, 1997), 66.

105. One can also argue that white social climbing is the core of the social question. Jill Locke, "Little Rock's Social Question: Reading Arendt on School Desegregation and Social Climbing," *Political Theory* 41, no. 4 (2013): 545–55.

country." Call this the "quasi-nation within a non-nation" thesis.[106] The second is to make an exception among minorities: unlike white immigrants, who are the most "audible" minorities, blacks "stand out because of their 'visibility.'" Arendt alleges that "while audibility is a temporary phenomenon, rarely persisting beyond one generation, the Negroes' visibility is unalterable and permanent."[107] The linguistic assimilation of the children of European immigrants is thusly distinguished from the multigenerational segregation of black Americans.[108] The gist is that the South, as opposed to the entire country, is steeped in the conformity and homogeneity of the nationlike social.

The other major reason that Arendt aligns the issue of desegregation with the social is that the modern school is a site of social discrimination. Her essay "The Crisis in Education" translates the authority of the older over the newer into the responsibility of adults to protect children from harm; her claim is that the abdication of parental authority transforms the school into a society in miniature, where children assemble into discriminatory cliques rather than as political equals.[109] Arendt is paternalistically concerned with protecting black adolescents at Little Rock schools from a far more dangerous situation, where the nine teens seeking admittance to Central High faced a macrocosmic race society in its moblike extreme. While her accusation that the parents of the Little Rock nine brought their children into a political struggle for the sake of social climbing is entirely off the mark, Arendt is exactly on target in diagnosing racial antagonism as phenomenologically social.[110]

---

106. I am playing on Cash's "nation within a nation" thesis. See W. J. Cash, *The Mind of the South* (New York: Alfred A. Knopf, 1941), viii.

107. Arendt, "Reflections on Little Rock," 199; see also Arendt, *Between Past and Future*, 175. Critical race theorists would challenge this statement on the grounds that racialized perception is conventional and learned. See Hanchard, *Party/Politics*, 192; see also Alcoff, *Visible Identities*, 191–92.

108. Charitably read, Arendt is describing how European immigrants assimilated into a "whiteness" that constitutively excludes "blackness." Cf. Desmond King, *Making Americans: Immigration, Race, and the Origins of the Diverse Democracy* (Cambridge, MA: Harvard University Press, 2000), 39–47.

109. Arendt, *Between Past and Future*, 189.

110. The standard defense is that Arendt misapplied her analysis of Jewish pariahs and parvenues to the black civil rights struggle and later admitted her mistake to Ralph Ellison. See, e.g., Elisabeth Young-Bruehl, *Hannah Arendt: For Love of the World*, 2nd ed. (New Haven, CT: Yale University Press, 2004), 316. Gines argues, however, that Arendt assumed that blacks were so desperate to associate with whites that they would act against their children's best interests. Gines, *Hannah Arendt and the Negro Question*, 22.

Authority inheres in the relationship of old-timers and newcomers in Arendt's essay on the crisis of education, whereas authority is at issue between federal and state governments in her essay on Little Rock. School desegregation involves "not the well-being of the Negro population alone, but, at least in the long run, the survival of the Republic"—a "survival" of the federalism of the constitutional founding.[111] For Arendt, "states' rights" means that the plurality of the states is "among the most authentic sources of power, not only for the promotion of regional interests and diversity, but for the Republic as a whole."[112] Leaving to one side the controversy on how far Arendt's position resembles that of southern segregationists,[113] I would like to pursue an alternative line of critique—namely, that Arendt fails to link the social question to the national foundations set in *Brown v. Board of Education*. Indeed, Arendt did understand *Brown* to be a departure from U.S. federalism. What she does not see, or perhaps does not want to acknowledge, is that the movement's treatment of black citizenship as social citizenship sets into motion the racial re-constitution of the entire U.S. public.

At some remove from Arendt's concern with federal division, the Warren Court declared that national community is at stake. The Court, drawing on psychological research, argued that the right to educational opportunity is violated by segregated schools, which breed among black students "feelings of inferiority as to their status in the community that may affect their hearts and minds in a way unlikely ever to be undone."[114] The Court, adopting the standpoint of the nation-state, noted that "today [education] is a principal instrument in awakening the child to cultural values, in preparing him for later professional training, and in helping him to adjust normally to his environment."[115] Citizenship as a means to cultural, professional, and normalizing ends is a protection from an internalized sense of inferiority, a sense that demonstrably correlates to racial segregation.[116]

---

111. Arendt, "Reflections on Little Rock," 200.

112. Ibid., 210.

113. Gines, *Hannah Arendt and the Negro Question*, 37, 127; Locke, "Little Rock's Social Question," 545. Arendt rejects state-mandated segregation and federally mandated desegregation. Her proposed alternative is voluntarily integrated schools.

114. 347 U.S. 483, 494 (1954).

115. Ibid., 493.

116. The effective guarantee of such citizenship would have required a massive expansion of federal administrative capacities, which U.S. founders established (weakly) in the "nationally integrated institutional systems" of courts and parties. Stephen Skowronek, *Building a New American State: The Expansion of National Administrative Capacities, 1877–1920* (Cambridge: Cambridge University Press, 1982), 24.

Insofar as it interprets education in terms of community standing, *Brown* makes the equal protection of well-being into a criterion of nation-state inclusion. Insofar as it treats education as a national resource, *Brown* benevolently preoccupies the public realm with the production, consumption, and distribution of social goods. Civil rights in this sense of European "social rights"[117] do ensure, as Arendt contends, "that the pursuit of private happiness [is] protected" by public power.[118] However, I must add that all rights claims—including claims to civil, economic, and social rights—involve political conflict. Like the interest claims of Madisonian factions, rights claims based on protected categories (age, sex, race, etc.) are always made against another with reference to their own legitimacy, enforcement, and limits. The juridical recognition of the NAACP-represented claims against state governments, for instance, implies that black Americans have rights contestable across all levels and sectors of the federal edifice. At this conjuncture of the social and the political, black contestations can prevent the welfare state from fully socializing citizenship or treating their "clients" as if they lacked voice.[119]

Brown recognized the black citizen as political actor *qua* social difference or as appellant in constitutional contest *qua* legally protected identification. The decision in this respect countered the strict division of realms in *Plessy v. Ferguson*. *Plessy* placed laws providing for segregated railway cars "within the competency of the state legislatures in the exercise of their police power." State police power, the Court declared, also justifies "the establishment of separate schools for white and colored children." Whereas *Plessy* interpreted the Fourteenth Amendment as inapplicable to "social, as distinguished from political, equality,"[120] *Brown* directly equated social inequality with political inequality. Rejecting the claim of *Plessy* that segregation only connotes hierarchical conditions in the "subjective" opinion of blacks,[121] *Brown* claimed that the subjective condition of blacks denotes that segregation is harmful according to the "objective" knowledge of social science.

---

117. T. H. Marshall, *Class, Citizenship, and Social Development* (Westport, CT: Greenwood, 1973), 71–72.

118. Arendt, *On Revolution*, 125.

119. See Iris Young, *Justice and the Politics of Difference*, rev. ed. (Princeton, NJ: Princeton University Press, 2011), 81–88.

120. 163 U.S. 537, 544 (1896).

121. If segregation stamps blacks with a "badge of inferiority," "it is not so by reason of anything found in the [Louisiana 'Jim Crow' law], but solely because the colored race chooses to put that construction upon it." Ibid., 551.

The Warren Court legitimizes the rights-bearer's conflict and, conversely, de-legitimates the segregationist's states' rights claim. *Brown* affirms the existence of U.S. citizenship without state mediation to deny that the wishes of southern governments are material, as adherence to the national principle and departure from the federal principle in their Madisonian meanings would necessitate. *Brown* withdrew the federal support of the states' power, established by the founding and reworked under postbellum constitutional amendments, to racially exclude. The broader dynamic at work is that the civil rights re-founding moved racial conflicts over enfranchisement/emancipation into the space of authorization once reserved for regional conflicts over disenfranchisement/enslavement. Put otherwise, the racial foundations of the nation-state replaced those of the federal republic.

Here I must address several challenges to my contention that the racial foundations of citizenship have been nationalized. The first objection is that the federal arrangement has endured since the founding. Take Daniel Elazar, a scholar of U.S. federalism, who avows that "the federal system in its essence and in its crucial details had been restored" by the 1880s, even if "the theory of secession had been buried and government activities had expanded on all planes and in all sections of the country."[122] This remarkable continuity is rooted in the consensus on federalism that framed both the dissolution and the restoration of the union. Likewise, this consensus makes desegregation into "a problem of implementing generally accepted principles of social and political equality for American citizens born black."[123] Elazar limits racial and regional conflict to the problem of cooperation between federal and state governments in the enforcement of legislation like the Civil Rights Act of 1964.

On the consensus view of American political development, widely held principles are gradually extended to more and more segments of the population (white women, black men, etc.). A conflict-oriented approach, however, would identify the disagreements surrounding any so-called consensus or, more accurately, any compromise reached by competing factions. Anthony Marx, for example, contends that Brazil never created a biracial order along the lines of segregation or apartheid because that country never had to ameliorate intense, intraracial conflict. The United States, by contrast, adopted an infa-

---

122. Daniel Elazar, "Civil War and the Preservation of American Federalism," *Publius* 1, no. 1 (1971): 47.

123. Daniel Elazar, *American Federalism: A View from the States*, 3rd ed. (New York: Harper and Row, 1984), 32–33.

mous compromise in 1877 to end the northern occupation and reconstruction of the South—all in the shadow of intraracial, interregional civil war.[124] Postbellum "consensus" was, in fact, a continued response to the intensification of North/South conflict to the point of friend/enemy distinction.

Although it ended legal slavery, reconstruction was no re-foundation of black citizenship. Instead, the failure of reconstruction replayed the racial logic of colonial Virginia at the national level. As the reader will recall, Virginian elite whites allied with poor whites, whom they considered more dangerous than black slaves. Analogously, Marx argues, northern whites allied with southern whites, whom they considered a greater threat to peace than emancipated blacks.[125] If Elazar is right to underscore that the federal structure is consistent across ante- and postbellum periods, he is wrong to downplay how blacks paid the price for postwar reconciliation. What stability the legitimation of regional conflict over slavery could not secure, southern black disenfranchisement provided for the late nineteenth-century federal restoration.

The question of postbellum U.S. citizenship brings us to our next challenge—that the United States has always been a modern nation-state with a *Herrenvolk* democracy.[126] The objection, basically, is that U.S. racial foundations have been stable. Bear in mind that the federal arrangement of the founding neither defined citizenship nor spelled out the relationship between state and national membership.[127] This intentional ambiguity, which allowed for the localization of citizenship across regions and states, lasted until *Dred Scott v. Sanford* declared that the denial of state citizenship entailed the denial of national citizenship.[128] Against the Taney Court's reworking of U.S. federalism, the framers of the reconstruction amendments wanted national citizenship to predominate. The Fourteenth Amendment, for instance, proclaimed "all persons born or naturalized in the United States" to be "citizens of the United States and the States wherein they reside." It threatened states with a reduction in House representation for denying voting rights to adult male citizens, reversing the logic of the three-fifths compromise that rewarded southerners for holding slaves.

---

124. Anthony Marx, *Making Race and Nation: A Comparison of South Africa, the United States, and Brazil* (Cambridge: Cambridge University Press, 1998), 134–35.

125. Ibid., 133.

126. Mills, *The Racial Contract*, 28, 96.

127. Rogers Smith, *Civic Ideals: Conflicting Visions of Citizenship in U.S. History* (New Haven, CT: Yale University Press, 1997), 115.

128. 60 U.S. 393 (1857).

Hence it is true that whites monopolized U.S. citizenship prior to the 1950s and 1960s, but it is also true that even the idea of a national citizenship that is irrespective of state mediation is relatively new. For black America, national citizenship began as legal citizenship without effective citizenship. In an undeclared state of exception, the suspension—neither the application nor the repeal—of reconstruction amendments invited something like the racial *status quo ante* back to the South.[129] The infamous compromise of 1877 substituted the exceptional citizenship of blacks present in the nation for the exceptional population of slaves represented in the House. Practices of citizenship distinguished the normal norm (U.S. citizenship for white males) from the exceptional norm (black male citizens without citizenship) to diminish the danger that black enfranchisement posed to the postreconstruction peace.

The reconstitution of U.S. federalism under a postreconstruction legal regime cut short the administrative inroads made into the social question. Du Bois in *The Souls of Black Folk* eulogizes the Freedman's Bureau, the federal bureaucracy established in 1865 to secure land, education, and legal protection for emancipated southern blacks.[130] That Du Bois starts his study of black exclusion from the white nation after the civil war is a sign that the abandonment of reconstruction was the social condition of reunification. That the first national welfare program in the United States provided pensions for Civil War veterans is yet another sign that the nation is the political form of the social.[131] Southern states, although no longer slave states, subordinated and later segregated black Americans.[132] And while far from a final answer to the social question, the civil rights movement authorized black contestations of exclusion and, more generally, agonistic racial conflict.

Not everyone in the post–civil rights era acknowledges this racial refoundation, even if more or less everyone who argues about race draws on its authority. The institutionalization of racial division is what authorizes contestants of any "race" to argue over what counts as "discrimination." An ironic

---

129. On the notion of suspension, see Schmitt, *Political Theology*, 9. I borrow from Schmitt in a loose sense; no sovereign with the authority to suspend constitutional law declared a state of exception into existence.

130. Du Bois, *The Souls of Black Folk*, chap. 2.

131. Theda Skocpol, *Social Policy in the United States: Future Possibilities in Historical Perspective* (Princeton, NJ: Princeton University Press, 1995), chap. 2..

132. The legal order that segregated blacks from whites emerged around the turn of the twentieth century. See C. Vann Woodward, *The Strange Career of Jim Crow*, commemorative ed. (Oxford, UK: Oxford University Press, 2002), chap. 3.

consequence has been the re-affirmation of racial majority rights or claims of "reverse discrimination" under the Fourteenth Amendment in affirmative action cases. *U.C. Regents v. Bakke*, decided in favor of a white male appellant, found that "diversity ... of which racial or ethnic origin is but a single though important element" can serve as a compelling state interest for affirmative action programs at public universities.[133] The Court ruled, *in nuce*, that any diversity-oriented admissions procedure that meets the exacting standards of strict scrutiny is constitutional, but that the University of California medical school policy strayed too far from the baseline of "color-blind" equal protection.

Bakke set a precedent for the University of Michigan cases, the next major decisions on affirmative action. While it struck down the University of Michigan's undergraduate admissions program in *Gratz v. Bollinger*,[134] the Court cited "the educational benefits that flow from student body diversity" in upholding law school admission policies at the same university in *Grutter v. Bollinger*.[135] The color-blind and racial-recognition strands of *Bakke* now split into separate rulings, as a fine line separates the factoring of race according to an unconstitutional point system in *Gratz* and the constitutionally permissible goal of achieving a critical mass of underrepresented minorities in *Grutter*. The euphemistic language of "diversity" cannot disguise the fact that the Court in *Bakke, Gratz, Grutter*, and—most recently—*Fisher v. University of Texas* has again and again conceded to the legitimacy of racial division.[136] The usage of race in antidiscrimination law—as in the "Negroes" of *Brown* or the "white race" of *Bakke*—legitimates race as a *form* of conflict, whatever the policy outcome might be.

It is well understood that conservatives have "hijacked" the civil rights movement's language of nondiscrimination, but it bears underscoring that they have done so to deny that movement's legitimation of black struggle. U.S. conservatives thereby elevate the liberal democratic at the expense of the radical democratic. The liberal state can only constitute its "universality" in opposition to social particulars (religion, race, etc.),[137] just as liberal color-blindness treats race as a "natural" attribute that should not bear on public

---

133. 438 U.S. 265, 315 (1978).
134. 539 U.S. 244 (2003).
135. 539 U.S. 306, 343 (2003).
136. 579 U.S. ___ (2016).
137. Karl Marx, "On the Jewish Question," in *The Marx-Engels Reader*, ed. Robert Tucker (New York: Norton, 1978), 33.

life.[138] This depoliticization, however, must be a second-order politicization for the reason that the contestation of specific racial policies presupposes the legitimacy of racial conflict. It appeals to the very racial foundations it seeks to overturn, confirming that the civil rights movement has pluralized and proliferated racial conflict in all its forms.

I exploit the ambiguity of Arendt's contention that "the United States is not a nation-state in the European sense" to explain how the United States became a nation-state in a distinctively American sense. The key factor to this development has been how the civil rights movement unified the citizenry around black/white division. The re-founding has served as a source of constitutional authority for the interest-group paradigm of U.S. racial politics, within which the ordinary politics of white authoritarian nationalism fit. Yet it might also function as a constitutional restraint against the white re-monopolization of U.S. citizenship or the extraordinary politics of white authoritarian nationalism. It took both the legal authority and popular power to rework U.S. federalism into U.S. nation-statism on racial matters. On matters other than race, such as the general exclusion of the *populous* from modern democratic governance, the foundations of the federal republic remain largely intact.

Conclusion: The Foundations of Racial Conflict and Popular Participation

I extended the Arendtian concept of foundation to cover the civil rights movement in the spirit of public freedom—the overriding concern of Arendt's *oeuvre*. My critique of Arendt, in turn, has indicated how her political theory can be made more relevant to critical theory (say, questions of black American contestation, white American regionalism, and racialized U.S. citizenship). I used Arendt's understanding of the American Revolution as a nonsocial revolution to be the baseline against which I have qualified the civil rights movement as a social revolution. The civil rights movement's authorization of racial division appears to be revolutionary in light of the American Revolution's discounting of that possibility.

Table 2.1 summarizes my comparison of U.S. foundations in terms of social order, political conflict, racial foundation, and constitutional authori-

---

138. Olson, *The Abolition of White Democracy*, 72.

TABLE 2.1 CONSTITUTIONAL FOUNDATIONS COMPARED		
Moment	*American Revolution*	*Civil rights movement*
Social order	Slavery	Segregation
Political conflict	Enmity	Contestation
Racial foundation	Federal	National
Constitutional authorization	State conflict	Racial conflict

zation. Along the first two analytic dimensions, slavery is the institutional codification of the public enmity of enslaved blacks, while segregation is the institutional target of the public contestation of black citizens. Along the second two dimensions, the federal arrangement legitimizes state conflicts over racial enslavement, while the national arrangement legitimizes racial conflicts over social condition.

I now address the question of contemporary U.S. racial foundations. In what respects is the civil rights movement a foundation of freedom—what Arendt would call a *constitutio libertatis*—for racially mediated U.S. citizenship? In what ways has it become a foundation of unfreedom, the re-constitution of black domination and exclusion? Finally, just how stable might the foundations of the civil rights movement be?

The civil rights movement has had the primary effect of constraining and sustaining racial antagonisms within agonistic institutions. The founding institutionalized the conflict between northern and southern states in a deadlock that it took a civil war to break. Analogously, the re-founding institutionalized the conflict between race-consciousness and color-blindness, the contradictory tendencies of the civil rights movement itself.[139] Mainstream U.S. racial discourse has been caught between liberal and radical democracy ever since. In substituting "culture" for the supposedly more divisive term "race,"[140] and in preferring economic to racial descriptions of interests, liberal democracy seeks to manage a color-blind system of cultural and interest-group pluralism. By contrast, radical democracy struggles for racial and other varieties of social justice and, at the second order, seeks to preserve, if not expand the sphere of legitimated conflict. While the for-

---

139. Desmond King and Rogers Smith, "'Without Regard for Race': Critical Ideational Development in Modern American Politics," *Journal of Politics* 76, no. 4 (2014): 960–66; cf. Howard Winant, *Racial Conditions: Politics, Theory, Comparisons* (Minneapolis: University of Minnesota Press, 1994), 31.

140. Claire Jean Kim, "Unyielding Positions: A Critique of the 'Race' Debate," *Ethnicities* 4, no. 3 (2004): 347.

mer project would eliminate racial divisions once and for all, the latter project accepts that racial divisions must be endured—perhaps indefinitely.

This intra-democratic conflict looks different to each side. For the liberal democrat, the question is whether racial policy is geared toward an individualistic equality of opportunity or a group-differentiated equality of results.[141] For the radical democrat, the question is whether race is engaged through liberal administration (equality of opportunity and/or equality of results) or popular contestations of inequality and exclusion. Agonistic institutions endow oppositions with legitimacy and, in the conflict under consideration, prevent either color-blind or race-conscious projects from winning decisively. That difference-sightedness is the oppositional project to the dominant project of difference-blindness, however, suggests that the post–civil rights era "conflictual consensus" is more liberal than radical democratic.[142]

The rise of the liberal over the radical democratic in the constitutional re-founding replayed the rise of administration over participation in the constitutional founding. We have already encountered Arendt's claim that the eighteenth-century French and American revolutionaries sought "[1] a constitution to lay down the boundaries of the new political realm and define the rules within it . . . so that [2] their own 'revolutionary' spirit could survive the actual end of the revolution."[143] Arendt holds that the French failed on both counts, whereas the Americans succeeded in the first task, only to fail at the second. Her diagnosis is that the U.S. founding provided no organs of popular participation within the body politic; it only assigned the task of administrating the interests of the many to the few who engage in constitutionally authorized conflict. This republican moment in Madisonian terms is the very definition of democracy ("representative democracy") for most late-modern Americans.[144]

Representative government limits the people's role to choosing administrators (if the representative is a "delegate" of the represented) or rulers (if the representative is a "trustee" of the represented).[145] Arendt seeks a distinctively modern way out of this distinctively modern bind in the self-organized

---

141. See, e.g., Hugh Davis Graham, *The Civil Rights Era: Origins and Developments of National Policy, 1960–1972* (Oxford, UK: Oxford University Press, 1990), 321.
142. See Chantal Mouffe, *The Return of the Political*, rev. ed. (London: Verso, 2005), 150–53.
143. Arendt, *On Revolution*, 117.
144. Ibid., 269.
145. Ibid., 228–29. I have used political science terms rather than Arendt's own to describe her position on representation.

councils of the European Revolutions of 1848, the Paris Commune of 1871, the Russian Revolution of 1917, and the Hungarian Revolution of 1956. The council system anticipates the reconciliation of action and authority: each local level of participation would entrust "the best" to participate at the next level up, and so on, thereby constituting a multitiered government from the bottom up.[146] It would combine central features of liberal constitutionalism, republican participation, and anarchist localism.

This "lost treasure" of the revolutionary tradition, as Arendt calls it, is ongoing popular participation in pre- and postrevolutionary times. It appeared not only in New England town hall meetings and Jefferson's postrevolutionary writings, but also when former slaves appropriated coastline from South Carolina to Florida without waiting for the Union's promise of the proverbial "40 acres and a mule."[147] Governed by local councils and protected by federal troops, black communities self-organized and self-authorized the alternative to representative democracy. Their spaces of freedom, akin to the Temporary Autonomous Zones of today's new social movements, would not survive for long in the face of official indifference and hostility.[148] Like the opportunity of integrating town halls into the constitutional founding, the opportunity of integrating black councils into postbellum federalism was squandered.

Charitably read, Arendt did not want to squander the opportunity to incorporate the civilly disobedient of the 1950s to the 1970s. A constitutional amendment, per Arendt's suggestion, could support the new left, who are still struggling to keep the terrain of legitimated racial contest open. Without their efforts, the new right would have already closed that terrain around "white citizenship," what Joel Olson calls "the *possession* of status rather than the *exercise* of one's power in public affairs."[149] The 1970s to 1980s new right is continuous with the liberal democratic transformation of whiteness from a legal status to a statistical advantage. Manning Marable, in this vein, sees even the participatory aspects of the civil right movement as the

---

146. Ibid., 270.
147. I am referring to the promise of General Sherman's Special Field Order No. 15 of 1865. Vincent Harding, *There Is a River: The Black Struggle for Freedom in America* (New York: Harcourt Brace Jovanovich, 1981), 269–76; cf. Robin Kelley, *Freedom Dreams: The Black Radical Imagination* (Boston: Beacon, 2002), 115.
148. The annulment of Special Field Order No. 15 eventuated in the return of the land to its former owners. On Temporary Autonomous Zones, see Richard Day, *Gramsci Is Dead: Anarchist Currents in the Newest Social Movements* (London: Pluto, 2005), 36.
149. Olson, *The Abolition of White Democracy*, 76, italics original.

fulfillment of "bourgeois democracy": "sit-ins were no rejection of the American Dream; they were the necessary though ambiguous steps towards [its] culmination."[150] The movement in these ways contributed to the normalization of black inequality and white advantage.

My conclusion that the civil rights movement was a social revolution will likely ring false for revolutionary socialists, utopian socialists, or even social democrats.[151] Admittedly, the civil rights movement is reformist at best when judged on the criteria of eliminating white over black hierarchy or ensuring substantive equality between blacks and whites. From a radical democratic perspective, however, I praise the movement for turning black social conditions into grounds of legitimated opposition as well as connecting regional black to U.S. national to global struggles.[152] The civil rights movement rekindled the U.S. nation precisely by racially dividing the racially united nation that arose from the ashes of reconstruction. As an enactment of participatory freedom, it dramatically widened the space of constitutionally authorized contestation over racialized conditions of unfreedom. The movement in these regards normalized racial conflict and re-founded U.S. citizenship.

The problem of the civil rights legacy is not that the successful institutionalization of administration is necessarily detrimental to the revolutionary spirit, but that the failure to institutionalize local participation into the constitution definitely is. What modern democratic polities need is not only better administrative arenas, but more arenas in which populations can "people" themselves. We need to remember that the risks of the re-founding bear a special resemblance to those of the founding, then: outside of organs of popular participation, racial divisions will appear as census populations or, more recently, interest groups.[153] With the decline of 1960s to 1970s radical democratic mobilizations, the nation-state rises to the occasion as a liberal democratic regime in which the few manage the interests of the many.

The 1970s and 1980s new right developed on the terrain of U.S. racial democracy, a terrain split by liberal democratic and radical democratic ten-

---

150. Marable, *Race, Reform, and Rebellion*, 63.
151. On social revolution versus political revolution, see Day, *Gramsci Is Dead*, chap. 4.
152. Black activism, of course, long predated the civil rights movement. However, the emergence of the black counterpublic as a national and international force accelerated after World War II. See Winant, *The World Is a Ghetto*, 158.
153. Census categories change under group-organized pressures. For example, lobbyists are responsible for the addition of various Asian nationalities to the census since the 1980s. Thomas Kim, *The Racial Logic of Politics: Asian Americans and Party Competition* (Philadelphia: Temple University Press, 2007), chap. 4.

dencies. The new right, like its descendent Trumpism, aspires to both authoritarianism and populism. The Trump administration has so far acted as if only whites can fully embody the *demos* and as if only the claims of white Americans are fully legitimate. How far Trumpism will erode existing elements and introduce new elements into U.S. racial foundations is, at this time, uncertain. It is more certain that social movements, both ordinary and extraordinary, are our best chance of making achievements of the civil rights era unassailable. Still, the possibility remains that the 2016 Trump election will be to the civil rights movement what the 1876 Hayes election was to the civil war—the disavowal, or even the undoing, of an extraordinary racial event.

3

Racial Removal Contracts and the *Nomos* of the New World

> The odium of colonialism . . . is nothing other than the odium of appropriation.
> —CARL SCHMITT, *The Nomos of the Earth*

> This emigration should be voluntary: for it would be as cruel as unjust to compel the aborigines to abandon the graves of their fathers, and seek a home in a distant land. But they should be distinctly informed that, if they remain within the limits of the States, they must be subject to their laws. . . . Submitting to the laws of the States, and receiving, like other citizens, protection in their persons and property, they will, ere long, become merged in the mass of our population.
> —ANDREW JACKSON, "Farewell Address"

We saw in the previous chapter how the twentieth-century civil rights movement founded a nation-state that responded to the failures of reconstruction. The U.S. nation-state also had antecedents related to the antebellum governance of Amerindians. The case at hand is the U.S. appropriation of southeastern Indian lands in a time of mass Indian removals. As northwestern polities like the Potawatomi, Sac, and Foxes were being dislocated from their territories north of the Ohio River, southeastern polities like the Creek, Chickasaw, Choctaw, Cherokee, and Seminole were being removed across the Mississippi River.[1] Some 100 million acres of indigenous land east of the Mississippi were exchanged for some thirty million acres west of it during the presidency of Andrew Jackson alone. The result was the resettlement of more than 60,000 indigenous people in lands known as "Indian Territory" or "Indian Country."

---

1. I use the terms "polities," "nations," and "tribes" similarly to speak of southeastern Indian political wholes. I use the terms "indigenous," "native," "Indian," "American Indians," and "Amerindian" interchangeably.

This extraordinary set of land appropriations is distinguished from an enormous "land grab" in that it reset the Amerindian racial and spatial coordinates of the U.S. federal system. I argue that nineteenth-century removal treaties replaced southeastern American Indians within a rearticulated spatial order: the racial state would substitute the "civilized" for the "savage" Amerindian and would place the southeastern polity again within an exceptional zone, Indian Country. Such removal treaties contributed to a shift in federal-Indian policy, which initially dealt with Amerindians as nations capable of making war and peace, but which increasingly managed Amerindians as populations in the postremoval period. Removal contracts would deploy fictions of indigenous consent to forward this project of Indian "domestication."

This chapter shows how a spatial order of state, federal, and Indian governments was simultaneously a racial order of white, Indian, and black peoples. This public order involved the racial formation of Amerindian replacement and the public constitution of land appropriation. This second case thus raises a Schmittian series of concerns that cut across the Arendtian series of questions posed by our first case. The state decisions on southeast land appropriation run perpendicular to the citizen actions of the constitutional re-founding. However, our present consideration of public order intersects with our previous consideration of public freedom at the point where the U.S. public is racially and federally constituted.

On a broader scale, this chapter situates southeastern Indian removal within a *nomos* of the Western Hemisphere. Here *nomos* refers to Carl Schmitt's notion of a land appropriation that "constitutes the original spatial order" and serves as the source of "all further law."[2] On Schmitt's usage, "*nomos* indicates an action and a process whose content exists in a *nemein*," a taking that precedes the dividing up and producing on particular lands.[3] *Nomos* as land appropriation grounds the legitimacy of a new concrete order, despite this legitimacy's often questionable legality from the perspective of

---

2. Schmitt, *Nomos of the Earth*, 48; for Arendt's critique of this work, see Anna Jurkevics, "Hannah Arendt Reads Carl Schmitt's *The Nomos of the Earth*: A Dialogue on Law and Geopolitics from the Margins," *European Journal of Political Theory* 16, no. 3 (2017): 345–66.

3. Schmitt, *Nomos of the Earth*, 326, 328–29. Schmitt's understanding of *nomos*, a term conventionally translated as "law," is idiosyncratic. In a personal correspondence, Naomi Campa derives *nomos* from the verb *nemo*, which means to distribute and to pasture animals; Campa notes that the idea of one's portion or one's pasturage resonates with the usage of *nomos* as "custom" rather than *nomos* as "law."

the existing order. The concept of *nomos* in Schmitt's post-Weimar thinking functions analogously to the concept of sovereignty in Schmitt's Weimar-era thinking. Both moments of extraordinary politics have the power to rupture the previous order and initiate the constitution of a new one.

Schmitt himself is preoccupied with the seventeenth- to eighteenth-century *nomos* of European interstate relations. The Eurocentric spatial order legitimated conflicts between European sovereigns in terms of formal conventions of war; "bracketed," legalized intra-European wars would consequently lack the intensity of creedal, civil, and colonial wars.[4] Conflicts involving non-European states on non-European soil, Schmitt claims, had a different juridical status and existential valence. These took place on the other side of global "amity lines," beyond which European values need not apply and "force could be used freely and ruthlessly."[5] Amity lines distinguished closed European territories (the normal zone) from non-European lands open for colonial appropriation (the exceptional zone).

Amity lines, in other words, revealed that the Eurocentric global order *logically* depended on the existence of lands "open" to European appropriation. This is why for Schmitt the 1648 Treaty of Westphalia marked the end of the beginning of the *jus publicum Europaeum*, and the 1823 Monroe Doctrine marked the beginning of its end.[6] The Monroe Doctrine, in "closing" Latin American republics to Spanish and Portuguese (re)colonization, took for granted "the freedom to appropriate land on [the United States'] own behalf, since there were still wide open spaces of American soil."[7] Following Frederick Jackson Turner, Schmitt identifies the 1890s with the closing of a U.S. frontier predicated on "the existence of an area of free land, its continuous recession, and the advance of American settlement westward."[8]

Schmitt's view is that both U.S. and European continental orders defined themselves in contradistinction to lands "open" to colonial appropriation. His view, however, overextends an analogy between the European and U.S. spatial orders. The latter's territorial concepts for Indian lands were derived

---

4. Ibid., 140–43.
5. Ibid., 94. Schmitt distinguishes French-English amity lines from Spanish-Portuguese *rayas*.
6. On Schmitt's usages of dates, see Rasch, *Sovereignty and Its Discontents*, 131–33.
7. Schmitt, *Nomos of the Earth*, 286.
8. Frederick Jackson Turner, "The Significance of the Frontier in American History," in *Rereading Frederick Jackson Turner: "The Significance of the Frontier in American History" and Other Essays*, ed. John Mack Faragher (New York: Henry Holt, 1994), 31.

from, but irreducible to, those elaborated in the former.[9] Nineteenth-century southeastern Amerindian lands, like twentieth-century unincorporated territories, had a *sui generis* status within U.S. constitutional law; they had, for instance, at least since the founding period, fallen on the "closed" side of U.S. territorial claims. It was precisely their status as exceptional zones that prompted efforts to further domesticate them. Making southeastern polities a part of—yet also an exception within—the federal order, the settler colonial state displayed its ambivalence toward indigenous sovereignty.[10]

On these grounds, I distinguish the continental expansionism of the U.S. federal republic from the overseas expansionism of modern European nation-states. The European spatial order "closed" European territories against the backdrop of lands "open" to European appropriation. U.S. federalism, by contrast, differentially included Amerindian polities into a "network" of "powers and counterpowers,"[11] that is, extended a pluralistic institutional order over defensively articulated indigenous sovereignties. U.S. colonialism did not open an exceptional zone within which European logics of discovery and effective occupation reigned. It instead crafted an American set of exceptional norms—including treaty federalism and indigenous consent—for the exceptional zone of Indian Territory. It created *one* federal order out of settler and indigenous entities wracked by land-based conflicts. Its aim was to eliminate rather than regulate the existence of war within this concrete spatial order.

This is not to deny that the Western Hemispheric order was colonial, racist, and—above all—"Americentric." The Eurocentric spatial order was oriented toward the balance-of-power among European sovereigns, the premise of colonial expansion policies from the seventeenth to nineteenth centuries.[12] The Americentric spatial order, on its part, was oriented toward the U.S. federal authority over "American states" (in both domestic and foreign senses) and Indian tribes (simultaneously "foreign" and "domestic"). The Monroe Doctrine centered the United States vis-à-vis European states as the decider on hemispheric order, much like Jackson's removal policies centered the federal government vis-à-vis state governments as the decider

---

9. That is, Indian lands were not unqualified national-state territories, colonies, protectorates, or "free" space. Schmitt, *Nomos of the Earth*, 184, 87.

10. This formulation of "colonial ambivalence" is from Kevin Bruyneel, *The Third Space of Sovereignty: The Postcolonial Politics of U.S.-Indigenous Relations* (Minneapolis: University of Minnesota Press, 2007).

11. Michael Hardt and Antonio Negri, *Empire* (Cambridge, MA: Harvard University Press, 2000), 166.

12. Schmitt, *Nomos of the Earth*, 161.

of federal order.[13] In the case of the American continents, the U.S. republic would decide on a spatial order of "free and independent" republics and hence what counted as hemispheric disorder.[14] In the case of continental expansion, the federal state would decide on a spatial order of indigenous and state governments and hence what counted as federal disorder.

Although divided over Indian removal, the U.S. government was the effective decider on the order of antebellum U.S. federalism. This chapter tracks how the federal executive's vision of Americentric spatial order prevailed over that of the federal judiciary. Section I contends that the judiciary excepted Amerindian territories from norms only applicable to the European spatial order. For this zone of exception, the Supreme Court crafted exceptional norms that would partially secure indigenous lands and partially recognize Indian sovereignties. Section II covers the executive's alternative to a legal-constitutional solution—what I term "racial removal contracts" negotiated within the federal-Indian treaty system. Racial removal contracts enacted the fiction of southeastern indigenous consent to being treated as administrated populations. In conclusion, I consider how the resettled southeastern polities were situated inside/outside the federal system on which the emergent *nomos* of the New World centered.

Section I: Racialized Exceptions from the *Jus Publicum Europaeum*

This section examines how the Supreme Court ruled on the constitutional status of Indian land during the nineteenth century. The Court in addressing this territorial question offered extended explanations as to why European international law could not be directly incorporated into U.S. constitutional law. On the basis of a spatial distinction between Old and New Worlds, Chief Justice John Marshall created racial norms for U.S. law in the space cleared by racial exceptions from European norms. This operation is normative in that exceptional norms govern the relationship between Amerindian and federal governments. It is existential in that it judges the applicability of

---

13. Monroe introduced the idea of a U.S.-centered *Großraum* into international law. Ibid., 281; see also Schmitt, *Writings on War*, 88.

14. James Monroe, "President's Message (December 2, 1823)," in *Annals of Congress*, 18th Congress, 1st sess., 19. Hereafter cited as "Monroe Doctrine," followed by the page number from the *Annals*.

normal norms in light of Schmittian claims about potential violence. I find that Marshall's placement of Indian polities within an Americentric spatial order—one consistent across the "anti-Indian" *Johnson v. McIntosh* and the "pro-Indian" *Worcester v. Georgia*—conforms to this logic of norm/exception distinction.

Johnson v. McIntosh: *Paradigm of Racial Exceptionality*

The Supreme Court in the 1823 case *Johnson v. McIntosh* incorporated certain principles from the *jus publicum Europaeum* into U.S. constitutional law. *Johnson* ruled in favor of William McIntosh's postrevolutionary land grant from the federal government and against Thomas Johnson's rival claim, which was based on a revolutionary-era land purchase from the Illinois and Piankeshaw. The United States, the Court reasoned, received the authority to extinguish native title from the 1783 Treaty of Paris, that is, the Crown. England, in turn, had held this authority because "discovery gave title to the government by whose subjects, or by whose authority, it was made, against all other European governments."[15] *Johnson*, Robert Williams argues, sustained the "fiction that discovery was the basis of the English Crown's original assertion of prerogative rights of conquest in America."[16] The supreme law of the "land" partook of those English "discourses of conquest" that had proven useful in the colonization of Ireland as well as against rival Spanish claims to the Americas.[17]

While Williams, like Schmitt, stresses the continuity of U.S. and European colonization efforts, I would emphasize the unique legal challenges of regulating U.S.-Indian intercourse. Such challenges prompted the Supreme Court to craft legal rules based on a complex set of racial and spatial distinctions. Now, we know from scholars of Amerindian politics that constitutional relations of Amerindian and U.S. governments exceed narrowly construed frameworks of "race relations."[18] I hold, though, that questions of native dispossession belong to both emergent literatures on settler colonialism

---

15. 21 U.S. 543, 573 (1823).
16. Robert Williams Jr., *The American Indian in Western Legal Thought: The Discourses of Conquest* (Oxford, UK: Oxford University Press, 1990), 315. Williams observes the doctrine of discovery was highly contested in the U.S. revolutionary period, only becoming constitutional law with *Johnson*.
17. Ibid., 46–47.
18. David Wilkins and Heidi Kiiwetinepinesiik Stark, *American Indian Politics and the American Political System*, 3rd ed. (Lanham, MD: Rowman and Littlefield, 2011), chap. 2.

and established literatures on transatlantic racialization. What I call "racial exceptionality," then, is a colonial and racial paradigm of federal-Indian relations. Before coming to *Worcester*, an 1832 case directly relevant to Indian removal, I argue that *Johnson* is an important precedent for this paradigm.

Johnson marked a civilizational discontinuity between East Indian and Amerindian polities, while assuming a civilizational continuity between European and U.S. polities. On the one hand, the Marshall Court intellectually and normatively distinguished the advanced from the backward. The United States' title derived from a European discovery that, as Schmitt describes this conceit, "lay in a higher legitimacy. [Discoveries] could only be made by peoples intellectually advanced enough to apprehend the discovered by superior knowledge and consciousness."[19] On the other hand, the Court spatially and institutionally differentiated Amerindians from East Indians: "we speak of their sachems, their warriors, their chiefmen, their nations or tribes" in the American context, but not of their "princes or governments" as "we" do in the East Indies.[20]

However, even if European and U.S. spatial orders share a mode of "consciousness," European international and U.S. constitutional law are only partially continuous. Marshall recalled a land appropriation—a taking from "wild" peoples and a parceling of "wild" places—that followed "bloody wars" between an "[advancing] white population" and "[receding] Indians."[21] This concrete necessity of colonial warfare makes it impossible to decide "on abstract principles" "whether agriculturists, merchants, and manufacturers" can rightfully "expel hunters from the territory they possess, or to contract their limits."[22] Delimiting the legal issue thusly, Marshall did not reject the classification of societies into the "progressive" series of hunter, agricultural, and commercial. If anything, he presupposes that settlers battled "hunters" and initiated civilized land usage. His question is rather how the exceptional norm of discovery arose to regulate this colonial process of expropriation.

A colonialist rendition of civilization and savagery enables Marshall to articulate a distinctively American form of conquest as an exception to

---

19. Schmitt, *Nomos of the Earth*, 132.
20. 21 U.S. 543, 599–600 (1823). This distinction responded to the plaintiff Johnson, who claimed territories purchased from "Indian princes" did not require a Crown patent. Johnson was playing on the dual meaning of the English word "Indian."
21. Ibid., 589–90.
22. Ibid., 588.

European norms. In the *jus gentium* as it derives from Roman law, Marshall opined, either "the conquered inhabitants can be blended with the conquerors, or safely governed as a distinct people." But what worked for Rome could not work for New World settlers fighting "fierce savages, whose occupation was war, and whose subsistence was drawn chiefly from the forest." Therefore the settlers faced three choices: (1) abandoning their colonies, (2) "enforcing [their] claims by the sword, and by the adoption of principles adapted to the condition of a people with whom it was impossible to mix, and who could not be governed as a distinct society," or (3) living under the threat of being massacred.[23] All three options are framed by the possibility of interracial violence against which Marshall judges the applicability of rules and their exceptions.

The second option, which Marshall implied the settlers took, is a clear instance of the logic of racial exceptionality. The first operation of racial exceptionality is to except the "savage" *from* the civilized rule: Marshall declared that "the actual condition of the two people" necessitates ruling counter to "natural right" and "the usages of civilized nations." The second operation is to craft an exceptional rule *for* the native as a substitute for the normal rule: the "concomitant principle" is that "the Indian inhabitants are to be considered merely as occupants, to be protected, indeed, while in peace, in the possession of their lands, but to be deemed incapable of transferring the absolute title to others."[24] "While in peace" means that the validity of rules—normal (Western "absolute title") or exceptional (Indian "occupancy")—depends on concrete cases of violence. If the rule of discovery is applied due to civilizational affinities, racial enmity opens an exception to the rule of conquest in the New World.

Racial exceptionality is the logical structure of Marshall's claim that normal norms regulate intra-civilized affairs and exceptional norms regulate "civilized" and "savage" relations.[25] The racial exception of the Amerindian spatially distinguishes the American from the European legal order. Marshall never deemed Indian lands simply "open" to U.S. appropriation, as Schmitt's interpretation of the spatial concept of the Western Hemisphere would suggest. Indian occupation instead fell short of both European dominion and no title at all. True, Marshall proposed that American lands

---

23. Ibid., 589–90.
24. Ibid., 591–92.
25. Ibid., 572.

unclaimed by European powers were "vacant lands" for the purposes of European discovery; the corollary proposition, though, is that Indians held (inferior) titles independently of (superior) titles, like that of the United States, derived from the discovery doctrine.[26] In 1823, the year James Monroe issued his eponymous doctrine, John Marshall situated Indian lands within a U.S. racial and spatial order—one governed by exceptional norms and geared toward colonial settlement.

Worcester v. Georgia: *The Background Conflict*

Contemporary liberals tend to cast *Worcester v. Georgia* as a principled protection of Amerindian sovereignty against land-hungry southerners and, on this ground, distinguish it from *Johnson v. McIntosh*.[27] Critical theorists, by contrast, tend to assail both cases as bare assertions of U.S. sovereignty over indigenous territories. I find in the spirit of liberalism that *Worcester* differed doctrinally from *Johnson*, but I find in the spirit of critical theory that both *Johnson* and *Worcester* deployed the same exceptionalist logic. Just as *Johnson* introduces the U.S. rule of Indian occupation into the space excepted from the European doctrine of conquest, *Worcester* introduces the U.S. rule of federal paternalism into the space excepted from the European doctrine of protection.

We turn now from *Johnson*'s questions of U.S. territorial holdings to *Worcester*'s questions of U.S. federal order. *Worcester* was a failed federal intervention into conflicts between southern state and southeastern Indian governments over land. Its immediate context was Cherokee removal, which some factions of Cherokee felt was inevitable. Smaller and less murderous Cherokee removals preceded the late 1830s "Trail of Tears" as the federal executive accelerated and aggrandized the land appropriation process.[28] Two decades earlier, Cherokee ceded eastern territories for Arkansas land to which several thousand Western Cherokee removed, largely in response to

---

26. Ibid., 596, 584. *Johnson* translates *terra nullius* as "vacant land," "vacant territory," and "vacant soil."

27. See, e.g., Gerard Magliocca, *Andrew Jackson and the Constitution: The Rise and Fall of Generational Regimes* (Lawrence: University of Kansas Press, 2007), 43; James Tully, "Aboriginal Property Rights and Western Theory," in *Theories of Empire, 1450–1800*, ed. David Armitage (Aldershot, UK: Ashgate, 1998), 366.

28. Cf. David Stannard, *American Holocaust: The Conquest of the New World* (Oxford, UK: Oxford University Press, 1992), 12–24.

General Andrew Jackson's threat that only a removal treaty could guarantee federal government protection or annuities.[29]

The remaining Eastern Cherokee, who would later split into proremoval Treaty and antiremoval National parties, sought to modernize. The goal was to be governed by the normal norms of international law rather than the exceptional norms for Americentric order. As the first of the southeastern polities to have their own written script, Cherokee made the strongest claim to (what American policymakers considered) civilization.[30] As the southeastern polity that had furthest formalized its government, their nation also made the strongest claim to (what European international law recognized as) sovereignty. By 1817, Cherokee had the most nationalized government, which—in Weberian terms—wielded the most centralized use of legitimated violence. By 1827, their written constitution had separated executive, judicial, and legislative powers. Finally, this southeastern polity more than any other had differentiated its kinship, religious, and political spheres prior to removal.[31]

The Cherokee constitution of July 1827 represents the wager that modernization would serve the antiremoval cause. The constitutional convention presided over by John Ross, the National Party leader, placed "the sovereignity [sic] & jurisdiction of this Government" over the "common property of the nation" front and center.[32] This is no self-enclosed sovereignty; unlike the strategically excluded state governments, the federal government is both inside and outside of the Cherokee constitution. Article I, section 1 bounds Cherokee territory according to the nation's interpretation of federal treaties, while Article III, section 19 declares that "all acknowledged Treaties shall be the Supreme law of the land." Ultimately, however, *Cherokee* decided on the constitutional interpretation and incorporation of treaties, meaning that *that* nation is both inside and outside the U.S. racial and spatial order. The Eastern Cherokee exploited the ambivalences of U.S. federalism to maintain "the

---

29. This cession happened in 1817. The Arkansas lands were traded for Indian Country land in 1828. Francis Prucha, *The Great Father: The United States Government and the American Indians*, vol. I (Lincoln: University of Nebraska, 1984), 234–35.

30. In the early 1820s, Sequoyah invented a Cherokee alphabet; by the late 1820s, the Cherokee were printing *The Cherokee Phoenix*, a bilingual Cherokee-English newspaper.

31. Duane Champagne, *Social Order and Political Change: Constitutional Governments among the Cherokee, the Choctaw, the Chickasaw, and the Creek* (Stanford, CA: Stanford University Press, 1992), 124, 138–39.

32. "Constitution of the Cherokee Nation, 1827 Jul. 24, New Town Echota," *Tennessee Documentary History, 1796–1850*, accessed April 18, 2017, http://diglib.lib.utk.edu/cgi/t/text/text-idx?c=tdh;cc=tdh;sid=70c00e216e581ff6c26c8d8237ad1425;q1=cherokee%20nation;rgn=main;view=text;idno=tl217.

greatest possible territorial holdings beyond the immediate purview of that system."[33]

Modernization strategies aimed at the federal government only heightened conflict closer to home, however. Georgia protested that the 1827 constitution set up an impermissible *imperium in imperio*, another sovereignty within its sovereignty. To be clear, the Georgians were not trying to remove Cherokee due to their radical Otherness or out of disrespect for indigenous forms of government. Theirs was a conflict of rival polities, more institutionally and sociologically alike than ever, claiming sovereignty over the same land; a formal settler/native antagonism supervened over all kinds of substantial similarities. For instance, even though less than 10 percent of Cherokee families owned slaves,[34] the 1827 Cherokee constitution used more racially explicit language than the contemporaneous 1798 Georgia constitution.[35] What Georgian official and popular forces feared was that the Cherokee's constitution, like their agricultural practices, signified "permanence" and—dare I say—"settlement."[36]

Worcester v. Georgia: *Racial Exceptionality Redux*

Worcester v. Georgia raised the question of the spatial ordering of state and indigenous governments in 1832. Samuel Worcester lived among Cherokee as a representative of the federally funded American Board of Commissioners for Foreign Missions. Worcester and three coreligionists were arrested for violating an 1830 Georgian statute requiring "all white persons residing within the limits of the Cherokee nation" to obtain a permit from the governor or take an oath of allegiance to Georgia.[37] The 1830 act was related to an 1829 act, which extended "all the laws [of Georgia], both civil and criminal" over Cherokee territory and declared all Cherokee law "null and void, and of no effect, as if the same had never existed."[38] The juridical question of

---

33. Bruyneel, *The Third Space of Sovereignty*, 50. The quote refers to how Northern Cherokee negotiated their postbellum relationship to the United States.

34. Champagne, *Social Order and Political Change*, 128.

35. The Cherokee constitution spoke of "negroes" and "mulattoes," whereas the Georgia constitution spoke about "free citizens" and "slaves." "1798 Georgia Constitution," *GeorgiaInfo: An Online Georgia Almanac*, accessed April 18, 2017, http://georgiainfo.galileo.usg.edu/topics/government/related_article/constitutions/georgia-constitution-of-1798.

36. Patrick Wolfe, "Settler Colonialism and the Elimination of the Native," *Journal of Genocide Research* 8, no. 4 (2006): 396, italics removed.

37. Act reproduced in 31 U.S. 515, 521–25 (1832).

38. Act reproduced in ibid., 525–28.

Worcester was which "races" would be allowed to inhabit this land under whose jurisdiction. The existential question was if the Court would legitimize the Georgian efforts to legislate the Cherokee government out of existence. To this question, Marshall replied in the negative. The Cherokee are "a distinct community occupying its own territory . . . in which the laws of Georgia can have no force."[39]

James Tully, who reads Marshall as affirming indigenous sovereignty, defends *Worcester* as the case that set a "normative framework" for U.S. treaty federalism.[40] Treaty federalism in the United States (and Canada) institutionalizes reciprocal trust in treaties that "are like 'international' treaties between crowned heads of state in Europe."[41] It is a "cross-cultural 'middle ground' composed of early modern Aboriginal and common-law conceptions of the constitutional relations between their two systems of property."[42] Tully insists this normative framework has legal precedent, but his moral purposes undermine his historical ones. Splitting norms from their violations, Tully admits this "normative framework has been violated, either by ignoring or denying it, on more occasions in the past than it has been honored in Canada and the U.S."[43] Regular violations of a framework, though, lead me to suspect that violations are the work of the frame itself.

Unlike Tully, we cannot clearly distinguish norms from violations in the case of exceptions that constitute racial norms.[44] Both Marshall cases respond to concrete political questions of Amerindian placements vis-à-vis the U.S. federal system more than abstract normative questions about native title. Whereas *Johnson* denies that Indian polities could extinguish Indian title, *Worcester* denies this same right to a state government. *Worcester* only partially affirmed indigenous sovereignty because it only treated relationships between native and federal governments like relationships between European sovereigns up to a point—the point of racial exceptionality. Again, the selective incorporation of European public law into the U.S. constitution is decisive.

Marshall, as Tully contends, sought European analogues of federal-indigenous alliances. Following Emeric de Vattel, Marshall suggested that weaker

---

39. Ibid., 561.
40. Tully, "Aboriginal Property Rights and Western Theory," 365.
41. Ibid., 368. Tully claims that the Canadian analogue to *Worcester* is the Royal Proclamation of 1763.
42. Ibid., 346.
43. Ibid., 365.
44. Mills, *The Racial Contract*, 122.

states retain their sovereignty on their entrance into unequal alliances with stronger states.[45] However, Vattel's rule that tributary and feudatory states must "honor" their protectors makes little sense outside of the early modern European spatial order.[46] The Indian tribe in the American colonial situation is *forced* into an exclusive relationship of intercourse with its European protector. Revisiting the colonial history of *Johnson*, *Worcester* granted that "Indian nations had always been considered as distinct, independent political communities ... with the single exception of that imposed by irresistible power, which excluded them from intercourse with any other European potentate than the first discoverer of the coast of the particular region claimed."[47] We have seen this logic of racial exceptionality before. Its first operation carves out the Indian exception from the European rule of protection precisely at the point that the "first discoverers"—that is, figures from the doctrine of discovery—of *Johnson* slip back into *Worcester*. Racial exceptionality is again derived from and oriented to the concrete possibility of violence.

Reminiscent of *Johnson*'s claim that the United States acquired Crown "discovered" lands, *Worcester*'s claim is that the United States acquired "discoverer"-like relations with Indians. However, as in *Johnson*, U.S. constitutional law is irreducible to European public law in *Worcester*. The federal protection afforded by *Worcester* in 1832 is distantly related to Vattel, yet directly related to *Cherokee Nation v. Georgia*, an 1831 case. *Cherokee Nation* limns a Cherokee "domestic dependent nation" within the federal spatial order—as a "nation," yet not foreign and as "domestic," but not a state government.[48] The Cherokee "relation to the United States resembles that of a ward to his guardian," Marshall clarified. "They look to our government for protection; rely upon its kindness and its power; appeal to it for relief to their wants; and address the president as their great father."[49]

Worcester, like *Cherokee Nation*, poses the federal duty to protect Cherokee as the corollary of the federal right to carry on exclusive intercourse with

---

45. 31 U.S. 515, 561 (1832).

46. Emeric de Vattel, *The Law of Nations*, new ed. (London: G. G. and J. Robinson, 1797), bk. 1, chap. 1, secs. 5–8. Marshall's description of Indian tribes as "tributary" and "feudatory" was conventional, but his reference to "the Indian race," i.e., all tribes, was novel. Robert Clinton, Carole Goldberg, and Rebecca Tsosie, *American Indian Law: Native Nations and the Federal System*, 4th ed. (Newark, NJ: LexisNexis, 2003), 75.

47. 31 U.S. 515, 559 (1832).

48. 30 U.S. 1, 18 (1831). *Cherokee Nation* invoked the commerce clause of the U.S. constitution to classify native polities as neither a foreign state nor a state government.

49. Ibid., 17–18.

them. Marshall ruled that "the whole intercourse" with this nation is "vested in the government of the United States," placing the Cherokee nation in an extraterritorial relation to Georgia.[50] More subtly, Marshall affirmed that the Georgian government, like the Cherokee government, is part of the federal spatial order, which the southern state has disrupted. *Worcester* said to Georgia what *Cherokee Nation* said to "foreign nations": we, the federal government, consider your "attempt to acquire [Indian] lands" as "an invasion of our territory, and an act of hostility."[51] Likewise, the Marshall Court said to Georgia what the Monroe Doctrine said to Europe: your disruption of this U.S.-centered spatial order is regarded "as a manifestation of an unfriendly disposition towards the United States."[52] In short, Marshall speaks as (if he were) the decider on federal order.

Normative readings of *Worcester* overlook the ways that the Marshall Court deeply racializes the federal-Indian relationship.[53] To oversimplify—but just a little—contemporary liberalism only counts inherent or permanent ascriptions as racial. Its concept of race centers on mid- to late nineteenth-century phrenology, ethnology, and other pseudo-scientific racisms. Whether Indians are inferior or superior to whites, though, is of little concern to Marshall insofar as the concrete stakes of *Worcester* are racial and spatial order. The more relevant question, to use contemporary terms, is whether Marshall is a "racial naturalist" or a "racial historicist" or, more specifically, whether he grounds indigenous/settler difference in the order of nature or the order of culture.[54]

I claim that Marshall's opinions on Indian condition in *Worcester* are symptomatic of the racial historicism of nineteenth-century U.S. colonial governance. At pains to distinguish the two cases, Marshall repositioned the possibility of violence ("the actual condition of the two people") from *Johnson* as the condition of treaty alignments in *Worcester*. *Worcester* explained that "fierce and warlike in their character, [Indian nations] might be formidable enemies, or effective friends."[55] The replacement of the need to conquer enemies (*Johnson*) with the possibility of friendship or enmity (*Worcester*) signals

---

50. 31 U.S. 515, 561 (1832). My thanks to Carole Goldberg for this insight.
51. 30 U.S. 1, 17–18 (1831).
52. "Monroe Doctrine," 22–23.
53. See, e.g., Smith, *Civic Ideals*, 36, 239.
54. Goldberg, *The Racial State*, chap. 4. See also Fred Lee, "Post–Naturalistic Racialization in the 'Post–Racial' United States: The Shifting rather than Declining Significance of Race," *Theory & Event* 20, no. 3 (2017): 661.
55. 31 U.S. 515, 546 (1832).

that "Indian" has acquired a more historicist, less belligerent valence for Marshall. Now friend/enemy decisions, more than naturalistic distinctions, ally the Crown and indigenous polities or the United States and the Cherokee. Federal-Indian treaties, Marshall pointed out, presuppose that Cherokee can decide on their friendship with as well as discern their boundaries with the United States.[56]

With this increased emphasis on racial development, *Worcester* argued that modernization could only strengthen Cherokee land claims. Marshall explained that the Civilization Fund Act sought "the preservation of the Indian nations" by way of "civilizing and converting them from hunters into agriculturists." Cherokee progress "encouraged perseverance in the laudable exertions still farther to meliorate their condition. This [1819] act furnishes strong additional evidence of a settled purpose to fix the Indians in their country by giving them security at home."[57] The U.S. attempt to "fix" natives in their designated place drew on an aptly named "fund" of civilization; this fixity was precisely the "settled" permanence that Georgian settlers abhorred. Put in the terms of Schmittian *nomos*, Indians would be "preserved" if they could settle within lands distributed by the federal government and oriented toward the settler's modes of production. The second operation of racial exceptionality creates the federal-Indian rules of a paternalistic civilizing mission in the space of exception from the intra-European rules of protection. Remember that Worcester was a missionary authorized by the federal government to enter Cherokee lands.[58]

Worcester reveals Marshall to be both federal decider and colonial administrator. *Worcester* is even more Americentric than *Johnson* in that the Court declares itself to be the decider of the Indian's place within U.S. federalism. *Worcester* consequently foregrounds not only the substance, but also the sites of federal decision—including the authority of the Supreme Court and the rival authority of the Jackson administration. Marshall maintained that the civilizing project has "long been cherished by the executive" and has taken place "under the sanction of the chief magistrate" in part to chastise the great land appropriator Andrew Jackson.[59] The federal judiciary,

---

56. Ibid., 554–55.
57. Ibid., 557.
58. Rasch sees the U.S. civilizing mission as akin to Spanish conversion efforts and as an extension of European Christianity. William Rasch, "Human Rights as Geopolitics: Carl Schmitt and the Legal Form of American Supremacy," *Cultural Critique* 54 (2003): 131, 137–39.
59. 31 U.S. 515, 557, 562 (1832).

no less than the federal executive, sought out a baseline of homogeneity for the federal system. Marshall intervened to decide *where* the Indian shall be civilized, not if he should be. He would in accordance with federal treaties replace the cultural substance of Amerindians while protecting the Cherokee from Georgian land appropriation.

Worcester v. Georgia: *The Broader Debate*

Both the Supreme Court in 1832 and the Cherokee constitutional convention in 1827 opposed removal using the means available to them. While the Cherokee constitution linked formal homogeneity to sovereign claims in the register of legal institutions, *Worcester* linked substantive homogeneity to protection claims in the register of racial historicism. To reduce the meaning of race to hierarchy (superiority/inferiority) is to ignore all the ways that *Worcester* articulates race in juridical (norm/exception), spatial (Old/New World), and historical (ahead/behind) terms. In fact, I have argued, *Worcester* incorporated European public law according to the same racial paradigm and discourse as *Johnson* did. The paradigm of racial exceptionality seized on the nineteenth-century discourse on civilization as settlement that proved flexible enough to accommodate both the "pro-Indian" *Worcester* and the "anti-Indian" *Johnson*. This discourse also informed the broader debate on Indian removal, where Lewis Cass counterposed his formulation of "preservation through resettlement" to Marshall's formulation of "preservation through settlement."

Cass was an ethnographic authority on northern native polities and, as governor of the Michigan territories from 1813 to 1831, an ex officio commissioner of Indian affairs. His 1830 essay "Removal of the Indians" argued that population is regulated for "wandering tribes" by "the bounties of nature"; in "stationary societies," by contrast, "art and industry can increase almost indefinitely those products which minister to . . . wants."[60] The problem of Indian "degeneration" (population decrease) is exacerbated by their inflexible character, their "stationary and unbending" habits.[61] Should Indians remain east of the Mississippi River, "prefer ancient associations to future prospects,

---

60. Lewis Cass, "Removal of the Indians," *North American Review* 30 (1830): 64–65. Cass defines these nations by their male "hunter-warriors," diminishing the importance of southeastern Indian agriculture and its association with women. Anthony Wallace, *The Long, Bitter Trail: Andrew Jackson and the Indians* (New York: Hill and Wang, 1993), 48.

61. Cass, "Removal of the Indians," 67. Jackson held similar views. See "Annual Message to Congress (Dec. 7, 1835)," in *Documents of United States Indian Policy*, 3rd ed., ed. Francis Prucha (Lincoln: University of Nebraska Press, 2000), 71.

and finally melt away before our people and institutions, the result must be attributed to causes, which we can neither stay nor control."[62] If native peoples do "melt away" before advancing settlers, this would be the operation of natural causes and no fault of "our people and institutions." Indians settled in their habits are doomed, but Indians resettled in a stationary way of life just might be preserved.

For Cass, Marshall, and other participants in the Indian removal debate, protection mandated paternalism and paternalism aimed at preservation. Both anti- and proremoval policymakers claimed to be friends, brothers, and humanitarians looking out for Indian welfare. From this administrative perspective, Cass insisted that without settler guidance no one could protect natives "from themselves."[63] From this same perspective, Cass insisted that grand plans for removing Indians west of the Mississippi should secure the "assent" of the southeastern polities.[64] Though he might not know his own good best, the Indian should not be forced into doing what is best for him. Cass thought that Amerindians should—and indeed must—choose. We must turn to the removal treaties themselves to critique this powerful, depoliticizing fiction of native consent to their own replacement.

Section II: Racial Removal Contracts for the Sake of Land Appropriation

Section I concluded that the Marshall Court affirmed its authority over the federal spatial order when it legally protected southeastern Indian polities against the land appropriations of southern state governments. Working within the U.S. constitutional paradigm of what I called racial exceptionality, *Worcester* envisioned an Americentric order of fixed Indian lands inhabited by fluid Indian characters. Section II covers how the federal executive constructed an alternative Americentric spatial order to the one Marshall envisioned. Below I investigate how federal Indian treaties authorized the expropriation of southeastern Indian lands irrespective of constitutional law. "Racial removal contracts," as I call them, forced southeastern households to choose between removing to Indian Territory or assimilating into southern

---

62. Cass, "Removal of the Indians," 121.
63. Ibid., 83.
64. Ibid., 110. As Secretary of War from 1831 to 1836, Cass would oversee land appropriations under the 1830 Removal Act.

states. These contracts, and especially those terms that provided welfare and criminalized warfare, treated native polities as racialized populations and bureaucratic targets.

Racial Removal Contracts: Vehicles of Land Appropriation

Spatial, juridical, and cultural replacement would be less unilaterally imposed than contractually negotiated by the racial state and its Indian subjects. Racial removal contracts of the Jacksonian era included the subclause of Mills's racial contract that demarcates "wild" and "civil" spaces and individuals.[65] Building on Mills's idea of the racial contract and her own idea of the sexual contract, Carole Pateman uses the term "the settler contract" to refer "to the dispossession of, and rule over, Native inhabitants by British settlers in two New Worlds."[66] In the strictest case of Australia, the settler contract declared lands to be "empty" of civilized peoples, legitimate sovereignties, and licit indigenous presence. In the tempered cases of Canada and the United States, the settler contract recognized "pre-existing social orders," but only to the degree that they resembled "a modern state in the making."[67] However, this tempered logic cannot put the settler state, the standard by which native societies are declared civil, into question.[68]

I agree with Pateman and Mills that European settlers misrecognized indigenous peoples, institutions, and lifeworlds as illicit outgrowths of the wilderness. For both Mills and Pateman, settler societies presume that no other societies exist on the appropriated land in order to legitimize whatever means it takes to actualize that presumption.[69] The settler contract is more focused than the racial contract on questions of indigenous sovereignty and territory, however.[70] My conception of racial removal contracts differs from both Mills's racial contract and Pateman's settler contract in that I theorize a necessary rather than contingent role for indigenous consent. All signatories of Mills's racial contract are "white," although not all "whites"

---

65. Mills, *The Racial Contract*, 41–53.
66. Carole Pateman, "The Settler Contract," in Pateman and Mills, *Contract and Domination*, 38.
67. Ibid., 39–40.
68. Ibid., 59. Contemporary usages of the original contract metaphor continue to place the burden of proof on indigenous claimants rather than settler states. Robert Nichols, "Indigeneity and the Settler Contract Today," *Philosophy and Social Criticism* 39, no. 2 (2013): 176–78.
69. Cf. Wolfe, "Settler Colonialism and the Elimination of the Native," 401–2.
70. Nichols, "Indigeneity and the Settler Contract Today," 168.

are signatories; Mills acknowledges the possibility that "nonwhites" might sign on to the racial contract, but he conceives of their signatures as both optional and a function of indoctrination.[71] Similarly, Pateman's settler contract is asymmetrical to Pateman's sexual contract insofar as indigenous agreement is not constitutive of the former, while female agreement is constitutive of the latter.

On this question of who "signs," the racial removal contract is modeled on the sexual contract rather than the settler contract. On Pateman's account, the sexual contracts of employment and marriage incorporate women, thereby squaring away civil freedom and civil subordination in liberal democratic regimes: "If the claim that civil society was an order of universal freedom was to be plausible, women had to be incorporated through contract, the act that, at one and the same time, signified freedom and constitutes patriarchal right."[72] Analogously, the contractual incorporation of Amerindians into the Americentric spatial order made it plausible for the settlers to believe that their civil society was an "order of universal freedom." The representation of the colonizer's society as an order of civilization depended on the representation of the colonized as "freely" giving their consent.[73] It is not just that contracts legitimate certain forms of subordination; it is rather that some forms of dominance can only be established through the solicitation and signs of subaltern agreement.

Racial removal contracts did not pretend that indigenous societies did not exist and did not seek out the signatures of settlers alone. They instead "recognized" Amerindian polities (or factions thereof) on the condition that they would sign up for a federal project of "civilization" on federally reserved lands. (The fail-safe, as we will see, is that Amerindians who refused to sign would still be subject to state-level assimilation.) The irony is that racial removal contracts undermined the sociohistorical conditions under which the federal-Indian treaty system had served as a site for the exercise of Amerindian agency. That system came more and more to serve an institutional order of "cultural imperialism" (which treats the normal norms of the dominant as universal) and racial "domination" (which constrains the subaltern's ability to determine their own actions).[74]

---

71. Mills, *The Racial Contract*, 11, 89.
72. Pateman, *The Sexual Contract*, 227.
73. Cf. G.W.F. Hegel, *Phenomenology of the Spirit*, trans. A. V. Miller (Oxford, UK: Oxford University Press, 1977), 116. My thanks to Dana Miranda for the Hegel comparison.
74. Young, *Justice and the Politics of Difference*, chaps. 1–2.

Removal treaties, in short, were the vehicles of both indigenous agreement and indigenous dispossession, both spatial ordering and racial orientation. Such treaties helped establish a *nomos* that broke from the previous order of federal-Indian alliance. Before the early nineteenth century, when the United States achieved dominance over eastern North America, various powers—French, Spanish, British, and American—had fought over trade and military alliances with indigenous polities in the highly contested southeast. The withdrawal of their European allies around the turn of the century increasingly compelled the southeastern polities to make territorial concessions and curtail military opposition to the United States.[75] Declines of the fur trade and depletion of game also sapped the ability of Indian peoples to wage war, although decreased strength certainly put no stop to lower-intensity frontier violence.

A new spatial order, consisting of contractual relationships, was meant to resolve ongoing land conflicts. Interlocking with congressional laws, War Department regulations, and Supreme Court cases, Senate-ratified treaties were the source of federal removal policy in which Indians most directly participated. Although many, if not most, were of questionable procedural legality, removal treaties were nonetheless powerful instruments of policy craft.[76] They deployed a logic of exchange rather than a logic of alliance. Land exchanges, for their part, did much to transform friend/enemy relationships in the period of imperial competition into administrative relationships in the period of United States dominance. On William Hagan's periodization, the 1776–1816 era of "Foes and Friends" is followed by the 1816–1850 era of "Indian Removal."[77] Relationships between southeastern polities and the United States would increasingly appear to be relationships between population divisions and the racial state.

Treaty of Dancing Rabbit Creek: Choice and Consent

The Removal Act of May 28, 1830, authorized the executive branch to negotiate trades of Indian land in "any of the states or territories" for western pub-

---

75. Champagne, *Social Order and Political Change*, 74–75.
76. Most treaties were unpopular with native majorities (e.g., the Cherokee Treaty of New Echota of 1835) or violated native understandings of prior agreements (e.g., the Seminole Treaty of Fort Gibson of 1833). Ronald Satz, *American Indian Policy in the Jacksonian Era* (Lincoln: University of Nebraska Press, 1975), 106–7.
77. William Hagan, *American Indians*, 3rd ed. (Chicago: University of Chicago Press, 1993), chaps. 2–3.

lic domain.[78] The first deal negotiated under the aforementioned act, the 1830 Treaty of Dancing Rabbit Creek,[79] resettled the majority of Choctaw beyond the Mississippi River. This treaty exemplifies the consent-based logic of racial removal contracts, whose similar terms addressed the shared predicament of the southeastern polities. The Treaty of Dancing Rabbit Creek responded to the extension of Mississippian law over Choctaw territory, much like *Worcester* responded to the extension of Georgian law over Cherokee territory. The treaty offered each Choctaw household the choice of remaining east as an "individual" or the choice of removing west as (a part of) a collectivity, both of which would contribute to the Mississippian land appropriation.

We first consider the choice of being absorbed into a differently established racial order. Article 14 of the Treaty of Dancing Rabbit Creek permits "each Choctaw head of family being desirous to remain and become a citizen of the States . . . to do so." Heads of households wishing to remain would be allotted lands based on their household's size and would hold this property under Mississippian law. Racial discrimination, however, dis-incentivized this choice. Triangulated against blacks and whites, Mississippi Choctaw would become nonwhite, like-black subordinates by law.[80] Neither Indians nor blacks could testify against whites in most southern courts, so indigenous southern landowners would have little recourse against fraudulent sales and white squatters. (Most of the 6,000 or so Choctaw who stayed in Mississippi ended up as poor, isolated squatters on infertile land.) Antebellum southern laws would formally recognize Choctaw heads of households as property owners, but differentially enforce their rights to private property. Arrangements for collective property would have to be reestablished among the emigrants "out west."

Southeastern land appropriation divided the southern states and southeastern polities along the lines of the central spatial institution of property. Charles Hudson, who admits that southeastern Indian conceptions of property were sometimes ambiguous, flatly denies that their traditional order contained a notion of private property.[81] Modern Western economics began to penetrate southeastern indigenous orders through the lucrative fur and

---

78. 4 Stat. 411.
79. 7 Stat. 333.
80. Deborah Rosen, *American Indians and State Law: Sovereignty, Race, and Citizenship, 1790–1880* (Lincoln: University of Nebraska Press, 2007), 108–15.
81. Charles Hudson, *The Southeastern Indians* (Knoxville: University of Tennessee Press, 1976), 312.

slave trade, which in the colonial period cemented alliances with European powers and sparked violence in cases of fraud. Trade gave rise to new desires for European manufactured goods (guns, tools, clothing, etc.) that facilitated the adoption of new modes of production.[82] By the mid-nineteenth century, each southeastern polity had an influential class of American-educated merchants and planters who produced for the capitalist market. At the same time, the great majority still adhered to the tradition of holding land communally to produce for a subsistence economy.[83] The other side of southeastern Indian removal, then, was the extension of the property order of southern state governments or the legal-institutional homogenization of what had been Indian lands.

Now we will consider the choice of being expulsed into the new racial order of Indian Country—"no part of [which] shall ever be embraced in any Territory or State," as Article 4 put it. The Treaty of Dancing Rabbit Creek posed collectivity under federal protection as the alternative to individuation under state law. Removed Choctaw would acquire a dependent status most evident in the treaty provisions on violence. Article 5 obligates the United States

> to protect the Choctaw from domestic strife and from foreign enemies on the same principles that the citizens of the United States are protected, so that whatever would be a legal demand upon the US for defense or wrongs committed by an enemy, on a citizen of the US shall be equally binding in favor of the Choctaws, and in all cases where the Choctaw shall be called upon by a legally authorized officer of the US to fight an enemy, such Choctaw shall receive the pay and other emoluments which the citizens of the US receive in such cases, provided, no war shall be undertaken or prosecuted by said Choctaw Nation but by declaration made in full Council, and to be approved by the US.

Choctaw would acquire the wartime protections and obligations of U.S. citizens in exchange for their authority to decide on the friend/enemy dis-

---

82. Ibid., 436; cf. R. S. Cotterill, *The Southern Indians: The Story of the Civilized Tribes before Removal* (Norman: University of Oklahoma Press, 1954), 17.

83. Though they did own personal property, individuals did not privately own means of subsistence; laborers completed agricultural tasks in common on one household allotment of communal land before moving on to the next. Hudson, *The Southeastern Indians*, 295–97.

tinction. This authority could be provisionally exercised in cases of "self-defense against an open rebellion, or an enemy marching into their country, in which cases they shall defend, until the US are advised thereof."[84] *Contra* the Marshall Court's interpretation of Cherokee independence, the Treaty of Dancing Rabbit Creek would alienate the Choctaw *jus belli* to the United States,[85] whose approval that indigenous polity would have to secure to legally undertake war.

The United States wanted to monopolize the legitimated means of violence within a federal spatial order where, in Schmitt's words, "there will be no more enemies."[86] Conflating private force and armed combat, the treaty depoliticizes and criminalizes violence enacted by Choctaw. Article 6 prohibits Choctaw individuals or factions from "[committing] acts of violence upon the person or property of the citizens of the US or [joining] any war party against any neighbouring tribe of Indians, without the authority in the preceding paragraph [the U.S. approval of Article 5]." Reciprocally, the treaty depoliticizes and criminalizes violence done to Choctaw. Article 7 demands that "all acts of violence committed upon persons and property of the Choctaw Nation either by citizens of the US or neighbouring Tribes of Red People" be reported to an Indian agent, who will see to it that "every possible degree of justice is done." These articles disassociate violence from war (a possible consequence of the friend/enemy distinction) and associate it with crime (a disorder amenable to the administration of justice). They position Indian polities as populations that consent to U.S. administrative authority.

This shifting status of violence highlights the difference between removal treaties based on exchange and peace treaties based on alliance. Alliance treaties like the 1785 Cherokee Treaty of Hopewell criminalized some forms of violence,[87] but—unlike the 1830 Choctaw Treaty of Dancing Rabbit Creek—it classified other forms of violence as political. The Hopewell articles of peace, even if these put the Cherokee nation under the exclusive protection of the United States, presuppose that a nation decides on the friend/enemy

---

84. An unratified Chickasaw treaty of 1830 had a similar provision in Article 3. "Treaty with the Chickasaw, 1830," in *Treaties with American Indians: An Encyclopedia of Rights, Conflicts, and Sovereignty*, vol. II, ed. Donald Fixico (Santa Barbara, CA: ABC-CLIO, 2008), 464.

85. The *jus belli* is the right of collectivities to demand from "members the readiness to die and unhesitatingly kill enemies." Schmitt, *The Concept of the Political*, 46.

86. Schmitt, *Nomos of the Earth*, 157.

87. See, e.g., Articles 6–7 of 7 Stat. 18.

distinction for itself. In Article 8, Cherokee signatories pledge to not apply their "idea of retaliation"—that is, not to make war[88]—unless "there is a manifest violation of this treaty." In Article 13, "the hatchet shall be forever buried, and the peace given by the United States, and friendship re-established between the said states on the one part, and all the Cherokee on the other, shall be universal." The hatchet belongs to a combatant, not a murderer. The Treaty of Hopewell recognizes that Cherokee people have a political existence in the late eighteenth century, a period of inter-imperial competition in North America. By the mid-nineteenth century, a period in which the United States dominated the Southeast, all Choctaw violence is criminal disorder for the Americentric spatial order.[89]

As an instance of extraordinary racial politics, the U.S. appropriation of the Southeast is "the constitutive event of a new spatial order."[90] Removal treaties contributed to the construction of spatial and racial orders on either side of the Mississippi: on one side is an order of southern states and on the other is an order of Indian territories. Put differently, the *nomos* of U.S. westward expansion established two modes and sites of colonial assimilation: a practical variant of discriminatory absorption into the order of southern states as distinguished from a paternal variant of absorptive expulsion into the order of Indian Country. Southeastern Indian removal physically and geographically pushed the settler-Indian frontier back, but administratively and culturally pulled Amerindians across it in the same gesture. This event had contradictory "integrationist" and "segregationist" impulses.

The true cunning of the racial removal contracts is that the *nomos* of the New World is not imposed on southeastern Indians. Indigenous choice and consent are rather built into the operative terms of such contracts. "Consent" is the formal moment of ordering and orienting in which native polities accept or reject the treaty; this operation prioritizes bilateral federal-Indian agreement over unilateral settler force in the process of colonial dispossession. "Choice" is the substantive moment in which an indigenous head of household opts for individuating assimilation or collective removal, discriminatory absorption or absorptive expulsion. Each Choctaw household

---

88. The law of retaliation governed interclan revenge and international war alike. The principle was that deaths on one side should be balanced by deaths on the other. Hudson, *The Southeastern Indians*, 239.

89. Later, southeastern Indians—save for renegade factions of mostly Creeks and Cherokees—signed alliance treaties with the Confederate States of America. Just like that, southeastern polities went from west to south and from population to people. Prucha, *The Great Father*, 416.

90. Ojakangas, *A Philosophy of Concrete Life*, 153.

must choose. Not choosing is not a choice. Hence the racial removal contract is a form of consent that contains the choices of remaining or removing and the requirements of protectionism and paternalism. Racial and colonial distinctions, far from breaking promises, made these promises possible.

Contract-based colonialism in the removal period is compatible with, and also constituted through, what James Tully calls "treaty federalism." Treaty federalism takes for granted the settler state's recognition of certain markers of indigenous sovereignty. *Worcester v. Georgia*, for instance, cited the Hopewell treaty as evidence that the Cherokee nation independently decides on war and peace.[91] Likewise, in the contemporary era, Amerindian activists and their allies use the term "treaty" to connote a diplomatic relation of two fully sovereign nations.[92] As such activists are well aware, however, federal-Indian treaties are a far from unproblematic site for the exercise of indigenous agency.[93] I grant that Congress increasingly asserted "plenary power" over indigenous polities after the treaty system was unilaterally ended in 1871, when cultural assimilation and land allotment policies would be pursued with renewed force.[94] Long before that, however, racial removal contracts stipulated conditions of indigenous subjection to the U.S. federal order. Treaties that presupposed the ability of Indian peoples to decide on their future actions worked to erode the social and institutional conditions of that presupposition.

Second Seminole War: Resistance and Partisanship

The logic of consensual exchange tries to replace, but can only displace the logic of friend/enemy distinction: the Indian rejection of removal treaties is a refusal to consent to an Americentric ordering, if not a declaration of hostilities against the federal decider on that order. Seminole warfare illuminates how the United States outlawed indigenous enmity or, to redeploy Heidi Kiiwetinepinesiik Stark's phrase, criminalized indigenous resistance.[95]

---

91. 31 U.S. 515, 530 (1832).

92. Francis Prucha, *American Indian Treaties: The History of a Political Anomaly* (Berkeley: University of California, 1994), 409.

93. I bracket the question of whether Amerindian polities have "inherent sovereignty," i.e., the legal doctrine that tribal sovereignty antedates the United States. See Prucha, *American Indian Treaties*, 399; see also Bruyneel, *The Third Space of Sovereignty*, xiv–xv.

94. 16 Stat. 544, 570. This interpretation is from Bruyneel, *The Third Space of Sovereignty*, 65–66, 93.

95. Heidi Kiiwetinepinesiik Stark, "Criminal Empire: The Making of the Savage in a Lawless Land," *Theory & Event* 19, no. 4 (2016), accessed January 18, 2017, https://muse.jhu.edu

While the U.S. military fought the first Seminole War in the early days of southeastern land appropriation (from 1816 to 1818), it fought the second Seminole War near the end of it (from 1835 to 1842). Enraged southerners and the federal state wanted to eliminate an "illegitimate" racial order wherein Seminole held land and lived with runaway slaves that "belonged" to whites. The 1832 Seminole Treaty of Payne's Landing, signed by a proremoval faction, was outright rejected by an antiremoval faction, which initiated combat in 1835.[96] Drawn-out combat alternated with fitful respites until the United States unilaterally stopped its offensive in 1842. It was a sign of the times that the federal government felt no need to draw up a peace treaty.

Schmitt would have classified Seminole resistance to land appropriation as a case of partisan warfare. In Europe, the partisan appeared in the guise of defensive Spanish guerrillas who fought invading French armies during the Napoleonic wars; in the Americas, the partisan appeared in the countless "wars of the white conquerors against the American redskins from the 17th to the 19th centuries."[97] European partisans stood outside and against the order of European sovereignties, the juridical and territorial condition of their existence. The Eurocentric order limited and legitimated warfare between national-state armies, rationalized and legalized combat that met certain formal requirements. This spatial order marked that, with the decline of Church authority, pre-modern wars based on claims of *justa causa* had given way to modern *guerre en forme* between *justi hostes* sharing no common authority.[98]

Partisanship had different meanings in the United States, where nothing comparable to the European nation-states system regulated federal-Indian warfare. The Seminole partisan stood outside and against the U.S. federal system, which—as Chapter 2 argued—delegitimated all varieties of racial conflict prior to the civil rights movement. Seminole in the Everglade marshlands waged an all-or-nothing war for political existence, bare survival, and "naturally, dignity."[99] An infamous episode in the second

---

/article/633282. Seminole were an independent, breakaway grouping of Creek who fled to northern Florida after their defeat to Jackson in the War of 1812. Seminole and Creek were merged in Indian Country for the purposes of administrative simplification; eventually they regained their distinctiveness.

96. 7 Stat. 368.

97. Carl Schmitt, *Theory of the Partisan: Intermediate Commentary on the Concept of the Political*, trans. G. L. Ulmen (New York: Telos, 2007), 3–4.

98. Schmitt, *Nomos of the Earth*, pt. 3, chaps. 1–2.

99. Fanon, *The Wretched of the Earth*, 9.

Seminole War concerned the 1837 capture and imprisonment of Chief Osceola and his party, who had come under a white flag to negotiate. No "civilized" military officer would negotiate a peace agreement with a "savage" chief that day.[100] It is as if the Treaty of Dancing Rabbit Creek's criminalization of potential Choctaw violence were the exceptional norm crafted in the space of the U.S. military's exception of actual Seminole violence from the normal norms of "civilized" warfare. Please forgive the nonlinear temporality of this statement, whose relevant dimension is spatiality. Racial exceptionality, after all, can only qualify as normative relative to a concrete spatial order.

Racial Removal Contracts: Paternalism and Productivity

Amerindian participation within a federal treaty system that could not function without it was narrowly construed as indigenous consent to state management. For instance, the Treaty of Dancing Rabbit Creek was a replacement for a removal treaty drawn up by proremoval Choctaw and rejected by the U.S. Senate.[101] The paternalistic context of its formation resonates with the paternalistic premises of its content, as in Article 16's guarantee that the United States will remove Choctaw Indians "under the care of discreet and careful persons, who will be kind and brotherly to them," or in Article 17's confirmation that the federal government will continue to pay all annuities already in effect, notwithstanding officials who feared the annuities system impeded the conversion of Indians into "hard working farmers."[102] My contention is not that the federal government should not have covered travel expenses or paid annuities. On the contrary, it managed to bungle these provisions and, judged by professional standards of administration or common understandings of decency, it should have done better.[103] My point is rather that the Choctaw

---

100. A contemporaneous apologist wrote that "when we reflect that the General was dealing with savages, who had once forfeited their plighted faith, and deceived him [Osceola broke an earlier promise to return slaves] ... it is believed he will not only be justified by public opinion ... but will be commended for it." *Army and Navy Chronicle*, cited in Grant Foreman, *Indian Removal: The Emigration of the Five Civilized Tribes of Indians*, rev. ed. (Norman: University of Oklahoma Press, 1953), 351.

101. Prucha, *American Indian Treaties*, 168–70. This treaty was negotiated by Secretary of War John Eaton and Jackson's friend John Coffee.

102. Prucha, *The Great Father*, 309, 333.

103. This appeal to "professionalism" is admittedly anachronistic. Systematic, centralized planning was not the bureaucratic order of the day. Furthermore, jobs in the Office of Indian Affairs were the spoils of 1830s party competition. Satz, *American Indian Policy*, 64–65, 73.

treaty, like the contemporaneous *Cherokee Nation v. Georgia*, turns federal paternalism into the obverse of federal protectionism. Protectionism is marked by the vanishing Choctaw right of war, whereas paternalism is marked by the administration of Choctaw well-being.

The federal government spoke of Indian welfare in openly paternalistic tones, especially when addressing less powerful southeastern polities. In the language of the 1832 Treaty of Pontitock Creek, for instance, the Chickasaw "have determined to sell their country and hunt a new home" because they "find themselves oppressed in their present situation."[104] Oppressive in the current situation is not the extension of Mississippian law into Chickasaw land; oppression instead stems from an ignorance of "the language and laws of the white man" so deep that Chickasaws "cannot understand or obey them." Thus Andrew Jackson, as the president with the supposed knowledge to save the tribe from self-incurred oppression, has sent his treaty commissioner to negotiate a removal. Removal is necessitated by the supposed ignorance that precludes Chickasaws from assuming normative citizenship under English-language law. Howsoever deep their ignorance runs, however, the Chickasaw nation knows enough to consent to the superior wisdom of the Jackson administration.

The Treaty of Pontitock Creek is an intriguing disclosure of the epistemic premises of the mid-nineteenth-century racial state. It figures Chickasaw "ignorance" in a racial historicist fashion, entertaining the possibility of their "enlightenment." Article 11 invests proceeds of Chickasaw land sales "in such safe and valuable stock as [the President] may approve of, for the use and benefit of the Chickasaw nation." Yet the Chickasaw polity may resume control over their assets if after fifty years they "shall have improved in education and civilization, and become so enlightened, as to be capable of managing so large a sum of money to advantage" and "the President of the United States, with the Senate, shall be satisfied thereof." The guardian who knows best decides when the Indian ward's education is complete. To play on Mills's formulation, indigenous "local knowledge," while not ruled out altogether, must be certified by the epistemic authority of a more "global . . . rationality."[105]

Nothing in the 1830 Choctaw treaty so blatantly parses knowledge and ignorance, but official education and socialization projects are likewise built into its operative terms. Potential enlightenment appears in Article 20, where

---

104. 7 Stat. 381. Notice the patronizing language of "hunting."
105. Mills, *The Racial Contract*, 45–46.

"for the benefit and advantage of the Choctaw people, and to improve their condition, there shall be educated under direction of the President at the expense of the US forty Choctaw youth for twenty years." The United States will pay for institutions (churches that double as schoolhouses) as well as for resources, both human (teachers, blacksmiths, and millwrights) and material (blankets, rifles, axes, ploughs, looms, iron, steel, etc.). The Indian's conversion to Christianity, the settler's settled agriculture, and English-language education were the desiderata of the federal government. A consensus on the need and desirability of civilizing the Indian uncovers the not-so-hidden complicity of *Worcester v. Georgia* with the Treaty of Dancing Rabbit Creek. Both pronouncements participated in a colonialist discourse that I have argued was flexible enough to accommodate both anti- and proremoval policies. This colonialist discourse was also flexible enough to accommodate both racial naturalism and racial historicism.

In perhaps *the* generic operation of racial figuration, nineteenth-century civilizational discourse split Amerindians into "good" and "bad" varieties. "Noble savages" and "ignoble savages," who carried all the same characteristics with inverted valences, could transform into one another with surprising ease.[106] That said, savagery figured less prominently than civilization in the ideology of continental expansion.[107] That is, popular writers romanticized Indian "savagery" more than their official counterparts, who typically held that "*to civilize* meant to bring to a state of civility out of a state of rudeness and barbarism."[108] Officials differed in that Cass and other proremoval policymakers focused on "bad" Indians and persistent difference, while Marshall and other antiremoval policymakers emphasized "good" Indians and potential sameness. Francis Prucha notes that, despite the prevalence and authority of scientific racism, the Office of Indian Affairs agents believed in "the perfectibility of the Indians," which (in their imaginations) meant the "ability to attain the civilization of whites."[109]

The "improvable" savage, to be clear, is no less racialized a figure than the "inherent" savage. In either the racial naturalist or the racial historicist

---

106. For example, the instinctual spontaneity of the noble savage is the childlike laxity of the ignoble savage, just as the disciplined ethic of the model minority is the cutthroat competitiveness of the yellow peril.

107. Reginald Horsman, *Race and Manifest Destiny: The Origins of American Racial Anglo-Saxonism* (Cambridge, MA: Harvard University Press, 1981), 105; cf. Goldberg, *The Racial State*, 74.

108. Prucha, *The Great Father*, 136, italics original.

109. Ibid., 291.

case, Euro-American civilization is the standard by which Indian existence is evaluated. An imperious value-logic imposes the obligation to civilize the uncivilized and cultivate their (waste)land in the productive moment of Schmittian *nomos*,[110] according to which "the higher value has the right and the obligation to subdue the lower value, while the value per se righteously eliminates the disvalue."[111] In this vein, scholars of Indian removal have argued that southern whites wanted the valuable land of the Southeast without the devalued southeastern Indians populating it.[112] My addendum is that questions of value cannot be taken at face value if the social order and its spatiality are the respective source and scope of the validity of values. Prior to economic valuation (productivity, market price, etc.) is the economic ordering that standardizes it, and prior to normative valuation (prejudgment, propriety, etc.) is the racial ordering that normalizes it.

This question of the spatial ordering of the social is at the forefront of all varieties of Marxist accounts of indigenous North American dispossession. Michael Rogin, for one, claims that, like the early-modern nation-state in Europe, Andrew Jackson acted "as the agent for primitive accumulation" in "[liberating] land from communal use and [thrusting] it into the market."[113] The violence of primitive accumulation is the structural condition of Civilization's envy of and rage toward Savages (imagined to be) blissfully attached to Nature; in Rogin's reversal of this settler colonial fantasy, "civilized" whites rather than "savage" Indians were the childlike primitives.[114] Dealing with a distinctive, yet related case of "primitive accumulation," Glen Coulthard argues that the "experience of *dispossession*, not proletarianization" is the "dominant background structure" of aboriginal peoples' relation to the Canadian state. What colonialist and capitalist formations needed from aboriginal nations, on Coulthard's account, was commodifiable land

---

110. Even a Whig opponent of the 1830 Removal Act like Senator Thomas Frelinghuysen conceded that "when the increase of population and the wants of mankind demand the cultivation of the earth, a duty is thereby developed upon the proprietors of large and uncultivated regions, of devoting them to such useful purposes." "Debate on 1830 Removal Act (April 9, 1830)," in Prucha, *Documents of United States Indian Policy*, 49.

111. Carl Schmitt, *The Tyranny of Values*, trans. Simona Draghici (Washington, DC: Plutarch, 1996), 24.

112. See, e.g., Michael Green and Theda Perdue, *The Columbia Guide to American Indians of the Southeast* (New York: Columbia University Press, 2001), 87; Prucha, *The Great Father*, 195.

113. Rogin, *Fathers and Children*, 167.

114. Ibid., 9. Rogin's account is developed in Anne Norton, *Alternative Americas: A Reading of Antebellum Political Culture* (Chicago: University of Chicago Press, 1986), 211–13.

more than exploitable labor.[115] What they needed from enslaved blacks, particularly in the United States, was super-exploitable labor.

Rogin, who stays close to Marx on primitive accumulation, might accept my premise that processes such as, say, the valorization of capital can only function inside an already established concrete order. This is because primitive accumulation for Marx takes logical priority over market production and exchange in the same way that land appropriation for Schmitt takes logical priority over land division and land-based production.[116] That is to say that both Marx and Schmitt posit extraordinary ruptures as the condition of possibility for everyday processes. In a parallel to his critique of Marx's primitive accumulation, though, Coulthard might worry that Schmitt mistakes land appropriation as an "inaugural set of events" rather than as "an ongoing practice of dispossession."[117] To put aside Schmitt's position, and to reiterate my own, I claim that an extraordinary event persists in ordinary times and spaces long after its period of initial intensity. In the case at hand, land appropriation continues, but as a submerged element within the trajectory of the federal spatial order. This is why I situate the federal ordering of southeastern polities within a nineteenth-century U.S. ordering of the New World that, as we will see, anticipates a twentieth-century U.S. attempt to order the earth.

Both Coulthard and Rogin might reject my proposal that the federal ordering of territory is co-equal to the federal orientation toward productive practices. My thought is that federal officials (President Jackson, Indian agents, etc.) acted in the interests of southern social groups (land speculators, plantation owners, etc.)—but they created a U.S. racial and spatial order in which commodification is a moment rather than an underlying process. Put another way, the federal logic of taking indigenous lands into the sphere of U.S. territorial sovereignty is irreducible to the capitalist logic of expanding market relations into spaces not yet commodified. The emergence of slave-based agriculture within the "civilized tribes," like the expensive wars for unprofitable Seminole land,[118] cannot be directly tied to totalizing market

---

115. Glen Coulthard, *Red Skins, White Masks: Rejecting the Colonial Politics of Recognition* (Minneapolis: University of Minnesota Press, 2014), 12–13, 60, italics original.

116. Karl Marx, *Capital: A Critique of Political Economy*, vol. I, trans. Ben Fowkes (New York: Penguin, 1976), pt. 8; Schmitt, *Nomos of the Earth*, 333–34.

117. Coulthard, *Red Skins, White Masks*, 151–52.

118. R. S. Cotterill remarks that Seminole removal seemed unnecessary "because Florida was so vast, the Indian population so scanty [about 5,000] and white immigration so small." Cotterill, *The Southern Indians*, 232; cf. Prucha, *The Great Father*, 229.

rationalities. If anything, these phenomena signaled the problematic place of indigenous polities within the U.S. federal order. Hence Indian removal literally and symbolically replaced indigenous polities with respect to simultaneously discriminative and absorptive frontiers.

Federal Racial and Spatial Order: Division and Decision

The racial state obligated its on-the-ground representatives to spread civilization. No abstract normative order (command), civilization was the project of an institutional racial order (arrangement). Christian missionaries and converts, federal bureaucracy and funds, removal pressures and treaties: all converged on Indian lands to concretize the generic civilized/savage distinction as the racial distinction of American/Indian ways of life. The spatial ordering of American civilization, which in some ways appropriated the European concept of civilization,[119] blurred the very line between "civilized" and "savage" it articulated. Put in the language of Chapter 2, "civilization" is the domination of the social, and "to civilize" is the expression of its expansionist tendencies.[120] The American social again rears its evaluative face, this time wearing the mask of federally mediated expansion.

My account of American civilization continues to extend Arendt's Eurocentric story about the rise of the social. On Arendt's account, the "family" of national society takes over the (purportedly) unified interest once represented by the ancient head of the household and next by the feudal monarch; after decapitating the monarch, so to speak, European nation-states are left with modern bureaucracy, "the most social form of government" or "the rule of nobody."[121] What carries across the Atlantic is the point that the family is a convincing metaphor for the nation, as U.S. national society has phenomenological origins in the private household. The antebellum southern plantation imparted the "indigenous model"[122] to the somewhat disorganized, yet thoroughly bureaucratic racial state out west. It is as if U.S. racial foundations were, in Arendt's terms,

---

119. On the European concept of civilization, see Schmitt, *Nomos of the Earth*, 228–29, 234–35.

120. The social is "variously said to 'absorb,' 'embrace,' and 'devour' people or other entities" by Hannah Arendt. Pitkin, *The Attack of the Blob*, 4. The social articulates the Borg cry from the *Star Trek* universe: "Resistance is futile. You will be assimilated."

121. Arendt, *The Human Condition*, 40.

122. Rogin, *Fathers and Children*, 169. "Indigenous" is meant in the sense of "U.S. national."

"augmented" when the household paternalism exercised over slaves rose into the public realm as the federal guardianship over Indians.

Andrew Jackson, the patriarch of the Tennessee plantation who loomed over the national household as "the Great Father," ascended along the same path. Both administrative father and sovereign decider, Jackson intervened against Marshall into the conflict of native and state governments. The Court's oral tradition reports that Jackson, after learning about *Worcester*, responded, "Marshall has made his decision; now let him enforce it."[123] The president probably never uttered these words which, even if he had said them, would not have exactly captured his conflict with the Chief Justice. The question is less that of enforcement and more that of decision—that of two federal officers who decided differently. Put otherwise, one authority of the racial state excepted Amerindians from even the exceptional norms crafted by another.

The president effectively suspended *Worcester* in an undeclared state of exception. Jackson never denied that Marshall's decision was good law; he only denied that the law applied to the situation at hand. Ignoring the federal protection of settled boundaries in *Worcester*, the Jackson administration replaced southeastern Indian polities into exceptional zones contradistinguished from the normal zones of organized territories and states. Removal would be carried out under the exceptional norms of the federal-Indian treaty system, not the exceptional norms of the U.S. Supreme Court. Jackson's decisive exception of the Amerindian from constitutional law was existentially superior to Marshall's ambiguous exceptions of the Amerindian from the European law of nations. Having (not) declared an exceptional situation into existence, the sovereign decided on an alternative Americentric *nomos*.

The presidential ability to reorder federal space does not emanate from nothingness or nowhere. Rather, as Schmitt's later work would imply, sovereignty draws its authority from the existing concrete order.[124] The U.S. federal order that divided state, indigenous, and federal territories itself divided into multiple points of authority, decision, and policymaking

---

123. *Worcester* can be read as an advisory opinion with no concrete Cherokee rights to enforce, crafted to avoid the possibility that Jackson would refuse to carry out the judgment. Magliocca, *Andrew Jackson and the Constitution*, 49–50. Marshall is famous for such stratagems, e.g., the 1803 case *Marbury v. Madison*.

124. See, e.g., Carl Schmitt, *On the Three Types of Juristic Thought*, trans. Joseph Bendersky (Westport, CT: Praeger, 2004), 51.

Congress, for its part, supported the president, with almost every enactment of the 1830 Removal Act putting the power to organize Indian space within the presidential sphere.[125] This evidence bears ambivalently on how Chapter 2 related U.S. federalism to the American nation-state. On the one hand, U.S. federalism structured the removal crisis as well as its resolution, as the federal conflict between judicial and executive branches settled the regional conflict between state and native governments. U.S. governance in this respect was more federal than national in character. On the other hand, Jackson served as the ultimate decider on the expansion of the social nation and the location of the southeastern Indian polities. Here U.S. governance centered on the sovereign, as in a national-state arrangement.

On March 4, 1837, President Jackson said goodbye to the United States constructed by his decisions on the place of the Indian race. His "Farewell Address" claimed that "the States which had so long been retarded in their improvement by the Indian tribes residing in the midst of them are at length relieved from the evil." It was also the Great Father's way of saying "farewell" to the southeastern polities whose "well-fare" would be federally superintended. Jackson's removal solution to "the Indian question" would make future Indian administration that much easier: that "ill-fated race has been at length placed beyond the reach of injury or oppression," where "the paternal care of the General Government will hereafter watch over them and protect them."[126] After the rule of father Jackson himself, the United States would "watch over" Indian children in accordance with the higher-than-constitutional law of "improvement." Yet just beneath the surface of bureaucratic paternalism is colonial maternalism. The absorptive character of the social is like "a mother who constantly prevents her basically perverse child from committing suicide,"[127] who protects—as Lewis Cass said—Indians "from themselves."

---

125. 4 Stat. 411. The act authorizes the president to organize the public domain into districts for each of the removed polities (sec. II), guarantee that lands west of the Mississippi would be held in perpetuity (sec. III), ascertain the value of lands claimed by households east of the Mississippi (sec. IV), assist the Indians in removing to and resettling in their new lands (sec. V), and maintain the order of Indian Country (sec. VI).

126. Andrew Jackson, "Farewell Address, March 4, 1837," *American Presidency Project*, University of California, Santa Barbara, accessed April 18, 2017, http://www.presidency.ucsb.edu/ws/?pid=67087.

127. Fanon, *The Wretched of the Earth*, 149.

Conclusion: The *Nomos* of Westward Expansion and the *Nomos* of the New World

Section I of this chapter introduced the concepts of racial exceptionality and Americentric spatial order through an examination of the Marshall Court's decisions on Indian land. Section II then demonstrated how the Jackson administration established an alternative Americentric order using the same logic of racial exceptionality. Paradoxically, racial removal contracts solicited southeastern Indians' consent to their status as a depoliticized population. Equally paradoxically, the physical and geographical displacement of the southeastern polities coincided with their administrative and cultural replacement. In a twist on *Johnson*, wherein "the conquered inhabitants" could be neither "blended with the conquerors" nor "safely governed as a distinct people," U.S. federalism tried to transform natives into settlers while governing natives and settlers as distinct peoples. This conclusion explores the liminal position of southeastern Indians inside/outside this federal order and orientation.

Much as a Bolivarian confederacy could have included the United States in an egalitarian interpretation of the Monroe Doctrine,[128] U.S. federalism could have incorporated southeastern Indians in an egalitarian interpretation of federal "protection." Indian Country, for instance, could have been organized as a territorial government; imagine, if you will, present-day Oklahoma as an official Indian state. Jackson was not alone in seriously considering proposals to confederate the "more civilized" polities of Indian Country and to grant the "most civilized" polities (Cherokee and Choctaw) special congressional representatives. Ranging from the vague implications of Monroe's annual presidential message of 1824 to the detailed congressional bills debated in 1834 and 1838, sundry plans sought to further normalize the exceptionality of Indian Country.[129] What happened in the absence of authentic federal-republican integration is simple: Indian Country consisted in Indian polities subjected to U.S. military interventions, congressional laws, and executive administration.

Perhaps contrary to our expectations, southeastern polities largely opposed plans for something like American statehood. They did so out of mis-

---

128. Oscar Guardiola-Rivera, *What If Latin America Ruled the World? How the South Will Take the North through the 21st Century* (New York: Bloomsbury, 2010), 194–95.

129. Prucha, *The Great Father*, 302–9; Satz, *American Indian Policy*, chap. 8. The polities of an Indian territory or state could have shared an administration and a legislative council.

trust toward the federal government, self-interest (among the most powerful, they did not want equality with weaker polities), and the desire for national independence. It is probable, however, that they would have been amenable to representation by Indian national government. In Article 22 of the Treaty of Dancing Rabbit Creek, "the Chiefs of the Choctaw who have suggested that their people are in a state of rapid advancement . . . have a solicitude that they might have the privilege of a Delegate on the floor of the House of Representatives." Article 15 expresses the desire of the United States to centralize executive power in "an additional principle Chief of the whole to superintend and govern upon republican principles." This office could be seen as akin to the governorship of states, all of which are constitutionally guaranteed "a Republican form of Government" (Article 4, section 4). These articles take for granted that Indian integration into the federal spatial order is contingent on assimilation into states of civilizational advancement and republican forms of state.

The Choctaw, Creek, and Chickasaw nations—none of which had significantly reformed their governments before removal—later republicanized them. They republicanized without the removal pressures that had prompted Cherokee constitutionalism, but not without the postremoval pressures of modernization.[130] Such reformations can be situated within the uneven racial terrain of antebellum federalism. With respect to the previous chapter, I claim that the heterogeneity of the U.S. racial and spatial order allowed for the antebellum differentiation of slave and free states or, for that matter, the postbellum differentiation of *de jure* and *de facto* segregated states.[131] Indian Territory, a territorial ordering of indigenous polities with unclear constitutional status, provided the extreme case of antebellum racial heterogeneity. The excess and liminality represented by the racial institutional order of Indian Country prompted further normalization efforts. This case reveals that substantive civilization and formal republicanism were what Schmitt would call the "minimum of homogeneity" for a federal order divided into different kinds and regions of governance. Homogeneity, from this perspective, smoothes over the existential contradictions constitutive of any federal system.[132]

---

130. The minority planter classes of these polities and their federal official supporters were able to overturn traditional, locally driven, and undifferentiated political arrangements. Champagne, *Social Order and Political Change*, 206.

131. Cf. Carl Schmitt, *Constitutional Theory*, trans. Jeffrey Seitzer (Durham, NC: Duke University Press, 2008), 393.

132. On the antinomies of federalism, see ibid., 159, 388, 392.

Non-Indian efforts to bring about Indian institutional and cultural homogeneity were akin to the reform missions popular in the first half of the nineteenth century. The movement for Indian welfare, however, was not based in civil society, where other movements of its day (for causes like "unfortunates," women, temperance, and abolition) were organized.[133] It was rather the project of the racial state, a project directed by the Office of Indian Affairs. This federal bureaucracy, like the Indian territories under its supervision, presupposed a racial division of population. Established as a part of the Department of War in 1824, the office transferred to the newly formed Department of the Interior in 1849. Its origin in the War department marks the potential violence of racialized friend/enemy groupings. Its movement from War to Interior, in turn, marks the absorption of an external racial enemy as an interiorized racial population. The relocation of the Office of Indian Affairs corresponds to the replacement of peoples with populations effected by racial removal contracts. The shifting Indian frontier domesticated and made domestic the southeastern polities who would be criminalized for disturbing federal order.[134] Domestication only intensified as the postbellum United States enhanced its capacities to exert sovereignty over indigenous peoples.[135]

While grand forces of modernization and capitalism certainly played their part, concrete agents with proper names carried out the domestication project. In 1832, the first commissioner of the Office of Indian Affairs, Elbert Herring, envisioned the civil transformation of Indian Country. Herring conjectured that "the form of government and rude civil regulations among" Indians were "perhaps well enough suited to their condition, when hunting was their only employment, and war gave birth to their strongest excitements." Those times had passed, though. Education was the crux of reforming conditions and characters, whether in the form of displays of military force or training in the arts of civilization (for instance, the basic and vocational schooling of indigenous youth).[136] The next chapter on the Japanese intern-

---

133. Prucha, *The Great Father*, 283–84.
134. As early as 1829, Secretary of War John Eaton proposed that the United States serve as a "policeman among the transplanted tribes." Eaton, cited in Satz, *American Indian Policy*, 126–27.
135. Bruyneel, *The Third Space of Sovereignty*, 46, 52. I disagree with Bruyneel's claim that the removal period preceded the (postbellum) domestication period for the reason that removal itself was a kind of domestication.
136. "Annual Report of the Commissioner of Indian Affairs," in Prucha, *Documents of United States Indian Policy*, 63. President Jackson also called civilization the prelude to peace in Indian Country. "Annual Message to Congress (Dec. 8, 1829)," in Prucha, *Documents of United States Indian Policy*, 48.

ment will recount a strikingly similar effort to amitize a racial enemy on the part of the War Relocation Authority, an agency that—like the Office of Indian Affairs—ended up in the Department of the Interior. Commentators have noted that the appropriation of the Southeast expanded the southern order of slavery. However, the affinity of 1830s Indian removal and 1940s Japanese incarceration is the less intuitive, hardly explored connection. The common stakes of these projects were the concrete racial orders of the (geographically shifting) West.

Our remembrance of the U.S. Civil War, which divides the nineteenth-century United States into north and south, relegates Indian Territory to the realm of forgotten regions. While not exactly "the West," the indigenous zone of exceptionality "out West" owed its existence to the *nomos* of westward expansion. Against the remembrance of the 1840s as *the* decade of great land appropriations, Rogin reminds us that Manifest Destiny started in Indian land.[137] I might even venture to say that 1830s Indian removals extended the original land appropriation of the American Revolution. That land appropriation is a founding and indeed republican act is confirmed by the rich postrevolutionary associations of "empire" with territorial expansion, liberty, divine providence, progress, and U.S. international standing.[138] The first phase of the U.S. imperial project ended at the fin-de-siècle, when U.S. land appropriation overcame its continental limits to seize Caribbean and Pacific Islands. The second phase would conclude at the turn of our century, as the United States tried, but failed, to replace a declining Eurocentric global order with an Americentric *nomos* of the earth.

No liberal democratic "new world order" served as the capstone of the "American century." Instead, a multipolar world—a world ordered by competing *Großräume*—emerged in the wake of the bipolar Cold War.[139] It is a remarkable instance of forgetfulness that the Monroe Doctrine's hemispheric consciousness is clearly remembered for its fear of European colonization, yet only dimly remembered for its anxiety surrounding the Indian frontier. Monroe declares that the United States will defend its hemispheric spatial

---

137. Rogin, *Fathers and Children*, 307. Rogin is intentionally anachronistic here; the phrase "Manifest Destiny" is coined in 1845 by John O'Sullivan, the editor of the *Democratic Review*. Up until the Civil War, the discourse of Anglo-Saxon racial struggle was not yet popular. Thomas Gossett, *Race: The History of an Idea in America*, new ed. (Oxford, UK: Oxford University Press, 1997), 310–11.

138. Norbert Kilian, "New Wines in Old Skins? American Definitions of Empire and the Emergence of a New Concept," in Armitage, *Theories of Empire, 1450–1800*, 317–20.

139. Mouffe, *On the Political*, chap. 5; cf. Schmitt, *Nomos of the Earth*, pt. 4, chap. 3.

order against all challengers—European or Amerindian. In his address to Congress, Monroe reports that "General Ashley and his part, who were trading under a license from the Government, were attacked by the Ricarees" near the northern Missouri River. So Colonel Leavenworth led a regiment to retaliate against a Ricaree village, and "it is hoped that such an impression has been made on them, as well as on the other tribes on the Missouri, as will prevent a recurrence of future hostilities."[140] This violence on the northern frontier was meant to keep peaceful exchange in line with Monroe's Americentric vision of the New World. But it took the nomological cunning of Andrew Jackson—a military hero no stranger to using or threatening violence against Indians—to force the southern frontier westward through indigenous consent.

---

140. "Monroe Doctrine," 17.

4

Racial States of Exception and the Decision on Enmity

> The rule proves nothing; the exception proves everything.
> —CARL SCHMITT, *Political Theology*

> Now, therefore, by virtue of the authority vested in me as President of the United States, and Commander in Chief of the Army and Navy, I hereby authorize and direct the Secretary of War, and the Military Commanders whom he may from time to time designate, whenever he or any designated Commander deems such action necessary or desirable, to prescribe military areas in such places and of such extent as he or the appropriate Military Commander may determine, from which any or all persons may be excluded, and with respect to which, the right of any person to enter, remain in, or leave shall be subject to whatever restrictions the Secretary of War or the appropriate Military Commander may impose in his discretion.
> —FRANKLIN D. ROOSEVELT, Executive Order 9066

Even more than President Andrew Jackson's decisions regarding southeastern native polities, President Franklin Roosevelt's decisions regarding West Coast Japanese Americans illuminate the extraordinary contours of executive authority.[1] At the outset of its involvement in World War II, the United States treated Germans, Italians, and Japanese similarly. For instance, soon after the attack on Pearl Harbor, the FBI arrested 1,700 foreign nationals and the Department of Justice ordered enemy aliens in western states to surrender potential tools of espionage and subversion.[2] But military actions authorized by Executive Order [EO] 9066, signed by Roosevelt on February 19, 1942, sharply distinguished Japanese masses from German and Italian indi-

---

1. A previous version of this essay has been published as Fred Lee, "The Japanese Internment and the Racial State of Exception," *Theory & Event* 10, no. 1 (2007), accessed April 18, 2017, https://muse.jhu.edu/article/213866.
2. Sucheng Chan, *Asian Americans: An Interpretive History* (Boston: Twayne, 1991), 123.

viduals. The evacuation and internment of nearly 120,000 Japanese Americans (the entire Pacific Coast population of both aliens and citizens) "alienated" some 70,000 citizens into the "enemy" category.

The state initially declared Japanese Americans—including Issei (first-generation aliens), Nisei (second-generation citizens), and Kibei (Nisei educated in Japan)—to be enemy aliens alike. However, decisions to lump this population together, as in mass incarceration policies, gave way to decisions to split it along finer lines, as in camp leave policies. The crucial point is that both sets of decisions identified Japanese Americans according to the logic of Schmittian sovereignty. This chapter accounts for the wartime fate of Japanese Americans in light of a series of friend/enemy distinctions based on shifting criteria of racial and national membership. To track this series and these shifts is to address how liberal democratic polities decide on and manage racialized "danger" in extraordinary times. My primary question is how the state both enacts and resolves the racial state of exception.

I contend that a state project of racial amitization emerged out of a series of wartime decisions premised on racial enmity. This emergency project claimed to restore and, in actuality, reconstituted the normal conditions for the sake of which the state of exception is declared. In continuing to address Schmittian questions of public order, this chapter specifies racial formation as Asian American enmity/amity and public constitution as the state of exception. Both southeastern Indian removal and the Japanese internment created exceptional zones. Internment camps, like Indian Country, were liminal to the federal racial and spatial order, though the federal government never meant camps for relocated Japanese—unlike new territories for removed Amerindians—to be permanent. However, the Japanese internment involved a more explicit articulation of the state of exception as a response to what it treated as a potentially militarized threat. Hence the mid-twentieth-century racial state declared Japanese Americans to be enemies or friends, while its mid-nineteenth-century analogue treated southeastern nations as populations to be managed.

This preliminary sketch of the Japanese internment has already indicated the centrality of sovereignty for the national-security state. Theorists of racial "crises" overlook the moment of sovereignty at their peril,[3] as the extraordinary wartime powers of the state distinguish the internment from

---

3. See, e.g., Omi and Winant, *Racial Formation in the United States*, chap. 5; Goldberg, *The Racial State*, chap. 2.

a long line of anti-Asian laws and policies of which it is a part. Sovereign decision breaks through "a mechanism that has become torpid by repetition" or, in contemporary parlance, the legal reproduction of the liberal state apparatus.[4] Racial crises instantiated through measures such as EO 9066 exemplify Schmitt's concept of sovereignty as that which decides the existence of a critical situation and, I would add, the criteria by which it can be resolved.

For Schmitt, the sovereign decides the question of whether the "concrete situation" is the normal one of peace and order or the exceptional one of danger and disorder. The former presupposes the application of legal-constitutional norms, whereas the latter presupposes the suspension of legal-constitutional norms for the sake of protecting the constitutional order itself. According to Schmitt, the determination of when the exceptional situation exists is based on a decision rather than a norm; the sovereign, as he who decides the exception/norm distinction, cannot be bound by the norm.[5] Rather, the decision on the exception sets the limit of the law's application; it reveals that the sovereign belongs to, yet stands beside, the legal order in wielding the authority to suspend otherwise valid law. The "decisionist" reasoning is that the state cannot be hindered by law in defending itself against enemies who do not respect legality, international or domestic.[6] This is a statist logic of "existential threat."

As they are used here, "exception" and its cognates refer to the logical structure of state decisions shared by Japanese American confinement and release policies. As Edmund Fong argues, these events cannot be called "exceptional" in a manner consistent with American exceptionalism or subsumed within a narrative of "the WWII era as a watershed moment in the nation's turn away from racial ascription."[7] While less ascriptive than the original articulation, the rearticulations of the friend/enemy distinction constituted neither color-blindness nor progress. The state's adoption of racial historicism ("assimilation") is rather a projected resolution of the crisis initially conceived as racial naturalistic ("ascription"). Racial exceptionality in the sense elaborated in Chapter 3 came to supplement the racial state of

---

4. Schmitt, *Political Theology*, 15.

5. Ibid., 6.

6. On the development of this mode of reasoning, see Carl Schmitt, *Dictatorship*, trans. Michael Hoelzl and Graham Ward (Cambridge: Polity, 2014), 117–18.

7. Edmund Fong, "Beyond the Racial Exceptionalism of the Japanese Internment," *Politics, Groups, and Identities* 1, no. 2 (2013): 240.

exception: the state crafted exceptional norms for Japanese Americans distinguished from the normal norms of white citizenship.

The historicist racialization of Japanese Americans points to the limits of Giorgio Agamben's extended engagement with Schmitt. For Agamben, the "originary" inscription of biological life into the national-state is the Declaration of the Rights of Man, and the link between natality and citizenship—bare life and rights-bearing—reaches a breaking point in the Holocaust of European Jews.[8] My narrative, by contrast, begins with an Agamben-like biopolitical project and concludes with a properly Schmittian concern with an American "way of life," the more-than-mere-life of U.S. nationality. A challenge to critical race scholars who conceptualize race politics exclusively as a biopolitics, wartime release policies rearticulate "the Japanese race" on the nonbiological terrain of culture. In a related challenge to the common sense of continental political theory, I loosen the paradigmatic associations between the state of exception and National Socialist eugenics.[9]

In this vein of historical specificity, I would grant that the federally divided American state partially contradicts Schmitt's imagination of a unified, extralegal sovereign decision. Bonnie Honig drastically qualifies *the* decision in the United States, where "emergency power occasions the creation of new administrative powers and the redistribution of existing powers . . . from the more proceduralized domains of courts and legislatures to the more discretionary domains of administrative agency." Honig casts the administrator rather than the dictator as the figure of "discretionary decision" for U.S. liberal democracy.[10] In the spirit of Honig, I contend that multiple deciders, spread across institutional and geographic locations, made contradictory decisions on Japanese America over the course of the Pacific War. Additionally, as we will see, something like Honig's notion of discretionary power informs Fred Korematsu's legal contestation of executive powers exercised in Guantanamo Bay.

That said, I contend that emergency power in Honig's sense of administrative discretion is most apparent in the emergency project of Japanese

---

8. Giorgio Agamben, *Homo Sacer: Sovereign Power and Bare Life*, trans. Daniel Heller-Roazen (Stanford, CA: Stanford University Press, 1998), 127–30; cf. Michel Foucault, *The History of Sexuality: An Introduction*, vol. I, trans. Robert Hurley (New York: Vintage, 1990), pt. 5.

9. Work in both these directions has already begun in critical philosophies of race and postcolonial studies, e.g., Falguni Sheth, "The War on Terror and Ontopolitics: Concerns with Foucault's Account of Race, Power Sovereignty," *Foucault Studies* 12 (2011): 51–76; Achille Mbembe, "Necropolitics," *Public Culture* 15, no. 1 (2003): 11–40.

10. Honig, *Emergency Politics*, 67; cf. Schmitt, *Dictatorship*, chap. 4.

American assimilation. This emergency project only operates in relation to the exceptional zone of U.S. internment camps. Hence I rely on Schmitt in Section I to propose that the Japanese internment is the paradigm case of the racial state of exception in the United States. Several executive decisions amounted to a declaration that an exceptional situation existed in the face of "internal enemies." Section II then turns toward the release and resettlement policies that followed relocation and incarceration. Rearticulating the line between friends and enemies in ways that allowed thousands to cross it, the state attempted to incorporate released Japanese into the wartime society. This project of racial amitization expressed a will to unify the liberal democratic state as a homogeneous nation. I conclude with some of the deep paradoxes of liberal democratic regimes that surfaced throughout wartime Japanese American policy.

Section I: Evacuation and Internment; The Sovereign Decision on the Racial State of Exception

Readers of the vast post-9/11 literatures on sovereignty and security might be skeptical that this chapter can cast the Japanese internment in a new light.[11] While it is well established that this event exemplifies the state of exception, what remains underappreciated is that wartime releases followed the same friend/enemy logic of wartime internment. I hope that my wary readers, then, will receive the rehearsal of the familiar as a preparation for the performance of the unfamiliar. This section foregrounds the Schmittian moment of the Japanese internment in conventional historiographical contexts. I argue that, in the internment and analogous cases, our critical efforts should be centered on the authority and the decisions of the racial state.

The Prewar Configuration of Race and Nation

Many Americans feared the "yellow peril" within U.S. territory long before the Japanese attack on Pearl Harbor and the subsequent U.S. declaration of war on Japan. Mid- to late nineteenth-century Chinese immigration first provoked anxieties over "yellow hordes," with anti-Chinese agitation peaking

---

11. See, e.g., Verena Erlenbusch, "The Place of Sovereignty: Mapping Power with Agamben, Butler, and Foucault," *Critical Horizons* 14, no. 1 (2013): 44–69; Natsu Taylor Saito, "Symbolism under Siege: Japanese American Redress and the 'Racing' of Arab Americans as 'Terrorists,'" *Asian Law Journal* 8, no. 1 (2001): 1–29.

in the 1870s to 1880s. By the early to mid-twentieth century, the anti-Asian movement had prioritized Japanese Americans due to the victory of imperial Japan over czarist Russia and the advent of substantial Japanese immigration. In this period, California denied aliens ineligible to citizenship (i.e., Asians) land rights, and Congress, under the influence of eugenics research, barred Asians from legal immigration.

Homer Lea's *The Valor of Ignorance* captures the widespread anxiety over a militarized yellow peril, even if its influence on World War II policymaking is debatable (it was published in 1909). The decline of the Anglo-Saxon in America concerns Lea, who posits "racial similarity as the primitive basis of all national security."[12] In other words, Lea racializes the American nation as Anglo-Saxon and thereby figures non-Anglo Saxons as alien to the American state.[13] Japanese Americans, as racially heterogeneous elements, will play a precipitating role in the impending conflict between Japan and the United States: discrimination against Japanese Americans is "provocative of a legitimate *casus belli* on the part of the nation whose people have thus been treated, in variance with the rights and immunities granted them by various treaties."[14] Lea's claim that Japanese per se threatened U.S. security epitomized the connection between the domestic and overseas yellow peril.[15]

Even prewar contestations of Japanese exclusions could partake of U.S. nationalist discourses on war. The 1922 Supreme Court case *Takao Ozawa v. United States* upheld a district court's denial of Ozawa's claim to naturalization, which is why it is usually read as a decision on white prerequisites in naturalization law.[16] I would point out that Ozawa's 1916 brief for the Hawaiian district court also foregrounded the question of wartime allegiance: "In name, General Benedict Arnold was an American, but at heart he was a traitor. In name, I am not an American, but at heart I am a true American." Here Ozawa positioned himself as the loyal Japanese against the disloyal Anglo, an apparent other contradistinguished from a true other. He ap-

---

12. Homer Lea, *The Valor of Ignorance* (New York: Harper and Brothers, 1909), 125.

13. Lea understood Anglo-Saxon political institutions to be characteristic expressions of the Anglo-Saxon race. A similar understanding is found in Gustave Le Bon, *The Crowd: A Study of the Popular Mind* (London: T. Fischer Unwin, 1903), bk. 2, chap. 1.

14. Lea, *The Valor of Ignorance*, 179. An 1894 treaty, for example, gave Japan most-favored nation status.

15. Carey McWilliams, *Prejudice: Japanese Americans, Symbols of Racial Intolerance* (Boston: Little, Brown, 1944), 42.

16. 260 U.S. 178 (1922).

pealed, furthermore, to common understandings of war as the test case of national loyalty.

His appeal to common sense also challenged a racial prejudice—namely, that "Arnold" sounds more American than "Ozawa." It is the innermost heart of loyalty that must be made sensible to change the sound of certain names. Assimilation, in turn, signified loyalty:

> 1. I did not report my name, my marriage, or the names of my children to the Japanese Consulate in Honolulu . . . 2. I do not have any connection with any Japanese churches or schools . . . 3. I am sending my children to an American church and American school . . . 4. Most of the time I use the American (English) language at home, so that my children cannot speak the Japanese language. 5. I educated myself in American schools . . . 6. I have lived continuously within the United States for over twenty-eight years. 7. I chose as my wife one educated in American schools.[17]

Certainly the first item, which disassociates the Ozawa name from the Japanese government, and perhaps the sixth item, which distances Ozawa's body from Japanese territory, address questions of state membership. All of the remaining items, though, speak of associational choices (a lack of association with Japanese language, churches, schools, etc.). If the Ozawa family's assimilation into American society is the sensible sign that Ozawa was no Benedict Arnold, then this discourse on race and nationality intimately associated assimilation with allegiance.

Conceding that Ozawa was "well qualified by character and education for citizenship,"[18] the Supreme Court still denied that Japanese legally qualified as white.[19] Protestations of sameness and loyalty made no difference for Ozawa's naturalization case; nor did such claims find a sympathetic audience in the aftermath of Pearl Harbor. Just as the immigrant Issei were *de jure* barred from citizenship in the case of *Ozawa*, the native-born Nisei were *de facto* stripped of citizenship in World War II. The White House, for

---

17. Takao Ozawa, "Naturalization of a Japanese Subject," Japanese American Research Project (Collection 2010, Reel 39), Department of Special Collections, Young Research Library, UCLA.

18. 260 U.S. 178, 189 (1922).

19. The Naturalization Law of 1790 limited naturalization to whites. 1 Stat. 103. After the Civil War, Congress extended naturalization to blacks. 16 Stat. 254.

instance, responded coolly when the Japanese American Citizens League (JACL) wired to affirm its patriotism.[20] Desperate to counter suspicions of disloyalty and avoid compulsory internment, the JACL even proposed to organize a "suicide battalion" of Nisei volunteers to fight the Japanese army.[21]

The JACL would continue to pledge loyalty and favor assimilation as strategic responses to the racial state of exception. At a November 1942 emergency conference in Salt Lake City, Utah, the organization petitioned the federal government to suppress (what it considered) Japan supporters in the camps and induct Japanese Americans into the armed forces.[22] No less controversially, it hyperbolized its commitment to "Americanism":

> WE, AMERICAN CITIZENS OF JAPANESE ANCESTRY, in order to uphold and defend the Constitution of the United States of America and the principles for which it stands against all enemies, foreign and domestic; to foster and spread the true spirit of Americanism; to build the character of our people morally, spiritually and socially on American ideals and traditions; to speed the ultimate and complete assimilation of the Japanese American into the American cultural pattern . . . ESTABLISH THIS CONSTITUTION FOR THE [JACL].[23]

Modeled on the United States constitution, the JACL constitution cuts the citizen Nisei of the pronominal phrase "we, American citizens" from the alien Issei implied in the prepositionally downplayed "Japanese ancestry." Moreover, its republican return to the U.S. founding puts a nationalist spin on the friend/enemy distinction. Upholding and defending the state "against all enemies, foreign and domestic" is the first *raison d'être* of the JACL constitution, while "ultimate and complete assimilation" to "the American cultural pattern" is the second. As in *Ozawa*, the promise to eradicate difference is the pledge of true allegiance.

---

20. Roger Daniels, *Concentration Camps: North America; Japanese in the United States and Canada during World War II*, rev. ed. (Malabar, FL: Krieger, 1993), 40–41.

21. Masayo Umezawa Duus, *Unlikely Liberators: The Men of the 100th and 442nd*, trans. Peter Duus (Honolulu: University of Hawaii Press, 1987), 52.

22. Brian Masaru Hayashi, *Democratizing the Enemy: The Japanese American Internment* (Princeton, NJ: Princeton University Press, 2004), 129.

23. The 1930 constitution did not include this preamble; I am not sure if an amendment to the constitution occurred between 1930 and 1942. JACL Constitution, in "Supplement to Minutes: Japanese American Citizens League Special Emergency National Conference, November 17–24, 1942," Japanese American Research Project (Collection 2010, Box 296), 1.

The Initial Articulation of the Friend/Enemy Distinction

General John DeWitt of the Western Defense Command (WDC) also constellated assimilation and loyalty in his February 1942 recommendation to exclude all Japanese from the Pacific Coast. "The Japanese race," he pronounced, "is an enemy race." Even among the citizens "the racial strains are undiluted," and there is little "ground for assuming that any Japanese, barred from assimilation by convention as he is, though born and raised in the United States, will not turn against this nation when the final test of loyalty comes."[24] Whatever its source ("racial strains" or "convention"), unassimilated substance signals danger and, by implication, substantial assimilation might signify loyalty. Potential threat explicitly constitutes foreign enmity, against which actual loyalty tacitly constitutes national amity. Racial difference accrues to the Japanese through the silent articulation of the American as whiteness.

John DeWitt co-articulated race and nation in ways reminiscent of military and legal discourses.[25] Like Lea's book, DeWitt assumed that racial heterogeneity presented a potential threat and, like the *Ozawa* decision, he asserted the primacy of not-white/white division. What Lea and *Ozawa* respectively represented in the cultural and juridical domains, DeWitt represented in the political and military domains. Remember that for Schmitt, the friend/enemy distinction is the highest degree of formal disassociation between classes, religions, or any other kind of groups. A friend/enemy distinction can arise out of existent social antagonisms, as we saw in the case of racial enmity on the antebellum southern plantation. However, the Japanese internment taps a different dimension of Schmittian politics in that enmity emanates from sovereignty in this case. What articulated racial enmity here is, more than any previously existing antagonism, DeWitt's declaration that a racial state of exception existed.

Not all officials of the racial state need to agree in order for a racial state of exception to transpire. Internment scholars have narrated the processes by which Roosevelt, DeWitt, and other officials arrived at their decisions,[26]

---

24. John DeWitt, *Japanese Evacuation from the West Coast, 1942: Final Report* (Washington, DC: Government Printing Office, 1943), 34.

25. Unlike DeWitt, mid-twentieth-century anthropologists had come to reject the idea that biological "race" could explain differences in character traits or cultural practices. See, e.g., Franz Boas, *The Mind of Primitive Man* (New York: Macmillan, 1911), chap. 10; Ruth Benedict, *Patterns of Culture* (Boston: Houghton Mifflin, 1959), chap. 1.

26. See, e.g., Greg Robinson, *By Order of the President: FDR and the Internment of Japanese Americans* (Cambridge, MA: Harvard University Press, 2001), chap. 3; Roger Daniels, *The Decision to Relocate the Japanese Americans*, reprint ed. (Malabar, FL: Krieger, 1986), chaps. 2–4.

observing that key players within the Departments of War and Justice debated the feasibility, necessity, and constitutionality of mass evacuation. Like popular opinion on Japanese Americans, the most hostile of which was on the West Coast, official opinion on Japanese American policy lacked unanimity. Yet public opinion is far less important to my argument than public authority—the question of who concretely decides. DeWitt's authority blurred the distinction between commissarial dictatorship and sovereign dictatorship or, put loosely, the distinction between being bound to protect an existing order and being unbound in the creation of a new order.[27] His power was largely commissarial in its dependence on EO 9066's authorization of military commanders to exclude persons from proscribed military areas. Yet DeWitt exercised something close to sovereign power in his decision over whether, where, and how the normal or exceptional situation exists, that is, "what constitutes public order and safety" and "determining when they are disturbed."[28]

What, then, was decided? DeWitt decided that Japanese exclusion would qualify as a military necessity. Brian Hayashi observes that, like his successor General Delos Emmons and other military commanders, DeWitt extended this essentially contestable concept to cover wartime requirements ranging from hemispheric defense to U.S. civilian morale.[29] To be clear, though, the "military necessity" of Pacific Coast exclusion does not refer to a norm to be neutrally applied to a factual situation, but rather marks a decision on the exceptional situation and which constitutional norms will apply. DeWitt effectively proclaimed that state of affairs into existence by virtue of the authority invested in his military command. With this reinterpretation, I am shifting the question of military necessity from whether the state needed to do what it claimed was necessary to what the state did in claiming that necessity.

My strategy of argumentation differs from that of revisionist historians who have refuted DeWitt's claims on basically empirical grounds. Finding no evidence of military necessity, they propose that the actual conditions and causes of Japanese American incarceration were agricultural competition on the Pacific Coast, wartime hysteria over fifth column activity, and anti-Asian

---

27. Schmitt, *Dictatorship*, 118–19. I say "loosely" because Schmitt's commissarial/sovereign distinction refers to legal-constitutional orders, while I use "order" in the extended sense of public constitution.
28. Schmitt, *Political Theology*, 9.
29. Hayashi, *Democratizing the Enemy*, 78–79.

agitation.³⁰ Roger Daniels deems the rationale of military necessity to be a "fig leaf for a . . . [white supremacist] variant of American racism."³¹ In a related effort, Michi Nishiura Weglyn emphasizes that the prewar U.S. government certified "a remarkable, even extraordinary degree of loyalty among this generally suspect ethnic group."³² Despite differences in identifying and weighing evidence, though, most of this revisionist literature makes its judgments from within what I call the "security-rights circle."

The security-rights circle centers on the question of whether rights were justifiably sacrificed in the name of what EO 9066 described as "every possible protection against espionage and against sabotage to national defense."³³ The internment unjustly deprived Japanese Americans of rights because the purported "military necessity" amounted to nothing: this judgment, which has a strong commonsense appeal, turns within the security-rights circle. It accepts a crucial premise of the state—that security needs *can* justify the curtailment of rights—rather than seeks out critical alternatives to the logics of sovereignty. Worse yet, this judgment entertains the possibility that newly discovered "facts" might one day vindicate the military necessity argument.³⁴

Worst of all, the racial state has no difficulty admitting that West Coast Japanese posed no danger by any standard (realistic, reasonable, or otherwise). In responding to the 1980s Japanese American reparations movement, Congress acknowledged that "the evacuation, relocation, and internment of [Japanese American] civilians during World War II . . . were carried out without adequate security reasons."³⁵ What the state cannot admit is that the

---

30. This typology of explanations derives from Alison Dundes Renteln, "A Psychohistorical Analysis of the Japanese American Internment," *Human Rights Quarterly* 17, no. 4 (1995): 623–27; cf. Gary Okihiro, *The Columbia Guide to Asian American History* (New York: Columbia University Press, 2001), 101.

31. Daniels, *Concentration Camps*, 71, xvi.

32. A 1941 State Department investigation known as the Munson report is cited. Michi Nishiura Weglyn, *Years of Infamy: The Untold Story of America's Concentration Camps*, rev ed. (Seattle: University of Washington Press, 1996), 34–35.

33. Executive Order 9066 of February 19, 1942, Authorizing the Secretary of War to Prescribe Military Areas, *Our Documents*, accessed April 21, 2017, https://www.ourdocuments.gov/doc.php?doc=74&page=transcript.

34. For this right-wing line of argument, see Michelle Malkin, *In Defense of Internment: The Case for "Racial Profiling" in World War II and the War on Terror* (Washington: Regnery, 2004), 163.

35. Commission on Wartime Relocation and Internment of Civilians [CWRIC], *Personal Justice Denied: Report of the Commission on Wartime Relocation and Internment of Civilians* (Washington, DC: Government Printing Office, 1982), 3.

racial state of exception is made possible by something other than norms—that "military necessity" is grounded solely on the authority to draw friend/enemy and norm/exception distinctions. The perhaps disturbing implication of my critique is that the official justification of mass internment is not best refuted on factual grounds.[36] The upshot, though, is that we will criticize the U.S. security state on grounds deeper than the extent of its racial discrimination and rights violations. Outside of the security-rights circle, we will question whether the racial state can monopolize, or if it even deserves, the authority to declare states of exception.

Racial Distinctions of Regional and International Scope

The determination of a racial danger within a delimited zone of exception appeared in a series of WDC Public Proclamations in the period of March to August 1942. Public Proclamations No. 1 and 2 mentioned German and Italian aliens in addition to "any person of Japanese Ancestry" when establishing Military Areas 1 to 6 and strategic zones from which enemies might be prohibited. Public Proclamation No. 3 imposed a curfew on Japanese Americans within Military Area No. 1 and the prohibited zones. Public Proclamation No. 4 prepared for evacuation by forbidding "all alien Japanese and persons of Japanese ancestry" from leaving Military Area No. 1, where some nine-tenths of the population resided. The execution of Civilian Exclusion Orders then relocated all Japanese Americans from Military Areas 1 and 2 into assembly centers, while German and Italian aliens and citizens remained.[37]

The exclusion program almost inevitably turned into indefinite internment because states outside of the Military Areas would not allow Japanese to resettle freely within their borders. Established in March 1942, the Wartime Civil Control Administration (WCCA) handled the army-supervised transportations from the exclusion zones to the temporary assembly centers

---

36. What is more frightening: the idea that no determination of enmity is objective or the notion that objective determinations of enemies are possible? On the "objective enemy" of totalitarian ideologies, see Arendt, *The Origins of Totalitarianism*, 465.

37. Military Areas 1 and 2 were in Washington, Oregon, California, and Arizona. Military Areas 3 through 6 were in Idaho, Montana, Nevada, and Utah. Internment camps were in Tule Lake and Manzanar, California; Minidoka, Idaho; Heart Mountain, Wyoming; Topaz, Utah; Gila River and Poston, Arizona; Granada, Colorado; and Rohwer and Jerome, Arkansas. This paragraph follows the lead of Daniels, *Concentration Camps*, chap. 4. Referenced WDC Public Proclamations are in the Manzanar War Relocation Center Records (Collection 122, Box 28) Department of Special Collections, Young Research Library, UCLA.

and the longer-term concentration camps (named "relocation centers"). There internees were subject to the War Relocation Authority (WRA), a civilian administrative body created by executive order that month. The WCCA relocated the potential "danger" from the exceptional zone of the WDC Military Areas to the exceptional zone of the WRA internment camps.

What my Schmittian staging illuminates is that only by spatially confining the state of exception did the racial state maintain a tolerably normal situation elsewhere. This dynamic is misconstrued as the trade-off of security and rights, as when Clinton Rossiter argues that constitutional governments must be altered during crises "to whatever degree necessary to overcome the peril and restore normal conditions." Even if necessity justifies the curtailment of rights according to his own doctrine of "constitutional dictatorship,"[38] the racial determination of the "peril" puts the Japanese internment into question for Rossiter.[39] He is quick to point out that U.S. civil liberties on the whole "suffered less invasion in [World War II] than in either the Civil War or the World War, with one major exception [the internment]."[40] But the constitutive link between norm and exception goes unnoticed by Rossiter, who almost connects the protection of rights to the exceptional "invasion."

Regional demands for evacuation disturbed the relative calm of the immediate aftermath of Pearl Harbor. In February 1942, a delegation of West Coast congressmen recommended that the president pursue a complete program "for the evacuation, removal, resettlement, and rehabilitation of undesirable persons."[41] With the coastal states roiling, the appeasement of regional public opinion was also an attempt to preserve public peace.[42] Hence the decision that the West Coast must be impenetrable to racial enemies is

---

38. Clinton Rossiter, *Constitutional Dictatorship: Crisis Government in the Modern Democracies*, rev. ed. (New York: Harcourt, Brace and World, 1963), 5.

39. Ibid., 281 83.

40. Ibid., 276.

41. Letter reproduced in John Tolan, *National Defense Migration: Report of the Select Committee Investigating National Defense Migration, House of Representatives, 77th Congress, 2nd Session* (Washington, DC: Government Printing Office, 1942), 3.

42. Jacobus tenBroek and colleagues argue that popular pressure cannot be proved to have caused the decision to evacuate. Jacobus tenBroek, Edward Norton Barnhart, and Floyd Matson, *Prejudice, War, and the Constitution: Causes and Consequences of the Evacuation of the Japanese Americans in World War II* (Berkeley: University of California Press, 1954), chap. 4. I make no assumption of causal links in the decision-making process; I only assume that the decision took account of popular agitations.

strictly equivalent to the posture that the internment camps offered protection from white "vigilantes":[43] both from the Schmittian perspective are attempts to prevent civil disorder. The territorialized state opened an exceptional racial zone to displace potential conflict "outside" of itself.

The continental United States in this respect differed from Hawaii, where Japanese were less directly targeted under the martial law declared in December 1941.[44] General Delos Emmons, the military governor of Hawaii, resisted proposals for mass internment. His bureaucratic resistance—what Honig would call his "discretionary decision[ism]"—took advantage of a federal spatial and racial order divided into multiple deciders, levels, and regions.[45] From the point of view of wartime economics, Japanese escaped mass internment by virtue of their integration into the territorial economy (Japanese laborers made the reconstruction of the post–Pearl Harbor defense industry possible). However, from the perspective of wartime security, the military closed down Japanese-language schools and selectively interned community leaders (due to conflations of ethnic solidarities and national allegiances).

Martial law in Hawaii extended military authority into arenas of civil authority, whereas sovereign authority on the mainland set spatial limits on constitutional rights.[46] What accounts for this difference is that Hawaii "stood prepared" by two decades of military planning while the West Coast scrambled to indiscriminately exclude "the Japanese race."[47] John DeWitt, then a colonel in the Army's War Plan Division, had envisioned selective internment in the case of a U.S.-Japan conflict as early as 1921.[48] By this time, agricultural strikes had prompted the U.S. government and Hawaiian Sugar Planters' Association to coordinate their surveillance of Filipino, Puerto Rican, and especially Japanese laborers, who were suspected of spying for the

---

43. DeWitt cites incidents of vigilante violence in justifying his decision for evacuation. See DeWitt, *Japanese Evacuation from the West Coast*, 8–9.

44. For instance, the December 1941 curfew applied to all residents. CWRIC, *Personal Justice Denied*, 266–67. A counterexample is that only Japanese workers in restricted areas had to wear certain badges. Gary Okihiro, *Cane Fires: The Anti-Japanese Movement in Hawaii, 1865–1945* (Philadelphia: Temple University Press, 1991), 227.

45. Roosevelt in March 1942 approved a recommendation to intern some 20,000 Hawaiian Japanese. Emmons negotiated the figure down to about 1,500. Ronald Takaki, *Strangers from a Different Shore: A History of Asian Americans*, rev. ed. (Boston: Little, Brown, 1998), 379–80.

46. On this distinction, see Giorgio Agamben, *State of Exception*, trans. Kevin Attell (Chicago: University of Chicago Press, 2005), 4.

47. Okihiro, *Cane Fires*, 273–74.

48. These plans were revised in 1923 and were not the last to be made. Ibid., 124.

Japanese government. (Both U.S. and Japanese imperial projects considered Hawaii to be of high geostrategic value in an East-West "race war.")[49] Ironically, the Hawaiian wartime situation of less discriminatory military decisions (selective rather than mass incarceration) had prewar origins in more discriminating military intelligence, surveillance, and planning.

Soon after it declared that a state of war existed in order to combat the external enemy of Japan, the United States declared that a state of exception existed in order to confine the Japanese internal enemy. A marker of the U.S. distinction between German and Japanese enemies was—and remains—the description of the wartime actions of the former as "Nazi" and those of the latter as "Japanese."[50] In the former description, the Nazi state is distinguished from the German nation, while in the latter, the Japanese nation is identified with the Japanese state. It was likewise conventional in U.S. visual culture to use Hitler images to represent Nazism and to use animal imagery (e.g., monkeys) to represent Japan.[51] Allegiance also trumped identification in the Western, Eastern, and Southern Defense Commands' issuance of individual exclusion orders to German and Italian citizens and aliens.[52]

The United States treated neither all Europeans as friends, nor all Asians as enemies.[53] However, the racial enemy—as opposed to various national enmities—was definitely Asian. The 1943 repeal of the Chinese Exclusion Act and extension of naturalization to Chinese Americans would not have been possible if the Occidental/Oriental distinction were not relatively autonomous from the friend/enemy distinction.[54] The "Chinks" (the original yellow peril) acquired the qualities of noble Chinese people (friend Asians) as the state engaged the "Japs" (the militarized yellow peril) in combat. A *Time* magazine article from 1941, "How to Tell Your [Chinese] Friends from the Japs," encoded this newly minted distinction in the most imaginative ways (it confidently asserts that "most Chinese avoid horn rimmed spectacles").[55] Yet the fine line that divides the panels captioned "Chinese" and "Japanese" marks the common racialization of these nationalities. Transnational in constitution

---

49. John Dower, *War without Mercy: Race and Power in the Pacific War* (New York: Pantheon, 1986), 4.
50. Ibid., 34, 78.
51. See, e.g., "Mimic," cartoon, *Washington Post*, July 1, 1942.
52. CWRIC, *Personal Justice Denied*, 288.
53. For an account of non-Japanese Asian Americans during World War II, see Erika Lee, *The Making of Asian America: A History* (New York: Simon and Schuster, 2015), 251–63.
54. 57 Stat. 600.
55. "How to Tell Your Friends from the Japs," *Time*, December 22, 1941, 33.

and international in orientation, the Asian American racial formation is flexible enough to accommodate Asian enmity and Asian amity.

Racial Exceptionality in Constitutional Law

Ironically, an excluded Nisei could in certain contexts be included within the constitutional order as a lawbreaker. Hannah Arendt observes that "the best criterion by which to decide whether someone has been forced outside of the pale of law is to ask if he would benefit by committing a crime." The excepted person who disrupts the order of the exceptional zone is "a recognized exception to the norm," but the "fact is that this exception is provided for by law."[56] Public Law 503, which criminalized violations of the military orders authorized by EO 9066, extended the "benefits" of criminalization to Japanese Americans in March 1942.[57] It enabled the "criminals" Gordon Hirabayashi and Fred Korematsu to contest curfew and exclusion orders before the Supreme Court; for its part, the Court normalized the state of exception through what I have called the paradigm of racial exceptionality, even in the case of the noncriminal Mitsuye Endo's contestation of detainment orders.

Gordon Hirabayashi was indicted for violating the curfew imposed on Japanese Americans and for failing to register for a civilian exclusion order. Hirabayashi contended that Public Law 503 unconstitutionally delegated power to the WDC and that his constitutional rights to due process had been violated. *Hirabayashi v. United States* in 1943 limited its judgment to the curfew and set aside the more controversial issue of exclusion. Satisfied that the curfew had a rational basis, the judiciary basically deferred to the executive determination of military necessity.[58] Especially in wartime situations, state actions "which indicate that a group of one national extraction may menace . . . safety more than others" are "not to be condemned merely because in other and in most circumstances racial distinctions are irrelevant."[59] The Court admits that the curfew based on a "racial distinction" is an exceptional rule, one that occupies the space of exception from (what is presumably) the normal rule of race irrelevance.

---

56. Arendt had the Japanese internment in mind here. A substantial footnote describes the hypothetical scenario of a West Coast Japanese American whose violation of exclusion orders would have increased his constitutional rights. Arendt, *The Origins of Totalitarianism*, 286–87.
57. 56 Stat. 173.
58. 320 U.S. 81, 93 (1943). Rational basis is the lowest level of scrutiny the Court can apply.
59. Ibid., 101.

Normal/exceptional rules that correspond to normal/exceptional situations are also the stakes of *Korematsu v. United States*. In this 1944 case, Fred Korematsu argued that a civilian exclusion order (which he purposely violated) was an unconstitutional prelude to an unconstitutional deprivation of liberty (internment). Keeping with the strategy of *Hirabayashi*, *Korematsu* bracketed the issue of internment in order to limit its decision to the less contentious exclusion. Unlike *Hirabayashi*, though, *Korematsu* seemed confused as to if and how the case involved race.[60] On the one hand, the Court noted that "all legal restrictions which curtail the civil rights of a single racial group are immediately suspect" and subject to "rigid scrutiny."[61] On the other hand, the Court asserted that exclusion was not based on "racial prejudice": "Korematsu was not excluded from the Military Area because of hostility to him or his race. He was excluded because ... military authorities feared an invasion of our West Coast."[62]

Playing on the ambiguity of the term "hostility," the Court masked public enmity in the language of personal hostility.[63] The explicit message of "Korematsu was not excluded because of personal hatred towards his race" contains the hidden message of "Korematsu was excluded because of military determinations of racial enmity." *Korematsu* disavowed—that is, simultaneously denied and admitted—that racial enmity exceeded "racial prejudice" or the privatized face of social discrimination. The Court's invocation of "rigid scrutiny" seemed to classify the case as racial (this acknowledged racial enmity), yet its failure to apply rigid scrutiny to the evacuation gave just the opposite impression (this fell back on racial prejudice). *Korematsu* justified the exceptional rule of evacuation by suspending the normal rule of "strict scrutiny" in its very articulation.[64]

Ex Parte Endo, handed down concurrently with *Korematsu* in 1944, equivocated on the role of race in the continued detainment of Mitsuye Endo. The Court decided that the WRA had "no authority to subject citizens who

---

60. Eric Yamamoto, Margaret Chon, Carol Izumi, Jerry Kang, and Frank Wu, *Race, Rights and Reparation: Law and the Japanese American Internment* (Gaithersburg, MD: Aspen Law and Business, 2001), 159.

61. 323 U.S. 214, 216 (1944).

62. Ibid., 223.

63. Schmitt rightly claims that the public enemy "need not be hated personally, and in the private sphere only does it make sense to love one's enemy." Schmitt, *The Concept of the Political*, 29.

64. "Rigid scrutiny"—later called "strict scrutiny"—is the highest level of scrutiny that the Court can apply. Its application in civil rights litigation has required racial distinctions in law to serve a compelling state interest, e.g., the 1978 case *U.C. Regents v. Bakke*.

are concededly loyal to its leave procedures to detainment" because "loyalty is a matter of the heart and mind, not of race, creed or color."[65] Yet while loyalty is not a matter of race, the "Application for Leave Clearance" administered to Endo in February 1943 made race into a question of loyalty.[66] If the state should release anyone from custody, the Court reasoned, surely it was Endo, who spoke no Japanese, had never visited Japan, was a Christian, and—unlike Hirabayashi and Korematsu—had violated no criminal laws. *Endo* restored normal liberty of movement to an "exceptional" citizen after the racial state of exception suspended it for all West Coast Japanese.

The application of a normal rule to the "concededly loyal" silently sanctioned its suspension for those not "concededly loyal," whom the state would detain at its discretion while restoring normal conditions. *Endo* and *Korematsu* were delivered in December 1944, immediately after Public Proclamation No. 21 announced the closing of the camps. This timing attests to the Roosevelt administration's efforts to avoid the possibility of Court-ordered camp closures. Thereafter, the Court would have no reason to rule on the constitutionality of mass incarceration itself. It did, however, take the opportunity to legalize internment-related policies of curfew, evacuation, and detainment. More technically, the Court normalized the racial state of exception.

An "*a priori* legal loophole" in the cases above juxtaposes protection-worthy citizens against legally abandoned enemy aliens.[67] The Supreme Court filled-in rather than closed this legal-conceptual loop with a set of exceptional rules for nonwhite subjects and citizens. Therefore we cannot say—as the security-rights circle would have us believe—that *Korematsu* is a racist violation of rights, while *Endo* is a nonracial protection of rights. We must instead see that what Falguni Sheth calls "the Violence of Law" is a structural element of the self-preserving, other-managing racial state.[68] We must see that our internment-related cases—*Hirabayashi v. United States, Korematsu v. United States,* and *Ex Parte Endo*—fit the paradigm of racial exceptionality exemplified in Chapter 3's cases on indigenous lands.

The nineteenth-century cases crafted exceptional norms for native polities where normal norms of international law were not applied; the twentieth-century cases effected a parallel exclusion of Japanese Americans within

---

65. 323 U.S. 283, 298 (1944).
66. Section II describes how this application functioned as a loyalty questionnaire; the attainment of indefinite leave, which Endo did not request, required separate applications.
67. Sheth, *Toward a Political Philosophy of Race*, 52–53.
68. Ibid., chap. 2.

constitutional law. *Hirabayashi* and *Korematsu* decided on the threat of violence (espionage and sabotage) in ways that created exceptional norms (curfew and evacuation) in the space of racial exception from norms (race irrelevance and "rigid scrutiny"). *Endo* presented the inverse case of *Hirabayashi* and *Korematsu*: bearing no relation to violent threat, the exceptional norm (continued detainment) did not apply to the exception to the racial exception (the "concededly loyal" Mitsuye Endo).[69]

Executive decisions on the exception thereby achieved juridical normalization. Put otherwise, the normal norm/exceptional norm distinctions in the line of judicial decisions from *Hirabayashi* to *Ex Parte Endo* made normative the norm/exception distinctions in the line of executive decisions from the president to the WRA. Both lines of decision converged in what Giorgio Agamben calls "the state of exception as a paradigm of government."[70] Just as the Supreme Court drove at juridical normalization in this section of the chapter, the WRA will drive at concrete normalization in the next. New friend/enemy distinctions set the terms of release from internment camps, subordinating existent racial and national identifications "to the conditions and conclusions of the political situation at hand."[71] The racial state of exception would continue to unfold according to a sovereign logic, a series of decisions that would defuse dangers and reconstitute normalcy at the same time.

Section II: Release and Resettlement; Rearticulating the Racial Friend/Enemy Distinction

Curiously, temporary leave policies were set almost as soon as camp life began and indefinite leave policies were soon to follow. While standard historiographical and recent theoretical debates ask why Japanese Americans were incarcerated, I take the more interesting question to be why thousands of Japanese Americans were released throughout the duration of the war. My claim is that leave policies constituted an emergency project of Japanese American assimilation. In Omi and Winant's terms, this "racial project" resignified the meaning of the friend/enemy distinction as it reorganized the

---

69. "The power to detain is derived from the power to protect the war effort against espionage and sabotage," but the detention of loyal citizens "which has no relationship to that objective is unauthorized." 323 U.S. 283, 302 (1944).

70. The phrase is the title of Agamben, *State of Exception*, chap. 1.

71. Schmitt, *The Concept of the Political*, 38.

administration of the Japanese population.[72] The WDC originally declared that Japanese were the "enemy race," yet the meaning of this "were" begins to slide in WRA rearticulations of racial enmity. Mass evacuation from the West Coast meant that Japanese Americans were racial enemies, while leave clearance from the camps meant that Japanese Americans could become racial friends.

Rearticulating the Friend/Enemy Distinction

Political theorists debate whether the friend/enemy grouping for Schmitt is a sovereign recognition of already-existing limits or an unstable limit created by the sovereign decision.[73] My view is that it depends on which Schmitt you ask. At one extreme, Schmitt claims that democracies in particular presuppose substantive homogeneity: "A democracy demonstrates its political power by knowing how to refuse or keep at bay something foreign and unequal that threatens its homogeneity."[74] At the other extreme, Schmitt claims that national identities in particular are defined by sovereign decision: "The enemy is solely the public enemy, because everything that has a relationship to such a collectivity of men, particularly to a whole nation, becomes public by virtue of such a relationship."[75]

To grasp both polarities is to hold that for Schmitt public identities are simultaneously or even "undecidably" constative and performative. Putting aside the finer points of Schmitt's constitutional theory, according to which political unity is the state representation of national identity,[76] the crucial point for our purposes is that Schmitt thinks within the nationalist and statist horizon of the French revolutionary tradition. He assumes that, as Arendt puts it, "only in the presence of the enemy can such a thing as *la nation une et indivisible* . . . come to pass. Hence, national unity can assert itself only in foreign affairs, under circumstances of, at least, potential hostility."[77] Hence, too, national unity can only assert itself in domestic affairs under circumstances of potential threat or internal enmity.

---

72. Omi and Winant, *Racial Formation in the United States*, 124–27.
73. See, e.g., Chantal Mouffe, "Carl Schmitt and the Paradox of Liberal Democracy," in *The Challenge of Carl Schmitt*, ed. Chantal Mouffe (London: Verso, 1999), 50; Kam Shapiro, *Carl Schmitt and the Intensification of Politics* (Lanham, MD: Rowman and Littlefield, 2008), 44.
74. Schmitt, *The Crisis of Parliamentary Democracy*, 9.
75. Schmitt, *The Concept of the Political*, 28.
76. Schmitt, *Constitutional Theory*, 239, 247–48.
77. Arendt, *On Revolution*, 77.

Schmitt claims that the friend/enemy decision is the core of sovereign existence within the European system of nation-states. The state that holds the *jus belli* can decide on enemies outside of its territory and engage them in armed conflict if (it deems this to be) necessary; it can also decide on enemies inside of its territory to maintain the normal situation of "tranquility, security, and order."[78] The *jus belli* implies that there is no politics without the possibility of war and no actual war without the dimension of politics. War and politics are mutual presuppositions in a "political world [that] is a pluriverse," as a world state or any political "universe" would eliminate the possibility of friend/enemy distinction.[79] The obverse of the plurality of states with no common decider is the unity of the people with one sovereign.

Sovereign decisions denationalized and nationalized Japanese Americans on the Schmittian theater of war/politics. Where nationality presupposes the "presence of the enemy," as Arendt would have it, the racial state treated "the American people" of World War II as if they were one. I say "as if" to signal that the state posited the homogeneity it actually sought based on quickly shifting criteria of nationality. The initial decision to denationalize Japanese Americans in exceptional zones worked from fixed, naturalistic assumptions about race and nation. Later decisions to reintegrate Japanese Americans into mainstream society worked with comparatively fluid assumptions about identity; these policies renationalized racial friends and even further denationalized racial enemies on cultural grounds. The first rearticulation of the friend/enemy distinction spoke to spatial-social distributions of populations, while the second spoke to existential-statist determinations of "loyalty."

The First Rearticulation of the Friend/Enemy Distinction

Shortly after the completion of the West Coast "round up," the WRA began granting leaves to incarcerated Japanese Americans. High demands for agricultural workers led to seasonal leaves, but students were afforded the first major opportunity for more permanent relocations. Thanks to the initiative

---

78. Schmitt, *The Concept of the Political*, 46. The phrasing of this statement alludes to Art. 48, sec. 2 of the Weimar Constitution: "If in the German Reich the public security and order are being significantly disturbed or endangered, the President can utilize the necessary measures to restore public security and order, if necessary with the aid of armed force." Article reproduced in Schmitt, *Constitutional Theory*, 417.

79. Schmitt, *The Concept of the Political*, 53.

of the National Japanese American Student Relocation Council (NJASRC) some 4,000 individuals eventually left the camps for college; criteria of student leave clearance included admission to an institution, proof of financial means, and a favorable FBI investigation.[80] The pedagogical purpose of student leave was to advance young Japanese Americans along a normal educational trajectory. A related administrative purpose was to resettle students in a spatial pattern that encouraged their assimilation.

WRA policy aimed at low population densities of Japanese American bodies within collegiate student bodies. Prior to the internment, Nisei students had "concentrated" at a small range of West Coast public institutions. The relocation program, by contrast, "dispersed" and "scattered" Nisei to more colleges across the country, among them private schools that had never enrolled Japanese students before.[81] Moreover, the WRA and the NJASRC encouraged released students to avoid visible "clustering." For example, at the University of Nebraska in November 1942, Nisei voted to participate in groups with white students and never form a Japanese student association.[82] For a counterexample, Nisei who attended Boston University would gather for parties and picnics in spite of official admonishments to avoid attracting attention.[83] Both examples, however, indicate that the state administered racial populations as it simultaneously politicized racial association. Social assimilation would internalize somatically articulated difference ("Japanese bodies") at the same time that the friend/enemy distinction externalized symbolically articulated conflict (Japan vs. the United States).

Like the student release program, the worker release program spatially and racially reordered the United States. In July 1942, new policies qualified Nisei—neither Issei nor Kibei—with firm offers of employment for leave. In October 1942, the WRA director, Dillon Myer, substantially relaxed standards for indefinite release: leave clearance would thereafter consist in a loyalty investigation by the FBI, a determination of employment outside of the

---

80. Robert O'Brien, *The College Nisei* (Palo Alto, CA: Pacific, 1949), 65. The NJASRC was a private organization formed in March 1942 to raise funds for potential students and to pressure university administrations for their admittance.

81. In 1941, 60 percent of Nisei college students attended 7 large institutions, with the remainder attending 186 others; by 1943, the number of institutions rose to 279, with only one college enrolling more than 100 Nisei and two enrolling more than 50; by 1945, the number of institutions rose to 451, with two schools enrolling more than 100 Nisei. Ibid., 81–83.

82. Ibid., 117.

83. Gary Okihiro, *Storied Lives: Japanese American Students and World War II* (Seattle: University of Washington Press, 1999), 108.

camps, and an assurance that the community of relocation would not be hostile to Japanese.[84] The last requirement expresses a concern for the security of relocated workers as well as a desire to integrate relocated workers into white (or at least non-Japanese) communities. In the prewar ethnic economy, Japanese merchants distributed the produce of Japanese-owned farms, which sometimes employed Japanese laborers.[85] Thereabouts *ken-jin* (mutual aid societies), churches, temples, and the Japanese-language press served as major ethnic institutions.[86]

The WRA released internees far from the ethnic economies and *Nihonmachi* (Japantowns) on the Pacific.[87] Negotiating or even rejecting the official project of "dispersal,"[88] though, new communities formed outside of the exclusion zones, especially in Chicago, Denver, Salt Lake City, and New York City. There the lack of long-standing ethnic institutions almost guaranteed increased interactions with whites; likewise, the linking of leave to employment took Japanese Americans out of ethnic economies. By January 1945, nearly 36,000 Japanese Americans had taken advantage of this program, with the great majority being Nisei under thirty-five years old.[89] After Public Proclamation No. 21 ended the exclusion, about 60,000 Japanese Americans returned to the West Coast, as compared to the roughly 50,000 who would remain east of the Sierra Mountains. This was a notable shift in population distribution.

Without doubt, leave policies afforded educational and employment opportunities to thousands upon thousands of Japanese Americans. What must not be overlooked, however, is that both programs embraced a binary Schmittian logic. In contrast to General DeWitt of the WDC, who doubted to the end that "loyals" could be distinguished from "disloyals," Director Myer of the WRA believed that the release of the "loyals" presupposed just

---

84. WRA, "The Leave Program of the War Relocation Program," Manzanar War Relocation Center Records (Collection 122, Box 23), 3–4.

85. Japanese farms depended on Mexican and Filipino labor in the 1920s and 1930s. Roger Daniels, *Asian America: Chinese and Japanese in the United States since 1850* (Seattle: University of Washington Press, 1988), 134, 158; Eiichiro Azuma, *Between Two Empires: Race, History, and Transnationalism in Japanese America* (Oxford, UK: Oxford University Press, 2004), 189–90.

86. Daniels, *Asian America*, 166–72.

87. Roger Daniels, *Prisoners without Trial: Japanese Americans in World War II* (New York: Hill and Wang, 1993), 81.

88. Ellen Wu, *The Color of Success: Asian Americans and the Origins of the Model Minority* (Princeton, NJ: Princeton University Press, 2014), 41.

89. War Relocation Authority, *The Evacuated People: A Quantitative Description* (Washington, DC: Government Printing Office, 1946), 30.

that distinction.⁹⁰ These wartime decisions were consistent with a prewar pattern whereby federal officials and military officers assumed Japanese loyalty to Japan, while (officials who would become) camp administrators and social scientists assumed Japanese—and, more specifically, Nisei—loyalty to the United States.⁹¹ Put starkly, the Japanese were essentially enemies for DeWitt, but potential friends for Myer. Whereas DeWitt understood race as an irreducible and essential difference, Myer understood race as a malleable and contingent one.

Recall the racial naturalism/historicism distinction discussed in relation to Justice Marshall's opinions on Amerindians. This distinction between racial "stasis" and racial "developmentalism" is roughly the difference of racial understanding between DeWitt and Myer.⁹² DeWitt believed that naturalist "strains" in addition to historicist "convention" excluded Japanese from substantive inclusion within the American nation. Myer, on the contrary, thought the American nation could include Japanese Americans on the historicist condition that their nationality excluded Japanese substance. Common to DeWitt and Myer, though, is the idea that "American" and "Japanese" were mutually exclusive ways of life.

The WRA rearticulation of the friend/enemy distinction added increased discrimination to the initial WDC declaration that a racial enemy existed. Thus the continental and Hawaiian situations converged as the indiscriminate mass incarceration on the mainland caught up with the more selective internment on the islands. The first rearticulation of the friend/enemy distinction released individuals deemed harmless in the normalizing situation as friends, while it detained "dangerous" individuals in the camps as enemies or, at a minimum, not-friends or not-yet-friends. In certain study and work situations, the released were racial enemies no longer. Nonetheless, their friend status could be revoked at any time by FBI agents, who kept surveillance on the indefinitely released in major areas of resettlement.⁹³

---

90. On DeWitt's efforts to undermine the loyalty review program, see CWRIC, *Personal Justice Denied*, 198–201. On Myer's endorsement of the WRA assimilation policy, see Richard Drinnon, *Keeper of Concentration Camps: Dillon S. Myer and American Racism* (Berkeley: University of California Press, 1987), 55–58.

91. Hayashi, *Democratizing the Enemy*, 9, chap. 1.

92. Here it tracks the uneven transformation of race from "the stasis of 'Being' to the developmentalism of 'Becoming' . . . from racial subjection through technologies of the whip, sword, and gun to racial management via the funneling technologies of education, opportunities, and access." Goldberg, *The Racial State*, 95.

93. Drinnon, *Keeper of Concentration Camps*, 53–55.

Suspicions of racial danger would demand more than spatial distributions of populations to be quelled.

The Second Rearticulation of the Friend/Enemy Distinction

The U.S. demand that internees declare national-state allegiance rearticulated the friend/enemy distinction yet another time. Its immediate context was the army's proposal to recruit an all-Nisei combat team from mainland and Hawaiian volunteers. But as only loyal Nisei would do, the state provided the opportunity to cross the very friend/enemy line that it drew. The WRA administered an "Application for Leave Clearance" in February 1943 to all internees aged seventeen and older. Two questions about "loyalty," drafted for adult male Nisei, read as follows:

> *No. 27.* Are you willing to serve in the armed forces of the United States on combat duty, wherever ordered?
>
> *No. 28.* Will you swear unqualified allegiance to the United States of America and faithfully defend the United States from any or all attack by foreign or domestic forces, and forswear any form of allegiance or obedience to the Japanese emperor, to any other foreign government, power or organization?

Question 27 did not strictly apply to women, if "combat duty" is interpreted in light of the intention to recruit troops. Question 28 would ask Issei, aliens racially ineligible for naturalization, to assent to their already effective statelessness. Revised versions of these questions requested military service from females, while requesting nonobstructive behavior from Issei.[94] A synecdoche for the overall program of leave clearance, the revised questions made finer-grained distinctions of gender, generation, and citizenship.

As the intended audience of question 27, male draft–aged Nisei recognized the irony of being called on to perform the duties of citizenship while

---

94. The revised question 27 for female Nisei and Issei asked, "If the opportunity presents itself and you are found qualified, would you be willing to volunteer for the Army Nurse Corps or the [Women's Auxiliary Army Corps]?" The revised question 28 for Issei males and females asked, "Will you swear to abide by the laws of the United States and to take no action which would in any way interfere with the war effort of the United States?" For various versions of these questions, see WRA, "Army and Leave Clearance Registration at War Relocation Centers," Manzanar War Relocation Center Records (Collection 122, Box 24), 51–52.

enjoying none of the rights of citizenship. Question 27, from the perspective of the state, garnered a far from favorable response. The registration process yielded only 1,200 Nisei volunteers, a figure that fell below the expectation of 3,000 recruits. Still more troubling, the "will you forswear allegiance?" of question 28 works like the joke "so have you stopped beating your wife?": a declaration of loyalty posed in these terms entails an admission of prior disloyalty. Unsurprisingly, conditional expressions of loyalty (for example, "yes, if . . ." or "no, unless . . . ") only accounted for about 1,000 of the almost 75,000 responses to question 28. Some 68,000 answered with an unqualified "yes," whereas over 5,000 responded with an unqualified "no."[95]

Because of and in spite of the aforementioned figures, the army moved Nisei males from the ineligible status of enemy alien to the status of draft-eligible citizen in January 1944. The reinstitution of normal draft procedures led to the formation of the 442nd Infantry Regimental Combat Team, the highly decorated and highly publicized Japanese American unit that fought on the European front. Nearly 26,000 Nisei served in the military throughout the war.[96] Military service is yet another site of racial exceptionality on which the mainland and Hawaiian situations converged. The difference between the discrimination of *Korematsu* and the segregation of the 442nd Combat Team is that the former responds to a citizen's contestation of the state and the latter solicits a subject's self-inscription into the state.

If, as Bonnie Honig argues, the consent of the foreigner to naturalization represents a liberal regime as worth choosing,[97] the submission of the "foreigner-citizen" to the *jus belli* represents a nation-state as worth fighting for. The Nisei citizen-soldier is supposed to be the exceptional among the excepted, the "most loyal" of "the loyal." Hear this much from Tom Kawaguchi: "So in the 442nd, a lot of us felt that this was our only chance to demonstrate our loyalty; we would never get a second chance—this was it."[98] Although critical of the team being used as "cannon fodder," Shig Doi acknowledges that "the 442nd wrote the history for the Japanese" and "we paid dearly for it."[99] Having rejected the JACL's proposal to form a "suicide bat-

---

95. War Relocation Authority, *The Evacuated People*, 165.
96. Exempted from draft ineligibility, Hawaiian Nisei served in the 100th Battalion, which merged with the 442nd in June 1944. CWRIC, *Personal Justice Denied*, 256–58.
97. Bonnie Honig, *Democracy and the Foreigner* (Princeton, NJ: Princeton University Press, 2001), 94.
98. Kawaguchi quoted in John Tateishi, *And Justice for All: An Oral History of the Japanese American Detention Camps* (New York: Random House, 1984), 184.
99. Doi quoted in ibid., 161.

talion" near the beginning of the war, the state came to accept this visceral evidence near the end of it. The shedding and sacrificing of "Japanese blood" answered DeWitt's skepticism regarding "racial strains" that would fail the "final test of loyalty."

Nisei most squarely faced the paradox of consent that forced Japanese Americans to choose (or reject) the American state.[100] The ability of these "citizen-foreigners" to consent seemed independent from the state, but the very solicitation of consent presumed the state's forceful "alienation" of these already-citizens. Nisei were simultaneously included in and excluded from legal citizenship. In this respect, Nisei resembled Agamben's figure of *homo sacer*, the bare life caught in the liminal zones of the juridical order.[101] *Homo sacer* is the victim who may be killed but not sacrificed. However, the *jus belli* transforms this unconditional capacity to be killed into the Nisei male's conditional capacity to be sacrificed. Being sacrificed as a representative of the nation is conditioned on a willingness to kill and die for the state. It is, as with the spatial distribution of Japanese populations, the concrete existence of "Japanese bodies" that rearticulates meanings of friendship and enmity.

Conceived as a means of qualifying Nisei for military service, the loyalty questionnaire perforce further separated friends from enemies. Whatever it meant for its respondents, the completion of the loyalty registration helped streamline leave clearance procedures and physically segregate "disloyals." Throughout September and October of 1943, the WRA shipped "bad" Japanese to the maximum-security Tule Lake camp and transferred "good" Japanese out of it. Those segregated at Tule Lake included internees who answered no to question 28 (or refused to answer it), who had been denied leave clearance, who were of questionable loyalty according to the WRA or Justice Department, who requested expatriation or repatriation to Japan, or who simply desired to remain with family members.[102] Next, Congress granted Japanese American citizens the chance to renounce their citizenship altogether in the hopes of removing renunciants—the "most disloyal" of the "disloyal"—to Japan after the war. Public Law 405, bringing

---

100. The degree of literal force used varied by camp. The registration process ran relatively smoothly at Minidoka. At Tule Lake, internees continued to be arrested for refusing to register even after the War Department informed the WRA that registration was not compulsory. Nishiura Weglyn, *Years of Infamy*, 143–51.
101. Agamben, *Homo Sacer*, 71–80.
102. WRA, "Administrative Instruction No. 100," Manzanar War Relocation Center Records (Collection 122, Box 27), 1–2.

a logic of coercive/consensual citizenship to its conclusion in July 1944, allowed a U.S. citizen in a time of war to make "a formal written renunciation of nationality."[103]

By an act of consent, the citizenship that birth could not guarantee could be at least partially restored and, by an act of refusal, it could be almost wholly renounced. Official attempts to assimilate Japanese Americans delivered on the historicist postulate in *Ex Parte Endo* that "loyalty is a matter of the heart and mind, not of race, creed or color." However, the second rearticulation of the friend/enemy distinction *preserves* a racial distinction, albeit not the original identification of the Japanese "enemy race." The state recognizes the citizen-soldier as the extreme racial friend—not the friend regardless of race, but the racial figure who has nevertheless proven nationally loyal. It recognizes the renunciant as the extreme racial enemy or the citizen-soldier's despised twin. The exemplary disloyal who renounces his or her nationality at Tule Lake shadows the exemplary loyal who fights for the state in the 442nd Infantry Regimental Combat Team. Not coincidentally, both figures were segregated.[104]

Paradoxically, racial exceptionality for Japanese Americans is most pronounced precisely in virtue of the normalizing logic of "regardless of race." The friend/enemy antagonism intensified over the course of its rearticulations, each of which increasingly discriminated between loyals and disloyals. Social integration and existential loyalty would substantiate and homogenize nationality: dispersion of the population worked against separation, while submission to the *jus belli* qualified the presumption of disloyalty. This project of incorporating Japanese Americans was a turning point in the largely twentieth-century U.S. "progress" from racial naturalism to historicism. Through it, the state reconstituted the normal situation of race opposed to the racial state of exception.

Government lawyers' justifications of state security policies have unwittingly disclosed their stakes in ways that many security-rights commentators have not. Notice that Edwin Ferguson and Philip Glick's 1946 defense of detainment only invokes the maintenance of peace, order, and a particular way of life: "The leave regulations 'stemmed the flow'; they converted what

---

103. 58 Stat. 677. Most of the nearly 6,000 renunciants regained their citizenship through lawsuits initiated by the attorney Wayne Collins in 1945.

104. By 1945, the 442nd was attached to the (otherwise) all-black Ninety-Second Division. Umezawa Duus, *Unlikely Liberators*, 227–28. Japanese Americans, like Amerindians, also served in nonsegregated units.

might otherwise be a dangerously disordered flood of unwanted people into unprepared communities into a steady, orderly, planned migration into communities that gave every promise of being able to amalgamate the newcomers without incident.... The detention, in other words, was regarded as a necessary incident to this vital social planning."[105] Jacobus tenBroek and colleagues remark that these criteria "are hardly the categorical imperatives of military necessity. They are the social desiderata of welfare planners."[106] This judgment correctly describes the desiderata, yet incorrectly opposes them to military necessity. Its authors treat military necessity as a freestanding norm to deem state actions unjustified in the absence of a particular state of affairs. Outside of the security-rights circle, though, Ferguson and Glick's justifications appear as the normalizing standards applied to resolve the crisis of racial heterogeneity. What, if not "vital social planning," could the project of leave clearance achieve?

The Social-National Moment of Spatial Replacement

This wartime project of "amalgamating" Japanese was a distant relative to the nineteenth-century project of "civilizing" Amerindians to the extent that both aimed at federal racial-spatial order.[107] Japanese American assimilation, in this vein, was committed to "progressive" education, on behalf of which ideological state apparatuses would handle the interpellant operations.[108] Primary schoolteachers, upon reporting to the camps, were instructed to "promote understanding of American ideals and loyalty to American institutions" and to "provide sufficient contacts with the main currents of American life outside the area to prevent intellectual stagnation and inbreeding."[109] Yet educational, economic, and military conditions of leave wove Japanese Americans into the social fabric of the nation more tightly than any ideological sutures. Social planning targeted Nisei college students, workers, and soldiers on the premise that they could be made most alike. The state amitized the

---

105. Edwin Ferguson and Philip Glick, *Legal and Constitutional Phases of the WRA Program* (Washington, DC: Government Printing Office, 1946), 13. This passage is meant to justify the detainment; evacuation receives a separate justification.
106. tenBroek et al., *Prejudice, War, and the Constitution*, 251.
107. See Fanon, *Black Skins, White Masks*, chap. 6.
108. Louis Althusser, *Lenin and Philosophy and Other Essays*, trans. Ben Brewster (New York: Monthly Review, 1971), 162–65.
109. WRA, "The Teacher and the War Relocation Project," Manzanar War Relocation Center Records (Collection 122, Box 13), 9.

racial enemy under what it stipulated as the conditions of living and dying as American nationals rather than as Japanese foreigners.

Other social facts—such as the location of the Poston War Relocation Center on the Colorado River Indian Reservation—gesture toward the material connections between twentieth-century indigenous and Japanese American racial projects. The fact that the U.S. military occupation of the Pribilof and Aleutian Islands during World War II led to an internment of Aleut Indian residents of Alaska is uncanny.[110] Beyond uncanny is the fact that Dillon Myer served as the Bureau of Indian Affairs (BIA) commissioner from 1950 to 1953 after his tenure as the WRA director from 1942 to 1946. The bureaucrat Myer understood, and perhaps even experienced, politics as administration. As BIA commissioner, he removed Indians from reservations (by means of propaganda, education, and adoption) in the hopes of decollectivizing tribes and normalizing individuals. As we see in Chapter 5, Indian "termination" worked from racial historicist premises about the replacement of nonwhite bodies in concrete situations. Both postwar Indian termination and wartime Japanese assimilation correlated the closure of exceptional zones with the relocalization of racial populations.[111]

Chapter 3 staged the 1830s to 1840s removal of southeastern native polities as an antecedent parallel to the 1940s Japanese exclusion from the West Coast. The Wartime Civil Control Administration, which forcefully relocated Japanese, functioned as the equivalent of the War Department Indian agents, who removed Indians that "consented" to emigration. Bureaucratic homologies are even stricter in the postremoval periods. In February 1944, an executive order promoted the WRA from its position in the Office of Emergency Management into a cabinet-level position in the Department of the Interior—the department that in the 1940s and 1950s established the U.S. Fish and Wildlife Service and gained jurisdiction over Guam and American Samoa.[112] The WRA thereby moved into the neighborhood of its cousin, the BIA, which had traveled as the Office of Indian Affairs (OIA) into the Interior Department from the War Department in 1849. As for our "keeper of the concentration camps," as Richard Drinnon calls him, Myer relocated from one division of the Department of the Interior to the next when he put his

---

110. 102 Stat. 904. Aleut internment, the government claimed, protected them against Japanese militarism in the area.

111. Drinnon, *Keeper of the Concentration Camps*, 265.

112. Department of the Interior, "History of Interior," *U.S. Department of the Interior*, accessed May 1, 2017, http://www.doi.gov/whoweare/history.cfm.

assimilationist toolkit to work on Amerindians. If rebuilding state architecture remodels the administrative household of the nation, it cannot be surprising that reassignments of career politicians are often all in the family.[113]

Nearly two years after mass internment and about one year before terminal departures, an executive order transferred cabinet responsibility over Japanese Americans from the Secretary of War to the Secretary of the Interior.[114] The transfer of the WRA, like that of the OIA, squared away lines of bureaucratic authority with existing practices of amitization. One difference between WRA and BIA domestication projects is that 1830s and 1840s removals "concentrated" Indians, whereas 1940s relocations "dispersed" Japanese. A related difference is that state-enforced coercion and state-offered choices appear in inverted positions across the two cases: the southeastern Indian can choose to resettle west of the Mississippi River, while the West Coast Japanese is forcefully removed east of the Military Areas. The obverse of this inverse relation is that the indigenous ward is confined "out west" under indirect OIA control, whereas the Japanese internee is released eastward from direct WRA control.

The strongest point of analogy between the nineteenth-century removal contracts and the twentieth-century loyalty registration is that the state forced both sets of respondents to choose. The racial state set social and spatial coordinates that would incentivize both sets of respondents to make the "right" decisions or to suffer the consequences. In the former case, the state left each Indian polity "free" to consent to treaties that forced each native household to choose removing; in the latter case, the state went directly for individual consent and forced each interned adult to choose "allegiance." Hegemonic incorporation broke consenting indigenous polities down into choosing individuals, while it broke coerced Japanese populations down into consenting and choosing individuals. The southeastern Indian's consent to land appropriation and the Japanese American's consent to wartime policies alleviated bureaucratic anxieties over territorial disorder—not to mention liberal democratic anxieties over racial difference.

Alternatives to the Friend/Enemy Distinction

Kandice Chuh insists on the "simultaneous emptiness and significance" of racial and national identities and allegiances for the Nikkei internment.

---

113. Myer surrounded himself with a coterie of "loyal" bureaucrats, some of whom had followed him from the WRA to the BIA. Drinnon, *Keeper of the Concentration Camps* 19, 168.
114. Daniels, *Concentration Camps*, 151.

Her recognition of the logical arbitrariness, yet historical inscription of Americanness and Japaneseness is a reminder that the official meanings of such signifiers are not "all-consuming."[115] A critique of sovereignty, I have argued, demands that we call into question the state's authority to instantiate emergency projects in the names of security and order, to identify public enemies in the names of race and nation. It also demands that we search out alternatives to militaristic nationalisms from discourses that states will inevitably condition, but cannot fully consume.

Eiichiro Azuma reimagines prewar Japanese American transnationalism as a critical alternative to the Japan/United States and Oriental/Occidental binaries. He finds that Japanese immigrants negotiated more than transcended Japan's and the United States' rival projects of racial supremacy and imperialist expansion. More simply, Issei triangulated themselves with a distant national homeland and a localized racial regime. An example of this triangulation is the elite project of transforming lower-class immigrants into self-governing Japanese subjects-*qua*-normative American citizens; this partially converged with U.S. Americanization projects (developed for Southern and Eastern European immigrants) and Japanese modernization projects (launched in response to encroaching Western powers).[116] Similarly, Issei historians remembered Japanese Americans as "pioneers of racial development" (*minzoku hatten no senkusha*)—a phrase redolent of both U.S. and Japanese expansionism—to contest both anti-emigrant discourses in Japan and anti-immigrant sentiments in the United States.[117]

The Pacific War for Azuma was the negation of an Issei transnationalism interpellated by the Japanese state apparatus and situated in the U.S. political economy. Prior to the war, Japanese Americans had forged strategic alliances with the Japanese government, alliances fraught with tensions between the diplomatic aims of governments and the localized aims of immigrants.[118] However, the domestic politics and geopolitics of 1941 necessitated a turn from Japanese/American dualism to unitary Americanism, as any link to Japan would likely be misinterpreted as disloyalty to the United

---

115. Chuh, *Imagine Otherwise*, 75–76.
116. Azuma, *Between Two Empires*, 58. The citizenship project floundered on alien land laws, immigration restrictions, and other measures of anti-Asian exclusion.
117. Ibid., chap. 4.
118. Eiichiro Azuma, "Dancing with the Rising Sun: Strategic Alliances between Japanese Immigrants and Their 'Home' Government," in *The Transnational Politics of Asian Americans*, ed. Christian Collet and Pei-te Lien (Philadelphia: Temple University Press, 2009), 25–26.

States.[119] Azuma emphasizes the irreducibility of transnational dualism to the nation-statist binaries on which it ideologically depended and pragmatically worked. One could also mention here that Japanese Americans, who were more concerned with familial well-being than with state-defined interests, likely sustained weak allegiances to both the United States and Japan.[120]

Prewar transnationalism anticipates wartime resistances to transpacific Manichean binaries. In addition to arguing that internee cultural practices refused the forced choice of "Japan or America,"[121] Gary Okihiro reframes resistance to WRA camp governance in terms of human rights. This is not to say that the discourse of human rights is without universalistic conceits; it is to say that claims to human rights subvert friend/enemy distinctions entirely compatible with claims to civil rights. "The concept of humanity excludes the concept of the enemy," Schmitt argues. "There is no specific differentiation in that concept." For Schmitt, universal claims made "in the name of humanity" are always articulated from particular positions of friend/enemy engagement.[122] By contrast, Okihiro shows how particular articulations of the friend/enemy distinction gave rise to universalistic demands for human rights. At Tule Lake under martial law, for example, Japanese Americans could counterpose their common humanity to the Japan versus United States divide.[123]

Their struggle occurred on a World War II terrain of crisis, where the lack of national rights entailed the lack of human rights and the acquisition of human rights required the acquisition of national rights.[124] Human rights, especially as articulated by national minorities and stateless peoples, marked deep conflicts between sovereign prerogatives and individualistic protections.[125] A condition of dispossession from human rights or "the right to have rights," Arendt says, "is manifested first and above all in the deprivation of a place in the world which makes opinions significant and actions effective."[126]

---

119. Azuma, *Between Two Empires*, 186, 208–9.
120. Mae Ngai, *Impossible Subjects: Illegal Aliens and the Making of Modern America* (Princeton, NJ: Princeton University Press, 2004), 200.
121. Gary Okihiro, "Religion and Resistance in America's Concentration Camps," *Phylon* 45, no. 3 (1984): 220.
122. Schmitt, *The Concept of the Political*, 54.
123. Gary Okihiro, "Tule Lake under Martial Law: A Study in Japanese Resistance," *Journal of Ethnic Studies* 5, no. 3 (1977): 80–81; cf. Hiyashi, *Democratizing the Enemy*, 219.
124. Arendt, *The Origins of Totalitarianism*, pt. 2, chap. 9.
125. Serena Parekh, *Hannah Arendt and the Challenge of Modernity: A Phenomenology of Human Rights* (New York: Routledge, 2008), 21; for a radical democratic framing of human rights, see Honig, *Emergency Politics*, chap. 5.
126. Arendt, *The Origins of Totalitarianism*, 296.

Read in this light, Okihiro is unearthing nonnationalist approaches to worldliness taken by Japanese Americans denied a place in the interstate system. Okihiro's insight is that agonistic contestations for human rights and cultural solidarity move respectively "above" and "below" Schmittian antagonisms.

A postwar challenge to nationalist binaries undermines the unitary conception of sovereignty that undergirds them. I am speaking of Fred Korematsu's 2003–2004 *amicus* briefs in support of prisoners detained at Guantanamo Bay without due process. Korematsu, who intentionally violated a civilian exclusion order in 1942, draws the security-rights circle around World War II and post-9/11 detention measures: he accepts in principle that the state may restrict rights for the sake of national security, but he in practice rejects all justifications to this effect on the grounds of factual error or excessive restraint.[127] Korematsu concedes that the decision on the emergency falls within the domain of state authority, but he—like Honig—stresses the constitutional limits of executive discretion. His basic claim is that the U.S. constitution does not authorize the executive to suspend normal protections without any "check-and-balance" from another branch of government.[128]

The lesson of the Japanese internment, on this view, is that the judiciary must ensure that executive security measures respect civil rights, human rights, and the separation of powers.[129] The liberal democratic goal of bringing "enemy combatants" back within the fold of due process is a constraint on executive decision, which is also subject to congressional regulation.[130] The U.S. federal system for Korematsu includes multiple points of decision with partially overlapping jurisdictions. Constitutional divisions on both of our views make it difficult, if not impossible to pinpoint a unified office with final authority. Korematsu's federalism is a critical alternative to Schmittian sovereignty insofar as it challenges executive attempts to monopolize decisions on the exception and the enemy.

---

127. Examples range from the Alien and Sedition Acts in the early republic to the McCarthyist Loyalty Oaths of the Cold War. Brief of Amicus Curiae Fred Korematsu in Support of Petitioners, 542 U.S. 466 (2003), 4–24.

128. Cf. Arendt, *On Revolution*, chaps. 4–5.

129. Brief of Amicus Curiae, 542 U.S. 466 (2003), 4–5.

130. Korematsu et al. observe that detainees at Guantanamo Bay would have received better procedural protections under the Emergency Detention Act of 1950, a now-repealed Cold War law. Brief of Amicus Curiae Fred Korematsu, the Bar Association of San Francisco, the Asian Law Caucus, the Asian American Bar Association of the Greater Bay Area, Asian Pacific Islander Legal Outreach, and the Japanese American Citizens League in Support of Respondents, 542 U.S. 426 (2003), 15, 18–19.

Conclusion: The Racial State of Exception and the Liberal Democratic State

This chapter has rethought the national-security state of the Japanese internment as a constituent of the informal U.S. constitution. It has outlined the fracturing of sovereignty across multiple sites of decision as well as the relative coherence of the project of distinguishing friendships from enmities. Section I theorized the incarceration of Japanese Americans as a decision on the state of exception that coincided with an identification of the racial enemy. Section II tracked shifting friend/enemy distinctions into different moments of administrative discretion, tracing the transformation of the simplistic equation of race and disloyalty into the vexed question of the loyalty of the race. Section I concluded with an account of racial exceptionality as a mode of governance, and Section II concluded with an account of liberal democratic divisions of sovereignty. This conclusion addresses the liberal democratic paradoxes of the wartime administration of Japanese populations.

Our starting point is Schmitt's claim that liberal democracy is a contradiction in terms and, in order to govern at all, "liberal democracy must decide between its elements."[131] The contradiction for Schmitt is that liberalism embraces the formal equality of individuals, while democracy demands the substantive equality of the people. If Schmitt is right, the Japanese internment is the case of a liberal democracy deciding in favor of a biologically inflected *demos*, white America. A liberal democracy at war, in other words, suspended its individualistic elements when deciding on its identitarian conditions of existence. A "democratic" crisis of racial-national heterogeneity, while anticipated by fears of yellow perils, only became a concrete reality with DeWitt's declaration of enmity. DeWitt's decision, in turn, participated in a broader imaginary of international race war.[132]

Myers's decisions inserted increasingly fine-lined discriminations into this same Manichean imaginary. The liberal solicitation of individual consent, when juxtaposed to the nonliberal coercion of mass confinement, suggests that an actually existing liberal democracy can never decisively decide. At his most polemical, Schmitt accuses liberal individualism and liberal management of depoliticization. In the case of the internment, however, individualism and administration were the specifically liberal moments of

---

131. Schmitt, *The Crisis of Parliamentary Democracy*, 15.
132. Cf. Don Nakanishi, "Foreword," in Collet and Lien, *The Transnational Politics of Asian Americans*, xi–xii.

liberal democracy's affirmation of the friend/enemy distinction.[133] Even if it ultimately decided in favor of democratic sameness, the racial state restored some measure of liberal choice in order to rearticulate racial and national identifications as cultural formations. To mix metaphors, this compromise between a democratic repression and a liberal "return of the repressed" made consent into the crucial mediator of the transfiguration of enemy into friend.

The Japanese internment exemplifies what Chantal Mouffe terms "the democratic paradox," a mutually transformative coarticulation of liberalism and democracy.[134] Historically speaking, the tensions between liberal individualism and democratic identification in the Japanese internment point forward to the tensions between liberal legalism and democratic struggle in the civil rights movement. More conceptually, liberal resolutions of democratic conflict and democratic contestations of liberal compromises continue to enact a dialectic of depoliticization and repoliticization.[135] Although easiest to discern in extraordinary events, the liberal democratic paradox is constantly negotiated and reproduced in everyday life. There liberal devices such as individual rights are constantly renewed as sites of popular conflict, say, in affirmative action controversies.

Both the Japanese internment and the civil rights movement transpired at the essentially contested site of the *demos*, where on-the-ground contests constituted their democratic valences. Put in terms of public constitution, the racial re-founding combined social rights with popular insurgency, while the racial state of exception conjoined cultural assimilation with national homogeneity. Put in terms of racial formation, the civil rights movement recognized white/black division to internalize ascriptively conceived blackness, while the Japanese internment renegotiated white/Japanese division to externalize culturally conceived Japaneseness.

The democratic valences of the Japanese internment and the civil rights movement were also respectively constituted by Schmittian liberalism and Lefortian liberalism. Lefortian liberalism re-creates racial conflicts (e.g., legitimated oppositions over membership) in precisely those arenas in which Schmittian liberalism makes recourse to individual consent (e.g., individual choices of incorporation). As we found in Chapter 2, the nationalization of

---

133. Schmitt observes that "liberalism too, as a historical force, has failed to elude the political." Schmitt, *The Concept of the Political*, 69; see also 70–73.
134. Chantal Mouffe, *The Democratic Paradox* (London: Verso, 2000), 10.
135. This analysis draws on Carl Schmitt, "The Age of Neutralizations and Depoliticizations," trans. Matthias Konzen and John McCormick, in Schmitt, *The Concept of the Political*, 90.

civil rights has led to continual disagreements concerning black and white social conditions. As we will see in Chapter 5, the Anglo-conformist strand of U.S. nationality has provoked various nonwhite claims of cultural pride. I explain such developments using Lefort's notion that modern democratic power cannot be embodied in an empirical social division and, more precisely, I contend that the U.S. citizenry can no longer be (fully) identified with whiteness after the civil rights movement.[136]

At least for now, the Lefortian liberal democracy of the civil rights movement predominates over the Schmittian liberal democracy of the Japanese internment. That said, the internment bridged prewar anti-Asian racism with postwar color-blind integrationism.[137] Wartime liberal officials wanted to "salvage" good Japanese Americans from the wreckage of bad Japanese made worse by internment. Later, at the height of the black power movement, the model minority discourse made Asian cultural values into a "solution" to the purported problem of black cultural dysfunction.[138] This turn from Anglo-conformity to cultural pluralism is not as pronounced as it might sound, for multiculturalism is coequal to assimilationism as an indicator of U.S. racial historicism. Both projects assume that races are no less historically contingent and culturally defined than nations. Both projects also pathologize the refusal of recent immigrants, racial minorities, and colonial subjects to incorporate.

The typical modes of engaging the racial enemy differentiated the U.S. "Provisional Solution" from the German "Final Solution," twentieth-century liberal democratic from totalitarian regimes. Though I am aware of the politics of naming and remembrance, I have dwelled neither on the question of whether camps for Japanese Americans should be called "internment camps" or "concentration camps," nor on the question of whether forcing Japanese Americans into camps should be called "internment" or "incarceration."[139]

---

136. See Lefort, *Democracy and Political Theory*, 226.

137. Fong, "Beyond the Racial Exceptionalism of the Japanese Internment," 242.

138. "Success Story of One Minority Group in U.S.," *U.S. News & World Report*, December 26, 1966, 6–8. As Prashad puts this problem, "How does it feel to be a solution?" Vijay Prashad, *The Karma of Brown Folk* (Minneapolis: University of Minnesota Press, 2000), viii.

139. Officials described mass confinement with euphemisms like "relocation camps." "Japanese internment camps" only became a keyword after the 1950s. In the 1970s, scholars called these "concentration camps" to connote political imprisonment. Today, some Japanese Americans speak of "mass incarceration" to emphasize that their families were deemed "guilty by race." Lane Hirabayashi, "Incarceration," in *Keywords for Asian American Studies*, ed. Cathy Schlund-Vials, Linda Trinh Võ, and K. Scott Wong (New York: New York University Press, 2015), 133–38.

More relevant for my purposes is the type of racial project pursued by each racial state. The German project of physically eliminating the enemy operated from racial naturalist premises from start to finish. The U.S. wartime project, in substituting racial naturalist for racist historicist assumptions, would be satisfied with social assimilation.[140]

My account of internment camps is at odds with Giorgio Agamben's hyperbolic description of "*the* camp" as "the most absolute biopolitical space ever to have been realized."[141] The transformation of the exception into the rule, the disjuncture of birth-right citizenship and national-state membership, and the indistinguishability of laws and facts: all these features of concentration camps for Agamben constitute the space of modern politics itself. Yet specific to Agamben's paradigm case of National Socialist camps is the "absolute" character of the "biopolitical space," the relentless logic of bare life under the sovereign ban. Japanese internment camps operated according to an attenuated logic, negotiating multiple sites of sovereign decision and conflicting notions of racialized life. Racial states of exceptionality surpassed the racial state of exception in demanding that both cultural and bare life be sacrificed for a national way of life. The demand that Japanese Americans renounce their heritage for the sake of national homogeneity is strictly analogous to the demand that Japanese Americans shed their blood for the sake of friend/enemy existence.

Assimilation, as distinguished from genocide, is a life-and-death struggle of the figurative variety. Racial assimilation, however, involves an existential conflict that Schmitt could have recognized as such. What Schmitt would have a harder time recognizing is the administrative cast of friend/enemy decisions in the Japanese internment. Rossiter's doctrine that democracies in the throes of emergency politics will suspend constitutions "to whatever degree necessary to overcome the peril and restore normal conditions" is entirely apposite here. Just as pertinent is my addendum that some restorations of the norm are reconstitutions of normality. That an emergency project of normalization emerged from the state of exception is evidence of a convergence between the punctuation of the decision and the procession of the project, the substantive identifications of democracy and the individualist consent of liberalism. That the exception became the rule proves everything.

---

140. On the relationship of German and U.S. eugenics, see McWhorter, *Racism and Sexual Oppression*, 229–31.

141. Agamben, *Homo Sacer*, 171, italics added.

5

Racial Counter-Publics and the Power of Judgment

> Similarly, one can never compel anyone to agree with one's judgments—
> "This is beautiful" or "This is Wrong" . . . ; one can only "woo" or
> "court" the agreement of everyone else. And in this persuasive activity
> one actually appeals to the "community sense."
> —Hannah Arendt, *Lectures on Kant's Political Philosophy*

> As Alcatraz then was symbolic of the rebirth of Indian consciousness to both Indians and non-Indians, it is also symbolic today of our present relationship to the government. The island has armed guards and is barb-wired and bugged.
> —LaNada Boyer, "Growing up in *E'da How*"

The black power, red power, and Asian American movements lead our study back into the Arendtian realm of citizen action after our foray into the Schmittian realm of state decisions. These participants in the postwar "politicization of the social" fused economic, cultural, and even spiritual issues together in "new collective identities."[1] However, as Michael Omi and Howard Winant argue, they failed to remake the whole society due to their inability to specify racial dynamics as well as their inability to outflank the racial state.[2] I broadly agree with Omi and Winant's assessment, but—following Cristina Beltrán—I also want to reconsider the criteria by which social movement successes and failures are typically adjudicated.[3] "Success" in this context comes down to more than whether or not a social movement could achieve its stated aims.

Ultimately, I praise racial power movements as enactments of public freedom, howsoever fleeting such moments may have been. As for enduring

---

1. Omi and Winant, *Racial Formation in the United States*, 162, 153.
2. Ibid., 178–79.
3. Beltrán, *The Trouble with Unity*, chap. 5.

achievements, I contend that racial power instituted oppositional spaces within the U.S. public, albeit in "multicultural" ways of which racial power activists may not have approved. This chapter outlines how racial power antagonism broke out of and was subsequently bracketed within civil rights movement agonism. Like Chapter 2, this chapter explores how the racial state contained radical democratic demands within liberal democratic institutions. It adds that racial power antagonism differed from civil rights agonism not only in its orientation to opponents; racial power also had a distinctively antagonistic manner of judging its identifications and aims.

Racial power activists did not only conceive of—and perhaps merely conceived of—the political in terms of sovereign power.[4] Moreover, they did not make (mere) assertions of collective will, though they made individuated judgments with respect to collectivities. They judged, more precisely, in terms of the articulation of nonwhite/white antagonism, the subaltern demand for institutional changes, and—most importantly—the appeal to a community's common sense.[5] Movements appealed to common sensibilities rather than common standards, as the new communities (for which they called) could not be defined by the old society's standards (which they found wanting). This chapter, then, specifies racial formation as new social movement sensibility and public constitution in the mode of judgment.

Racial power activists had to judge who they were precisely because the answer to this question is unknowable. But the lack of names, norms, and other givens did not mean that anything went in responding to the identification question. Claims of racial identification appealed to communities' moral, aesthetic, and economic senses of themselves or, put otherwise, raised the social question as a question of sensibility. Activists appealed to what Arendt, following Immanuel Kant, calls common sense (*sensus communis*), an "extra sense" that "fits us into a community."[6] For Kant, common sense is the principle of validity for certain kinds of judgment; it is what a judgment of taste presupposes in claiming that "everyone *ought* to give [their]

---

4. A critique of the uses of sovereignty in contemporary recognition claims is Patchen Markell, *Bound by Recognition* (Princeton, NJ: Princeton University Press, 2003).

5. These criteria exclude white power, which imagines a return to the white monopolization of U.S. citizenship. Chicano/a and Puerto Rican movements meet the criteria, but are not included because I am comparing (relatively distinctive) black, Asian, and Amerindian formations.

6. Arendt, *Lectures on Kant's Political Philosophy*, 70. It is an "extra" sense or an addition to the other five senses.

approval to the object at hand."[7] For Arendt, however, *a* common sense puts into question the Kantian "everyone": with the circulation and reception of any judgment, who might travel under this sign? This question of intersubjectivity arose again and again for racial power activists who made claims about belonging together in the world.

Racial power activists also had to judge what they wanted because even the most "objective" determination of interest involves an appeal to what is between (*inter-est*) subjects (e.g., institutions, resources, norms).[8] Movement counter-publics, to use Nancy Fraser's keyword, were spaces of withdrawal for subalterns as well as grounds for contestations of the hegemonic public.[9] In both moments, appeals to common good partook of struggles for institutionalized power. Hegemonic struggles for leadership within subaltern counter-publics were coupled with counter-hegemonic demands for equality within the official public. Following Chantal Mouffe, I understand hegemonic struggle as what establishes a partially fixed social order and what guarantees the partial, unfinished character of that ordering.[10] Racial power counter-hegemony kept open the radical democratic possibilities that the liberal democratic institutionalization of the civil rights movement foreclosed.

In thinking judgment and hegemony together, I am proposing that the political theoretical turn to the sensible ("the aesthetic turn") could benefit from critical theoretical considerations of movement power. While Arendt is attuned to the publicly constitutive character of judgment, for instance, we must be skeptical of Arendt's misjudgment of black power as "proto-totalitarian." What Arendt feared most, to read her charitably, is that black power articulated violence in an antagonistic manner.[11] Mouffe's critique that Arendtian political theorists want agonism without antagonism is entirely ap-

---

7. Immanuel Kant, *Critique of Judgment*, trans. Werner Pluhar (Indianapolis: Hackett, 1987), 85–87, italics original.

8. Cf. Steven Klein, "'Fit to Enter the World': Hannah Arendt on Politics, Economics, and the Welfare State," *American Political Science Review* 108, no. 4 (2014): 861–63, 866–68.

9. Nancy Fraser, *Justice Interruptus: Critical Reflections on the "Postsocialist" Condition* (New York: Routledge, 1997), 82. I am also informed by Linda Zerilli's study of feminist counter-publics. Linda Zerilli, *Feminism and the Abyss of Freedom* (Chicago: University of Chicago Press, 2005), chaps. 2–4.

10. Mouffe, *On the Political*, chap. 2.

11. Arendt, *On Violence*, 21–22; cf. Arendt, *The Origins of Totalitarianism*, chap. 8. Nor would Arendt have appreciated the red power and Asian American movements, had she been cognizant of them. For a more critical assessment of Arendt's model of judgment, see Gines, *Hannah Arendt and the Negro Question*, chap. 7.

propriate in this case:¹² Arendt's own concept of judgment covers nonantagonistic relationships between the judging self, her community, and her "others." For this reason, I extend the Arendtian concept of judgment to cover racial power activists who appealed to subaltern common senses (antagonistically) excluded from and excluding of a dominant common sensibility.

An inversely symmetrical problem awaits on the other side of our theoretical conjuncture. If Arendt thinks of judgment without hegemony, Mouffe thinks of hegemony without judgment. Mouffe's account of hegemonic formation is missing the moment that the self appeals to an audience's senses of fairness, beauty, and usefulness. This absence is all the more striking because "common sense" for Gramsci, whom Mouffe follows on many questions, is a site of critical reflection—a nexus of popular belief, perception, and passion that movement leadership must help render "critical."¹³ Mouffe, who largely avoids humanistic conceptions of powers/faculties, creates a distance from Gramscian common sense that I would hope to close. The Gramscian intellectual who avows a relationship with a class formation is, on my account, akin to the racial power activist who avows a relationship with a racial common sense.

Critical race theorists argue that Asian American panethnicity, Amerindian pantribalism, and black transnationalism irrevocably changed racialized self-conceptions.¹⁴ I would add that post–civil rights era identifications marked the extension of radical democratic struggles into domains ostensibly private, neutral, or nonpolitical (e.g., housing). In other words, what Omi and Winant call "politicizations of the social" included judgments of how "we" can radically reconstitute everyday life. To literatures on 1960s and 1970s U.S. racial activisms, I would offer an account of how judgment co-articulated public identities and public institutions for selected movements.¹⁵ Table 5.1 summarizes these judgments as follows.

Modes of identification below are emblematic of their respective movements, but they do not exhaust that movement's range of identity repertoires.

---

12. Chantal Mouffe, *Agonistics: Thinking the World Politically* (London: Verso, 2013), 9–15. Mouffe claims that antagonism is prior to and a condition of possibility for agonism.

13. Gramsci, *Selections from the Prison Notebooks*, 323–31.

14. On nonwhite pride, see Ian Haney López, *Racism on Trial: The Chicano Fight for Justice* (Cambridge, MA: Harvard University Press, 2003), 2, 238.

15. See, e.g., Joane Nagel, *American Indian Ethnic Renewal: Red Power and the Resurgence of Identity and Culture* (Oxford, UK: Oxford University Press, 1996); William Wei, *The Asian American Movement: A Social History* (Philadelphia: Temple University Press, 1993).

TABLE 5.1 US/THEM DIVISIONS AND COMMUNITY APPEALS			
Section	*Movement*	*Us/them identifications*	*Appeal to common sense*
I	Black power	Diasporic nationalism	Ethics
II	Red power	Pantribalism	Aesthetics
III	Asian American	Panethnicity	Economics

Idioms of appeal, by contrast, have no specific affinity with any (relatively distinctive) movement; every movement posed demands in light of (nonexclusively) ethical, aesthetic, and economic criteria.[16]

Each movement has its own section below in order to highlight distinctive features, histories, and achievements. Section I considers how Malcolm X, a foundational figure for (what came to be called) black power, appealed to black nationalist senses of right and wrong. Section II is about an inaugural event of red power, the occupation of Alcatraz Island, where activists judged pan-Indian insurgency on aesthetic criteria. Section III turns to the anti-eviction campaign at the International Hotel, where Asian activists put economic needs at the center of a panethnic front. Across all three parts, the complex of identification, appeal, and demand relates movement counter-publics to the official public. In conclusion, I argue that U.S. multiculturalism is, among other things, a (semi-)official response to 1960s and 1970s racial empowerment movements.

Section I: The Associational Choices of Black Nationalism

Preceded by Martin Delaney, Marcus Garvey, and earlier black nationalists, Malcolm X anticipated Stokely Carmichael, Huey Newton, and later "community nationalists."[17] Far from a full reconstruction of X's life story,[18] this section studies an underappreciated moment in X's political thought—namely, the ethical appeal of his judgments of friendship and enmity. This section first recounts episodes in the *Autobiography* to show that X's judgments of "white devilry" depended on judgments of black common sense.

---

16. I align blackness with ethics, for instance, because Section I is about Malcolm X. If Section I were about Huey Newton, I would have aligned blackness with economics instead.

17. Tommie Shelby, *We Who Are Dark: The Philosophical Foundations of Black Solidarity* (Cambridge, MA: Harvard University Press, 2005), 103–7.

18. See, e.g., Wolfenstein, *The Victims of Democracy*; Manning Marable, *Malcolm X: A Life of Reinvention* (New York: Penguin, 2011).

It then accounts for analogous judgments in "The Ballot or the Bullet," a speech that marks the secularization of his racial nationalism. I argue that X's nationalism in both theological and secular variants aligns black associational choices with ethical self-relation.

Black nationalism came to the prison inmate then known as Malcolm Little through the Nation of Islam (NOI). This fraternal movement in the tradition of Prince Hall masonry offered a meta-history and its hermeneutic key:[19] as Elijah Muhammad taught, "when white men had written history books, the black man simply had been left out."[20] Little set off in search of histories assumed to be at least partially recoverable, unlike the "X" that would mark the spot of an irrevocably lost surname.[21] His research in the prison library uncovered how, "since the sixteenth century, the so-called 'Christian trader' white man began to ply the seas in his lust for Asian and African empires, and plunder, and power." He judged differences between countries, continents, and circumstances to be secondary in comparison to this global, white/nonwhite antagonism. Secular histories confirmed "that the collective white man had acted like a devil in every contact he had with the world's collective non-white man."[22]

NOI theology takes European relations to non-Europeans as evidence of the essence of radical evil rather than, say, the result of uncivilized European behavior. This is far from saying that the evidence is not intellectually tested—far from it, in Little's hyper-cognitive examination of facts. When Little first heard that the white man is the devil, for example, he literally imagined how many instances of whiteness fit this description. "The white people I had known marched before my mind's eye. From the start of my life," X remembers. "The state white people always in our house after the other [Ku Klux Klan] whites I didn't know had killed my father . . . , the white people who kept calling my mother 'crazy' to her face. . . . The ones in Boston, in the white-only dances at the Roseland Ballroom where I shined their shoes."[23] What Little learned is less my concern than how he learned it. He deemed "the white man is the devil" to be successful in accounting for examples of

---

19. Gilroy, *Against Race*, 223–24.
20. Malcolm X and Alex Haley, *The Autobiography of Malcolm X* (New York: Grove, 1965), 175.
21. Ibid., 201; cf. Patterson, *Slavery and Social Death*, 56–58. Malcolm Little changed his name to Malcolm X after he was released from prison. I refer to Malcolm as either "Little" or "X," depending on the time frame.
22. X and Haley, *The Autobiography of Malcolm X*, 177–79.
23. Ibid., 160–61.

European oppression from history books and examples of white discrimination known from personal experience.

X's trains of thought traveled the pathway of "determinative judgment," where the rule is given and the instance is subsumed under it.[24] Using one of Kant's categories, though, does not oblige us to inquire into its conditions of possibility. We will ask instead how X actually judged whether the generality was adequate to the subsumption of the particulars; as Kant would say, our question is more empirical than transcendental. However, the empirical character of the following analysis does not foreclose the possibility that X's judgment is exemplary of ethical judgment. How did he come to know the enemy of blacks in America? How could he claim that his judgments on enmity were valid for anyone else?

A liberated mind in an imprisoned body represented community sensibilities not literally present as the ground of judgment. Little imagined himself into the position of other community members, attempting to "enlarge" his perspective.[25] While NOI "teachings ring true—to every Negro," X explains that "among all Negroes the black convict is the most perfectly conditioned to hear the words, 'the white man is the devil.' You tell that to any Negro. Except for those relatively few 'integration'-mad so-called 'intellectuals' . . . you have struck a nerve center."[26] This sensory language of "[ringing] true" and "[striking] a nerve center" appeals to the very common sense of black community that it characterizes and constitutes. Reactions of "'integration'-mad so-called 'intellectuals'" and "the black convict" to NOI demonology are, respectively, paths cut off from or pathways into the potential generality of "every" or "any Negro." The certainty that "the white man is the devil" is thereby achieved on the basis of persuasion, a persuasiveness relative to black common sense. Here determinative judgment, where the rule is given and the instance is subsumed, turns on a "reflective judgment," where the instance is given and the rule is sought.[27]

We would do well to keep in mind the antagonistic form of Malcolm X's public imaginations. The contention that "the collective white man" is a devil

---

24. As Kant defined it, "if the universal (the rule, principle, law) is given, then judgment, which subsumes the particular under it, is *determinative*." Kant, *Critique of Judgment*, 18, italics original.

25. Arendt, *Lectures on Kant's Political Philosophy*, 42–43.

26. X and Haley, *The Autobiography of Malcolm X*, 175, 184.

27. As Kant defined this mode, "if only the particular is given and judgment has to find the [general] for it, then this power is merely *reflective*." Kant, *Critique of Judgment*, 18–19, italics original.

to "the world's collective non-white man" articulates the friend/enemy distinction in the NOI's distinctively theological language. Malcolm X of the NOI is caught between religious and ethical discourse, determinative and reflective judgments. In his post-NOI speech known as "The Ballot or the Bullet," Malcolm X decides in favor of ethical discourse and reflective judgment. His secular turn simultaneously calls for the transfer of decision-making authority to individuals in black communities. Racial national identifications achieved outside of the NOI fraternal order will require new organizational forms.[28]

The institutional demands of this speech bottom on self-determination and separation from whites (but maybe also other nonblacks). Self-determination means "community control," as in blacks collectively controlling their politics, economics, and morality.[29] Black people should form their own associations, invest in their own enterprises, and find pleasure in their own company. A community can only control itself if its members can control the institutionalized coordination of their activities; either a community self-determines its fortunes or its fate will be determined by others. The problem, as X construes it, is that "the white man controls his own school, his own bank, his own economy—but he also controls yours."[30] X proposes that self-controlled separation is the real alternative to other-controlled segregation and other-controlled integration. Black autonomy, on this conception, is the question of who—which embodied individuals—will occupy institutionalized positions of power.[31]

The aim of black autonomy is a nationalist project, but one that does not aspire to the statist universality and territorial boundaries of the nation-state. As Kirstie McClure might say, community nationalism elaborates "'the political' beyond its modernist enclosure within the territorially bounded juridical institutions of the state into the far more fluid and shifting domain of cultural representations and social practices."[32] Its social practices are

---

28. X delivered this 1964 speech as the leader of Muslim Mosque Inc., which he helped found after leaving the NOI. His final political efforts were with the Organization for Afro-American Unity, which was modeled on the Organization for African Unity.

29. Malcolm X, "The Ballot or the Bullet," in *Malcolm X Speaks: Selected Speeches and Statements*, ed. George Breitman (New York: Pathfinder, 1989), 38–39.

30. Ibid., 42.

31. Jane Gordon, *Why They Couldn't Wait: A Critique of Black-Jewish Conflict over Community Control in Ocean Hill-Brownsville (1967–1971)* (New York: Routledge, 2001), 23.

32. Kirstie McClure, "On the Subject of Rights: Pluralism, Plurality and Political Identity," in *Dimensions of Radical Democracy: Pluralism, Citizenship, Community*, ed. Chantal Mouffe (London: Verso, 1992), 123.

often localized projects such as supporting neighborhood businesses. Its cultural representations, as we will see, are typically transnationally and geopolitically articulated. So X does not seek to flatten black American experiences into a uniform U.S. citizen-subjectivity. That said, he does provide grounds other than citizenship for demanding civil rights.

Black civil rights claims are grounded on the creditor/debtor relationships of black counter-publics and the official U.S. public. Because the hegemonic interpretation of the civil rights movement "kept us out," black nationalists must provide "an interpretation that will enable us to come into [the civil rights struggle]." X interprets civil rights as something owed to a black nation from a white nation, claiming that "all we're doing there is trying to collect for our investment. Our mothers and fathers invested sweat and blood," unfree labor and military service in the United States.[33] This demand is entirely consistent with friend/enemy politics. There is just as little contradiction in X demanding rights from the national enemy of black nationalists as there is in Jefferson extracting labor from the slave enemy of white colonists.

X re-signifies "separation," "segregation," and "integration" in ways that distinguish the black nationalist movement from the civil rights movement; this is part of the black nationalist bid for hegemony within existing black counter-publics. As I argued in Chapter 2, Martin Luther King Jr.'s theological politics treats the opponent as an adversary. Malcolm X's politics—both theological and secular—treats the opponent as an enemy. The U.S. republic for King agonistically internalizes racial division; thus King cites freely from black and white political and theological traditions to authorize civil rights activism as "the best in the American dream and the most sacred values in our Judaeo-Christian heritage." For X, the U.S. nation-state antagonistically externalizes racial division. Struggling in the name of a "not-American" nation, X makes recourse neither to spiritual authority nor to the American political tradition. "I'm not an American," he avows. "I'm one of the 22 million black people who are victims of Americanism."[34]

My reading of X militates against overly psychological interpretations of his statements about white Americans. It is not enough to say X mistrusts whites, as some democratic theorists might; it is better to see that X judges

---

33. X, "The Ballot or the Bullet," 31–33.
34. Ibid., 26. Similar images of black community can be crafted in amoral language, e.g., Stokely Carmichael and Charles Hamilton, *Black Power: The Politics of Liberation in America* (New York: Random House, 1967), 60, 77.

oppressors to be enemies. Take his claim that "it's the white man who grins at you the most, and pats you on the back . . . [h]e may be friendly, but he's not your friend."[35] This bears the equally defensible interpretations of "white men may be privately friendly, but they are publicly hostile" and "white men may appear publicly friendly, but they are hypocritically hostile." Likewise, it is not enough to say that X debates questions of violent tactics and strategies in passages like this one: "We will work with anybody, anywhere, at any time, who is genuinely interested in tackling the problem head-on, nonviolently as long as the enemy is nonviolent, but violently when the enemy gets violent."[36] For the very question of political violence presupposes the existential division between enemies and friends.

As a consequence of its secularization, X's identification of friends and enemies is now structurally rather than substantively articulated. If whiteness is a structural location of domination over blacks, blackness is a structural location of subordination to whites. X no longer demonizes whites after his break with the NOI; the enemy who carries out the oppression, exploitation, and degradation of black communities "just happens to be a white man." Black people, for their part, are potentially friends insofar as they "all are going to catch the same hell from the same man" irrespective of religion, education, or class.[37] Although he spans the political/cultural divide of black nationalism,[38] X nonetheless privileges racial struggle over cultural substance. Blackness as an *effect* of racial oppression links black liberation in the United States transnationally with African, Islamic, and third world decolonization.[39]

Just as Malcolm Little did in deciding to associate with the NOI, Malcolm X makes a choice of black company through an appeal to common sense. X and Arendt might agree that (what appear to be) determinative judgments on the right/wrong distinction depend on reflective judgments on the company one keeps. For Arendt, ethical judgments appeal to the community of the self, the "two-in-one" who would like to remain on speaking terms. Socrates, the exemplar of Arendtian self-dialogue, validated the prop-

---

35. X, "The Ballot or the Bullet," 30.
36. Ibid., 38, 42.
37. Ibid., 24.
38. Michael Dawson, *Black Visions: The Roots of Contemporary African-American Political Ideologies* (Chicago: University of Chicago Press, 2001), 92. Revolutionary nationalists (e.g., Black Panthers) spoke about nations in terms of Marxist socialism, whereas cultural nationalists (e.g., US) spoke about nations in terms of ways of life.
39. Singh, *Black Is a Country*, 188.

osition that "it is better to suffer than do wrong" with the insight that "if I do wrong I am condemned to live together with a wrong doer in an unbearable intimacy."[40] So the Socratic example indicates, if only by implication, that "even if we are by ourselves, when we articulate or actualize this being-alone we find that we are in company, in the company of ourselves."[41] Roughly put, Arendt's Socrates grounds ethical "rules" on the sense of the self as an ethical association.

According to Arendt, the moral self appears in the emergency situation as the refusal to do wrong (e.g., "I cannot participate in this genocide"), while moral judgment appears in the everyday situation as an associational choice. Moreover, another's choice of their company informs our choice of that other's company. Hence "in the unlikely case that someone should come and tell us that he would prefer Bluebeard for company . . . the only thing we could do is to make sure he never comes near us."[42] The ordinary "I will not associate" falls short of the extraordinary "I cannot do wrong," although it extends the analogy of self and political association Arendt establishes elsewhere: "if you are at odds with yourself it is as though you were forced to live and have daily intercourse with your own enemy."[43] Almost adopting an antagonistic standpoint, Arendt implies that judgment contains a moment of imagining others the self would only live with under compulsion. Unlike the moral moment strictly speaking, which takes the self as its starting-and-ending points, this moment of dissociation gestures toward the world, where selves choose others they would be-with.

Antagonism for Arendt is implicit in the self being-without another individual, but for X antagonism is explicit in a people being-against another collectivity. X elevated an everyday choice of company into a friend/enemy decision—for 1964, the year of "The Ballot or the Bullet," was surely witness to an emergency situation.[44] X, however, held no sovereign power. As an associate of a called for community, he could only offer up his judgment regarding that community's disassociates. "Right now, in this country" are "22 million African-Americans—that's what we are—Africans who are in

---

40. Hannah Arendt, "Some Questions of Moral Philosophy," in *Responsibility and Judgment*, 90. That is, in the same way that friends speak with one another in political life, the individual speaks with herself in ethical life.
41. Ibid., 96.
42. Ibid., 145–46.
43. Ibid., 91.
44. That year urban riots/racial uprisings exploded across Harlem, Chicago, Philadelphia, and Rochester. Carmichael and Hamilton, *Black Power*, 155.

America," X insisted. "You'd get farther calling yourself an African instead of Negro.... Change your name to Hoogagagooba. That'll show how silly the white man is." The name "Hoogagagooba" is akin to the "African" clothing that veils visible "Negro" appearance in this story:

> A friend of mine who's very dark put a turban on his head and went into a restaurant in Atlanta before they called themselves desegregated. He went into a white restaurant, he sat down, they served him, and he said, "What would happen if a Negro came in here?" And there he's sitting, black as night, but because he had his head wrapped up the waitress looked back at him and says, "Why, there wouldn't no nigger dare come in here."

Ironically, X's friend affirms the connection of blacks across national borders by exploiting the white waitress's distinction between nationals and foreigners. The anecdote shows that the true distinction is between the gullible enemy and the cunning friend. Its content of segregated dining has an affinity with its formal appeal to the taste for clever subversion and the distaste for idiotic segregation. Its setting mocks the civil rights movement desire for integration into other-controlled institutions that "[call] themselves desegregated."[45]

Integration is hypocritical for requiring blacks to masquerade as what they are not—American nationals rather than diasporic Africans. X mocks "bourgeois Negroes out ... ordering quails under glass and stewed snails—why, Negroes don't even *like* snails! What they're doing is proving they're integrated."[46] Their (purported) distaste for snails is overpowered by their taste for integration; their inner sense is sacrificed to the altar of outward appearances. The "bourgeois Negro," on X's account, is the social climber for which Arendt mistook the parents of the Little Rock Nine in Chapter 2. This parvenu knows not what he does, but the pariah passing for "African" knows exactly what he is doing. Unlike Arendt's "conscious pariah," who openly and rebelliously enters into the political realm,[47] the passing pariah masquerades in the

---

45. Restaurants played a special part in X's polemics against civil rights movement sit-ins: blacks are not Americans because "sitting at the table doesn't make you a diner, unless you eat some of what's on that plate." X, "The Ballot or the Bullet," 26.
46. X and Haley, *The Autobiography of Malcolm X*, 279, italics original.
47. Hannah Arendt, "The Jew as Pariah: A Hidden Tradition," in *The Jewish Writings*, ed. Jerome Kohn and Ronald Feldman (New York: Schocken, 2007), 284.

social realm and subverts its exclusionary terms.[48] In the restaurant anecdote, the self hides in order to disclose the other: the black customer passes for what he is not ("Hoogagagooba") so that the white waitress can reveal who she is ("Bluebeard"). X counsels that only separation from the white segregationist could, in Arendt's wording, "make sure [she] never comes near us."

Arendt is critical of the hunt for hypocrisy in the public realm, where she sees appearance and reality as one and the same.[49] By contrast, X embraces the split of social appearance versus social reality, which his charges of hypocrisy take for granted. In Arendt's moral thinking, one self becomes two in a harmonious dialogue, whereas in X's moral associationalism, one nation is actually two locked in discordant struggle. Arendt holds that "if you are at odds with yourself it is as though you were forced to live and have daily intercourse with your own enemy," whereas X would hold that "if you are forced to live and have daily intercourse with your own enemy it is as though you were at odds with yourself." The thinking self for Arendt must remain on ethical terms with itself or suffer the antagonistic consequences. The racial nation for X must articulate the friend/enemy antagonism or suffer the ethical consequences. The racial enemy for X, like the immoral self for Arendt, is judged poor company indeed.

Emergency politics for both X and Arendt calls for an individual to exercise moral judgment. Arendt claims that the self who stops to think about right and wrong can be counted on in an emergency; this self, at a minimum, will not enact a radical evil. X would claim that the self who refuses to choose between wrong and right cannot be relied on in an emergency. For X is the arch-enemy to all those who "do not propose to take sides," which is what everyone who distinguishes right from wrong does.[50] During the Korean War, X contended to a draft board that "when the white man asked me to go off somewhere and fight and maybe die to preserve the way the white man treated the black man in America, then my conscience made me object."[51] X's refusal to associate with an American "way of life" is a gesture of friendship with other "victims of Americanism."

---

48. On this idea of masquerading, see Norma Claire Moruzzi, *Speaking through the Mask: Hannah Arendt and the Politics of Social Identity* (Ithaca, NY: Cornell University Press, 2000), 46.

49. Arendt, *On Revolution*, 96–98.

50. Carl Schmitt, *Political Romanticism*, trans. Guy Oakes (Cambridge, MA: MIT Press, 1986), 122.

51. X and Haley, *The Autobiography of Malcolm X*, 205; see also X, "The Ballot or the Bullet," 25.

Anticipated by the Civil Rights Congress's appeal to the United Nations,[52] X's demand for human rights is a site for potential alliances: "Any time any one violates your human rights, you can take them to the world court . . . where our African brothers," "our Asian brothers," and "our Latin-American brothers can throw their weight on our side."[53] X hopes that Africans, Asians, and Latin Americans can be persuaded to side with blacks in the United States, but he cannot be certain that they will do so. While the NOI X determinatively judges a binary opposition between the dark world and the white world, the post-NOI X reflectively judges a variety of localized struggles according to their globalized complexities.[54] A black oppositional space within the U.S. nation-state, the post-NOI X thinks, is exactly the place to start forging transnational solidarities. This goal is akin to the pantribal aspirations of the Alcatraz occupiers, to whom we now turn.

Section II: The Being-With-and-Against of Alcatraz Occupiers

Red power intensified the militant and pantribal tendencies of an American Indian civil rights movement tactically oriented to the enforcement of federal-Indian treaty rights.[55] An inaugural event of the red power movement, the 1969 to 1971 occupation of Alcatraz Island, arose from the localized struggles of Indians working and studying in the San Francisco Bay. I argue that Alcatraz occupiers constituted a pan-Indian common sense through the forging and sharing of aesthetic judgments, that is, judgments about the meaning and feeling of the sensible world. This idiom of counter-public constitution is approached along two distinct avenues: a "cultural" route exemplified by Adam Nordwall and an activist route exemplified by LaNada Boyer. These paths converged in the Alcatraz Proclamation, which made demands in the name of a "we" that claimed to represent the "everyone" of indigenous America.

---

52. Civil Rights Congress, *We Charge Genocide: The Historic Petition to the United Nations for Relief from a Crime of the United States Government against the Negro People* (New York: Civil Rights Congress, 1951).

53. X, "The Ballot or the Bullet," 35.

54. Cf. Ernesto Laclau and Chantal Mouffe, *Hegemony and Socialist Strategy: Towards a Radical Democratic Politics*, rev. ed. (London: Verso, 2001), 130.

55. Troy Johnson et al., "American Indian Activism and Transformation," in *American Indian Activism: Alcatraz to the Longest Walk*, ed. Troy Johnson, Joane Nagel, and Duane Champagne (Urbana: University of Illinois Press, 1997), 12. The "fish-ins" staged in the 1960s Pacific Northwest were a good example of such tactics.

Red power addressed the state more directly than contemporaneous black and Asian movements, largely for the reason that indigenous polities have a *sui generis* U.S. constitutional status. During the 1950s or the "termination era" of Indian administration, the federal government sought "for once and for all, to solve 'the Indian Question.'"[56] It disbanded more than 100 tribes in the face of overwhelming native opposition, and it transferred authority once exercised by federal and indigenous governments over some one million acres of land to state and local governments.[57] The resultant postwar relocation dispersed hundreds of thousands of Indians to urban centers like Cleveland, Dallas, Phoenix, Los Angeles, and San Francisco. Termination aimed for the "forced inclusion" of indigenous populations within U.S. territory into a uniform citizen-subjectivity.[58]

Termination policies, contrary to their designer's intent, led to the emergence of pan-Indian counter-publics, into which Adam Nordwall's biography will be our first point of entry. In the 1950s, Nordwall moved to the San Francisco Bay, where he ran a local termite extermination company and lived with his wife and children by the 1960s. He recalls that Bay Area Indians began to associate "partially out of loneliness and confusion in their new urban surroundings and partially out of an urge to share a cultural identity." Picnics in the park evolved into a "powwow circuit" that "made their own subtle political statement."[59] Pan-Indian cultures, often inspired by Plains Indian aesthetics, were at some remove from state-oriented activisms in the mid-twentieth century.[60] Yet their "subtle" politics visibly and audibly addressed the state, as the very act of association contested the latest intensification of the Indian assimilation project.

Adam Nordwall met fellow Chippewa (or Ojibwa or Ojibwe) Cy Williams while performing in a powwow at San Jose's Frontier Village, an amusement park whose name is redolent of westward expansion. Nordwall remembers that "I was doing my best in what I imagined then to be a good traditional

---

56. Nagel, *American Indian Ethnic Renewal*, 118.

57. Troy Johnson, *The Occupation of Alcatraz Island: Indian Self-Determination and the Rise of Indian Activism* (Urbana: University of Illinois Press, 1996), 7.

58. The General Indian Citizenship Act of 1924, which defined the U.S. citizenship of Amerindians, should also be mentioned in this context. Wilkins and Kiiwetinepinesiik Stark, *American Indian Politics and the American Political System*, 176.

59. Adam (Nordwall) Fortunate Eagle, "Urban Indians and the Occupation of Alcatraz Island," in Johnson et al., *American Indian Activism*, 53.

60. Stephen Cornell, *The Return of the Native: American Indian Political Resurgence* (Oxford, UK: Oxford University Press, 1988), 126; cf. Nagel, *American Indian Ethnic Renewal*, 202.

style. I realize now that my dancing was only a 'tinkle, tinkle, tinkle' Hollywood imitation in Cy's eyes." Neither rules of "traditional style" nor Williams's actual opinion settle the judgment that Nordwall's performance was a "Hollywood imitation"; rather, Nordwall *imagines* how his dancing was perceived through Williams's ears and eyes to arrive at his own judgment. The verdict is that Nordwall had poor taste before becoming friends with Williams. In much the same way, Nordwall saw the "little buckskin dolls" and "decals of animals or Indian faces" in Williams's car as "a link with home and a way for Cy to express what he felt like shouting." These "touristy trinkets" are invested with Nordwall's imaginings of what Williams feels about homelessness and home.[61]

Much like the black customer repurposes the turban in X's anecdote of the segregated restaurant,[62] the Amerindian "consumer" repurposes the signifiers of the U.S. culture industry. Nordwall suggests that "so great was the hunger for powwows that we would gather even when it meant serving a white man's need for a Hollywood version of Native America." The political metonymically and analogically links to the social: on the one hand, the powwow circuit that turns against termination is a metonym for social condition and, on the other, Nordwall analogously judges relocation problems and cultural practices in relation to Williams's affective reactions. "'Ah, the hell with it,' [Cy] would say in frequent frustration," Nordwall recounts. "[We] spoke often about the problems faced by relocated Indians, and gradually Cy began to pass on to me some of his great knowledge of traditional dancing."[63] In relating to Williams, Nordwall appeals to a common sense of the sensible—a common sense about how the world looks, sounds, and feels forged through the sharing of aesthetic judgments.

Hannah Arendt intimately relates aesthetic and moral judgment alike to the *sensus communis* (common sense). Judgment is that faculty that reflects on the immediate pleasure/pain experienced after the subject's encounter with a worldly percept. Common sense, in turn, is "what judgment appeals to in everyone, and it is this possible appeal that gives judgments their spe-

---

61. Nordwall, "Urban Indians and the Occupation of Alcatraz Island," 53. Williams himself called these items "Indi-onish." Adam Fortunate Eagle with Tim Findley, *Heart of the Rock: The Indian Invasion of Alcatraz* (Norman: University of Oklahoma Press, 2002), 25–26.

62. On this process of working both on and against a dominant cultural text, see José Esteban Muñoz, *Disidentifications: Queers of Color and the Performance of Politics* (Minneapolis: University of Minnesota Press, 1999), 31.

63. Nordwall, "Urban Indians and the Occupation of Alcatraz Island," 53–54.

cial validity.... [O]ne can only 'woo' or 'court' the agreement of everyone else."[64] For Arendt, the question "to which 'everyone' does judgment appeal?" is the question of "for which public is the judgment valid?" Judgment, she claims, "is valid 'for every single judging person,' but the emphasis is on 'judging'; it is not valid for those who do not judge or for those who are not members of the public realm."[65] To be clear, as McClure argues, a community bounded within an already-existing horizon of interpretation is no precondition of Arendtian judgment.[66] If common sense only strictly exists *in* the exercise of judgment, communities of common sense are constituted through the rendering, circulation, and reception of judgments.[67]

Judgments on Nordwall's "Hollywood imitation" of Indian dancing and William's "touristy trinkets" work to constitute a common sense for Indian urbanites. Nordwall judges the pleasure experienced while dancing at the amusement park to be inappropriate by imagining what Williams perceived; he also judges the mixed pleasure and pain aroused by the adornments of Williams's car to be appropriate through the same operation. By putting himself in Williams's place, yet reflectively judging for himself, Nordwall discloses his choice of Williams's company. As with Malcolm X, the choice of others whose standpoints Nordwall visits (fellow urban Indians) is counterpoised to the choice of "others" whose standpoints Nordwall does not visit (amusement-park visitors). Similar choices, I would venture, went into the formation of the United Bay Area Council of American Indian Affairs, which Nordwall and Williams helped found in 1961.[68] This pantribal council joined Bay Area Indian student radicals in undertaking the Alcatraz occupation.

Our second point of entry into the constitution of an urban Indian counter-public is more conflict-oriented from the start. A Shoshone-Bannock student at the University of California, Berkeley, LaNada Boyer came to Alcatraz Island on the route of Native American and third world campus

---

64. Arendt, *Lectures on Kant's Political Philosophy*, 72.

65. Arendt, *Between Past and Future*, 221.

66. McClure, "The Odor of Judgment," 76. McClure is arguing against communitarian readings of Arendt.

67. Arendt herself claims that "judging is one, if not the most, important activity in which... sharing-the-world-with-others comes to pass." Arendt, *Between Past and Future*, 221.

68. Two authors joke that "sometimes, invisibility and isolation seemed to be all [the members of the United Council] had in common." Paul Chaat Smith and Robert Allen Warrior, *Like a Hurricane: The Indian Movement from Alcatraz to Wounded Knee* (New York: New Press, 1996), 10.

activisms. Boyer learned long before her formal education that "as a result of governmental rule ... our reservation and people were suffering" and learned from her father, a tribal chairman, "about the continuing war against our people." The Indian Wars are not over for Boyer. Public hostilities, if not less obvious forms of state violence, seethe from the mid-1960s policies that relocated Boyer to the Bay: "the federal government's plan to 'drop us off' in the cities was another insidious method of depriving us of our reservation lands and membership in our tribes."[69] Boyer narrates a struggle hidden beneath the juridical order in the style reminiscent of that early-modern English discourse Michel Foucault calls the "war of the races."[70] Just as Puritans denied that the seventeenth-century English constitution could put an end to the warfare between conquered Saxons and conquering Normans, Boyer denies that twentieth-century U.S.-Indian relations could be anything other than a state of war.

How does Boyer judge that her palpable "anger and resentment" is an appropriate response to her "settler-colonial present"?[71] Boyer does not appeal to the U.S. racial state, which she would not trust to adjudicate indigenous claims.[72] The state undermines reservation Indian communities, although it inadvertently builds up urban Indian communities: "On the reservations, it was easy to divide Indians against Indians; but in a major city, we are so glad to see other Indians, we don't care what tribe they are."[73] A common response to the perception of a familiar-looking face, gladness binds and brings together urbanites across tribes. At the same time, the bounds of familiarity are stretched by the sensible signs of Indianness diversified under conditions of "civilization": "We did not all look or behave like our ancestors. . . . We were finally 'civilized Indians,' from liars and thieves

---

69. LaNada Boyer, "Reflections of Alcatraz," in Johnson et al., *American Indian Activism*, 88; see also LaNada Boyer, "Growing Up in *E'da How*—One Idaho Girlhood," in *The Schooling of Native America*, ed. Thomas Thompson (Washington, DC: American Association of Colleges for Teacher Education, 1978), 32.

70. Michel Foucault, *"Society Must Be Defended": Lectures at the Collège de France, 1975–76*, trans. David Macey (New York: Picador, 2003), 60. On Foucault's unacknowledged debt to black radical thought, see Brady Heiner, "Foucault and the Black Panthers," *City* 11, no. 3 (2007): 313–56.

71. Coulthard, *Red Skins, White Masks*, 121, 126.

72. For an account of how the state capitalizes on injury, see Wendy Brown, *States of Injury: Power and Freedom in Late Modernity* (Princeton, NJ: Princeton University Press, 1995), chap. 3.

73. Boyer, "Reflections of Alcatraz," 88; see also Boyer, "Growing Up in *E'da How*," 35, 41. "Supra-tribal consciousness" is prevalent in urban Indian interactions with urban whites; between urban Indians, tribal identification is primary. Cornell, *The Return of the Native*, 145.

to genuine Indian chiefs."[74] Boyer's judgments of racial antagonism and her affective responses to it, then, appeal to emergent community sensibilities for their validity.

Boyer and Nordwall alike report that urban Indians discovered a taste for each other's company, which made association pleasurable and antagonism articulate. Arendt observes that "we all know very well how quickly people recognize each other, and how unequivocally they can feel that they belong to each other, when they discover a kinship in questions of what pleases or displeases." Aesthetic "kinship" is based on the similitude of the immediate pleasure/pain that accompanies the apprehension of any sensible phenomenon, on an immediate reaction as distinguished from a reflective judgment. This mode of being-with-others, however, does not by itself qualify as specifically public. It takes the communication and circulation of the results of reflective judgment to disclose "not only how the world is to look, but also who belongs together in it" in a stricter political sense.[75]

For Boyer and Nordwall, judging-with-others as to "how the world is to look" is a mode of being-with-others in the world. However, for Boyer and not for Nordwall, judging-with-others as to how the world is *not* to look is a mode of being-against-others. For instance, Boyer arrives at Alcatraz with fellow occupiers to find that "we were on the island and it was beautiful," but this same island is ugly for Amerindians, "an infamous prison that carries . . . the bondage and captivity of our people."[76] The pleasure of insurrection comes adorned with the pain of unfreedom as the Alcatraz occupiers articulate friend/enemy antagonism in terms of the beautiful/ugly criterion. Now the latent disassociation of being "so glad to see other Indians" comes to the fore against the backdrop of the reservation where the government could manifestly "divide Indians against Indians." For Boyer, more than for Nordwall, urban Indians share an antagonism toward the U.S. racial state more than any cultural practices. Boyer's being-with is also her being-against.[77] This moment in Boyer's thought and its analogues in Malcolm X's stretch the Arendtian model of judgment to accommodate Schmittian friend/enemy antagonism.

Antagonism is clearly articulated at the start of the 1969 to 1971 occupation of Alcatraz Island, where Boyer argues the Indian assimilation project

---

74. Boyer, "Reflections of Alcatraz," 92; cf. Fortunate Eagle with Findley, *Heart of the Rock*, 44.
75. Arendt, *Between Past and Future*, 223.
76. Boyer, "Reflections of Alcatraz," 91, 100.
77. This being-with included Asians, Latino/as, and blacks in a 1968 "Third World Liberation Front" at UC Berkeley. Boyer, "Growing Up in E'da How," 36, 38.

"backfired."⁷⁸ In July 1969, San Francisco proposed to purchase this federal property for the purpose of building a theme park based on the United States space program. Bay Area Indians proposed a more terrestrial program, recalling that in 1964 Sioux activists had occupied Alcatraz on the grounds of the 1868 Sioux Treaty of Fort Laramie. Before a brief occupation of the island on November 9, 1969, Richard Oakes—a charismatic Mohawk activist from San Francisco State—read aloud the Alcatraz Proclamation before the assembled press. (The Alcatraz occupiers would draw even more national attention with the November 20, 1969 landing and continuous occupation.)

The witty proclamation stands out against the weighty declarations of its day. A sense of Indian humor, as Vine Deloria Jr. would put it, infuses the telluric identification of the proclaimers:⁷⁹ "We, the native Americans, reclaim this land known as Alcatraz Island in the name of all American Indians by right of discovery."⁸⁰ It is true, on strictly legal grounds, that U.S. constitutional law on Indian land is not directly based on the doctrine of discovery (with the exception of *Johnson v. McIntosh*) and that the Sioux Treaty of Fort Laramie could provide the occupants with little legal justification (the occupying force was pan-Indian, for starters). Nonetheless, the Alcatraz Proclamation deploys the "right of discovery" and federal-Indian treaties in a nonjuridical, yet entirely serious way.

These terms mark the reclamation of federal property as Indian territory in the context of what Boyer calls the "continuing war against [indigenous] people." They expose how removal treaties, termination policies, and the like achieved an ostensibly peaceful, actually aggressive deterritorialization of indigenous peoples. The federal government, then, is invited to accept the terms of reterritorialization unilaterally set in "the following treaty":

> We will purchase Alcatraz for 24 dollars in glass beads and red cloth, a precedent set by the white man's purchase of a similar island [Manhattan] about 300 years ago. . . . We will give the inhabitants of this land a portion of their own, to be held in trust by the American Indian Government—for as long as the sun shall rise and the rivers go down to the sea—to be administered by the Bureau of Caucasian

---

78. Boyer, "Reflections of Alcatraz," 92.
79. Vine Deloria Jr., *Custer Died for Your Sins: An Indian Manifesto*, rev. ed. (New York: Macmillan, 1988), 167.
80. Alcatraz Proclamation reproduced in Nordwall, "Urban Indians and the Occupation of Alcatraz," 61–64.

Affairs (BCA). We will further guide the inhabitants in the proper way of living. We will offer them our religion, our education, our life-ways, in order to help them achieve our level of civilization.

Stylized parodies of federal treaty provisions establish a spatial order (where the white man shall roam), a racial order (what cultural patterns whites shall maintain), and a governing order (the "BCA" of "the American Indian Government"). They ask white Americans to consider how the liberal logic of land appropriation would look if applied to themselves. The land appropriators preserve the colonial discourse of Indian children and white guardians discussed in Chapter 3—only this time around, "the last shall be first."[81]

The demand for land appropriation is constitutive of the split between the Alcatraz occupiers ("us") and the federal government ("them").[82] Each party to this conflict represents more than itself. "Indians of All Tribes" discursively represented themselves as the political representatives of "all American Indians" in their reclamation of Alcatraz from "the Great White Father and all His People." All these names designate various components of the territorial claim: "Indians of All Tribes" are its claimants, "all American Indians" are its "constituency," and "the Great White Father and all His People" are its addressees. For this reason, each "all" can be no empirical "every." Indianness for the red power activist, like blackness for the black nationalist, is an invitation into a sought-after community sense.

No invitation would qualify as such if it could not be refused. In fact, the Ohlone people of Northern California made a tribally specific counterclaim to the island, which the Alcatraz occupiers problematically failed to draw into a more general set of claims.[83] A more charitable interpretation of "Indians of All Tribes," though, would affirm the affinities between aesthetic and political representation (*Darstellung* and *Vertretung*). Take their figuration of the reservation system that some of the occupiers—including Nordwall, Boyer, and Oakes—had literally left: "We feel that this so-called Alcatraz Island is more than suitable as an Indian Reservation," seeing how it has no fresh water, adequate sanitation, resource rights, jobs, industry, health care, educational facilities, or good land. Alcatraz is "isolated from

---

81. Fanon, *The Wretched of the Earth*, 2. The "table-turn" is a common rhetorical move in Amerindian activism, e.g., "Civilizing the White Man," *American Indian* 1, no. 4 (1970): 2.
82. Cf. Adam Dahl, "Nullifying Settler Democracy: William Apess and the Paradox of Settler Sovereignty," *Polity* 48, no. 2 (2016): 297.
83. Johnson, *The Occupation of Alcatraz Island*, 161, 147.

modern facilities" and its "population has always been held as prisoners and kept dependent."[84]

The judgment that "the prison is like the reservation" is representative in the sense of what Arendt calls "representational thinking." A hypothetical case is instructive here. "Suppose I look at a specific slum dwelling," Arendt says. "I perceive in this particular building the general notion which it does not exhibit directly, the notion of poverty and misery." Arendt, judging as herself, would not necessarily have the same perception as that of an inhabitant of the building. However, Arendt must interpret what the building standing before her stands-for from the inhabitant's perspective, or even imagine "how [she] would feel if [she] had to live there," in order to assume that her judgment could be valid for others.[85] The judgment that the reservation is a prison likewise conjoins a representation of the reservation inhabitant by the urban occupier with a representation of the absent reservation by the present Alcatraz. One self thinks in the place of an other, just as one place stands for another.

Representational thinking is not, as the political scientific literature would suggest, "descriptive" or "substantive."[86] Representation that operates through the faculties of imagination and perception is what Hannah Pitkin would term "symbolic" insofar as its validity turns on the reception and assent of its audience.[87] That said, the opinion of an Alcatraz occupier retains a special kind of validity even if it disagrees with the opinion of a reservation inhabitant[88]—the validity of a reflective judgment that posits the very Amerindian common sense that it calls into existence. Seeing the ugliness of indigenous oppression in the barb-wired fences and guard towers of Alcatraz Island is a judgment about the meaning of the sensible. It is the judgment that, in Boyer's words, Alcatraz carries "the bondage and captivity of [her] people." It is an aesthetic claim that can be more or less persuasive to "everyone," not an authoritative claim from which there can be no appeal.

---

84. Prior to its transformation into a federal penitentiary in 1934, Alcatraz had served as a prison for the United States Army. Nordwall attributes the "political prisoner" metaphor to Richard Oakes and LaNada Boyer. Fortunate Eagle with Findley, *The Heart of the Rock*, 75.

85. Arendt, "Some Questions of Moral Philosophy," 140.

86. See, e.g., Suzanne Dovi, "Preferable Descriptive Representatives: Will Just Any Woman, Black, or Latino Do?" *American Political Science Review* 96, no. 4 (2002): 745–54. In descriptive representation, the representative resembles the represented; in substantive representation, the representative forwards the interests of the represented.

87. Hannah Pitkin, *The Concept of Representation* (Berkeley: University of California, 1967), 92–111.

88. Some reservation Indians feel that their urban counterparts are out of touch with reservation problems, but nonetheless have disproportionate access to the federal government. Nagel, *American Indian Ethnic Renewal*, 235.

Everyone is meant to be "all Indian Americans," but it could mean the "the Great White Father and all His People" too. The opening salvo of the Alcatraz Proclamation already places agonistic brackets around the antagonistic terms of land appropriation. Land is the material condition of proposed "Indian institutions," including a Center for Native American Studies, an American Indian Spiritual Center, an Indian Center of Ecology, a Great Indian Training School, and an American Indian Museum. Conflicts of varying intensities would be channeled into these counter-hegemonic institutions; even the pacific-sounding Indian Center of Ecology—with its mission to "train and support our young people in scientific research"—attacks the destructiveness of "the white man's way." Had the state acceded to these institutional demands, it would have legitimized the Alcatraz occupiers' counter-public.[89] Official legitimation could have further sublimated the "war of the races," to use Foucault's phrase, initially tamed by the transformation of self-authorized appropriations into state-oriented demands.

Negotiations could have brought Alcatraz occupiers and federal officials into a postcolonial common sense about Indian affairs. We must recognize, however, that the bracketing of antagonism between a counter-public and the official public preserves an undercurrent of public hostility, even when the desires and identities of each side change.[90] This bracketing is a promise that can be broken as easily as any federal-Indian treaty. Taking advantage of waning support and stalemated negotiations, government security forces removed the remaining fifteen occupiers on June 13, 1971. In 1977, the anti-eviction campaign at the International Hotel would come to a similar denouement just across the San Francisco Bay. The violent enforcement of property rights would again frustrate popular demands for a place in the world.

Section III: The Popular Front of the International Hotel Campaign

As ethnographic curios of the Cold War "model minority" discourse,[21] Asian Americans struggled to establish counter-public spaces and sensibilities. This

---

89. A polity sprung up around the occupiers living on the island, complete with an elected council, a security force, a public relations office, a radio program, a newsletter, an academy, an arts and craft school, health care services, a communal kitchen, and a nursery. Johnson, *The Occupation of Alcatraz Island*, chap. 5.

90. Public hostility often manifests itself as a lack of trust. See "National 'Indian' Park Planned for Alcatraz, Indians Angry," *American Indian* 1, no. 5 (1970): 1–2.

91. Robert Lee, *Orientals: Asian Americans in Popular Culture* (Philadelphia: Temple University Press, 1999), chap. 5.

is perhaps why the Asian American movement staked much on its equivalence with other racial empowerment movements. This section first examines how Fred Ho of the I Wor Kuen (IWK) tied Asian to black liberation within the globalized idiom of the "U.S. Third World Left."[92] It then turns to the International Hotel anti-eviction struggle in which the IWK supported the Katipunan ng mga Demokratikong Pilipino (KDP; Filipino for "Union of Democratic Filipinos") and the International Hotel Tenants Association (IHTA). Following KDP member Estella Habal, I argue that activists crafted a localized set of Filipino and Chinese equivalences out of the IHTA demand for housing. I conclude that an indeterminate identification of Asian America both enabled and put strains on the I-Hotel panethnic front.

Let us begin with Fred Ho of the I Wor Kuen (Cantonese for "righteous and harmonious fists"), a Maoist organization founded in 1969 in New York City's Chinatown. Ho arrived at radical politics when, as a Chinese American teenager, he became disillusioned with Anglo-conformist assimilation. Just as the suburbanite Adam Nordwall turned into a red power activist, the assimilationist Ho turned into a "revolutionary yellow nationalist": "We called ourselves Third World people in the US as we identified with the national liberation struggles waged in Africa, Asia, so-called Latin America and the Caribbean and the Pacific Islands."[93] In 1975, Ho joined the Nation of Islam as "Fred 3X," one of the few Asians to associate with the group. As with Malcolm X's narrative, Ho's story of religious conversion is not a story of ethnic rediscovery.[94] Ho differed from Malcolm X, though, in that Ho knew his surname and understood that a renunciation of pork required "[giving] up *cha siu bao* [pork buns]."[95]

Ho soon moved closer to the Marxist scene of East Coast Chinatown politics. In 1977, Ho joined the IWK after coming around to its position on how to liberate oppressed nations and nationalities. Black political thought

---

92. The phrase is from Young, who expresses reservations about the term: "The metaphor potentially works in favor of helping First World minorities . . . , but the political danger exists that it might perform significant work on, rather than for, Third World majorities." Cynthia Young, *Soul Power: Culture, Radicalism, and the Making of the U.S. Third World Left* (Durham, NC: Duke University Press, 2006), 14.
93. Fred Ho, "Fists for Revolution: The Revolutionary History of I Wor Kuen/League of Revolutionary Struggle," in *Legacy to Liberation: Politics and Culture of Revolutionary Asian Pacific America*, ed. Fred Ho, Carolyn Antonio, Diane Fujino, and Steve Yip (Edinburgh, UK: AK, 2000), 3.
94. Fred Ho, *Wicked Theory, Naked Practice: A Fred Ho Reader*, ed. Diane Fujino (Minneapolis: University of Minnesota Press, 2009), 47.
95. Ho, "Fists for Revolution," 4–5.

was central to debates on "the national question," even when the positions of black political thinkers came into question. Ho criticized a generation of black Marxists who "gave up building Black-in-form organizations, [abandoning] cultural work and the arts to the narrow cultural nationalists."[96] The IWK, taking a different tack, organized national in-form, socialist-in-content campaigns in Asian American communities and participated in Asian American cultural production. Cultural work for Ho refers less to the recovery of national traditions than to the imaginary register of nationalist struggles. Thus Ho glosses the African Marxist Amilcar Cabral's maxim "national liberation begins as an act of culture" with his statement that "oppressed people don't begin to fight their oppression until they resist the identity and historical image their oppressor makes of them."[97]

Ho invites his audience to understand his political autobiography in light of 1960s and 1970s U.S. third world left debates. He writes as if his associational choices were entailments of concepts (e.g., the national question), but an Arendtian reading would cognitively decenter Ho's narrative. My sense is that Ho judged associates through appeals to a plurality of common senses—Asian American socialist, black nationalist, and third worldist—that often circulated among similar sets of concrete individuals. It should be mentioned that Black Panthers introduced some Bay Area Chinatown youth to Mao's "Little Red Book" and that, according to Ho, "much of the Black Nationalist leadership looked at Asians as Third World brothers and sisters."[98] Asian Americans, on their part, sometimes performed blackness to reimagine their own identities, build multiracial solidarity, and resist cultural assimilation.[99] Ho himself, long after his NOI days, enjoyed a distinguished career as a composer and performer of "Afro-Asian New American Multicultural Music."[100]

I locate Asian America, black nationalism, and the third world as overlapping sites of appeal for 1960s and 1970s U.S. activists of color. For the most part, I have circumvented the debate on how much black power influ-

---

96. Ibid.; see also Ho, *Wicked Theory, Naked Practice*, 307–12.

97. Ho, "Fists for Revolution," 9; cf. Fanon, *Wretched of the Earth*, chap. 5.

98. Ho, *Wicked Theory, Naked Practice*, 291. A contrary view is Liz Del Sol, "Finding Our Common Interests: Personal Reflections about the Asian Movement," in *Asian Americans: The Movement and the Moment*, ed. Steve Louie and Glenn Omatsu (Los Angeles: UCLA Asian American Studies Center, 2000), 143.

99. Daryl Maeda, *Chains of Babylon: The Rise of Asian America* (Minneapolis: University of Minnesota Press, 2009), 96; cf. Gary Okihiro, *Margins and Mainstreams: Asians in American History and Culture* (Seattle: University of Washington Press, 1994), 34.

100. Ho, *Wicked Theory, Naked Practice*, 52.

enced Asian American and other contemporaneous movements. Laura Pulido is correct to stress "the individuality of each movement" while not "denying that non-Black people of color were greatly inspired by, and in some cases emulated, Black Power."[101] The very terms of this debate, however, suggest that there was an asymmetrical relation between blackness and other racial identifications. Blackness cohered the third world formation in a way that Asianness could not for reasons irreducible to, say, the authority of black activists among U.S. leftists.

The third world is an instance of Laclau and Mouffe's "chain of equivalence," a discursive formation that links a diversity of movement demands in all their multiplicity.[102] A particular link in the chain operates as the general equivalent for all other links or, as Laclau puts it, "its own particularity comes to signify something quite different from itself: the total chain of equivalential demands."[103] This function is fulfilled by a signifier with the ability to "float" across a variety of discursive ensembles; once pulled into a concrete chain of signification, it reconstellates the other signifiers around its common denomination (e.g., "democracy" for the Occupy Movement). The demands of the equivalential chain do not share an attribute that an abstract concept might name;[104] what these demands share is a constitutive lack named by an "empty signifier" (e.g., the lack of democracy on Wall Street).

Black liberation functions as the empty signifier or, to play on Marx, the universal racial equivalent for Ho's third worldism. Ho put himself in distinguished Marxist company in seeing more than black particularity in black power. "The struggle of black people in the United States," Mao argued, "is bound to merge with the American workers' movement, and this will eventually end the criminal rule of the US monopoly class."[105] Despite the fact that it was not addressing Asian Americans, Mao's statement made an impact on the IWK, the Wei Min She (WMS; Mandarin for "organization of the people"), and similar organizations.[106] The Asian American left's recep-

---

101. Laura Pulido, *Black, Brown, Yellow, and Left: Radical Activism in Los Angeles* (Berkeley: University of California Press, 2006), 60. On the distinctiveness of black and Amerindian struggles, see Deloria, *Custard Died for Your Sins*, chap. 8.

102. Laclau and Mouffe, *Hegemony and Socialist Strategy*, 156.

103. Ernesto Laclau, *On Populist Reason* (London: Verso, 2005), 96; see also Laclau and Mouffe, *Hegemony and Socialist Strategy*, 112.

104. Laclau, *On Populist Reason*, 97.

105. Mao Zedong, "A New Storm Against Imperialism," *Peking Review,* April 19, 1968: 5–6.

106. See Ho, *Wicked Theory, Naked Practice*, 286–87; see also Steve Yip, "Serve the People—Yesterday and Today: The Legacy of the Wei Min She," in Ho et al., *Legacy to Liberation*, 19.

tion of Mao, to be clear, does not signal their overidentification with or appropriation of blackness. It indicates that the Asian American movement had been inserted into a third world chain of equivalence held together by the demand for black liberation. In speaking of black Americans, Mao was speaking of Asian Americans too.

The U.S. third world left established reciprocal equalities ("we have distinctive, yet related struggles") between Asians, blacks, Latino/as, and Amerindians. Asian American activists like Ho used black liberation to link racial struggles in the United States with each other and with what they considered anti-imperialist struggles abroad (e.g., the Vietnamese Civil War). A comparatively localized discourse will accentuate the contingency of the name, yet affirm the necessity, of the empty signifier for Asian American alliances. I argue that the Bay Area struggle to keep the I-Hotel open turned the demand for low-income housing into the empty signifier of a distinctively Asian American chain of equivalence.

Estella Habal, a Filipina American activist and scholar, worked with the KDP on the I-Hotel campaign from 1975 to 1977. The KDP from its inception practiced a transnational politics that was simultaneously Philippine, Filipina/o American, and third worldist,[107] and its program divided into United States (prosocialist, antiracist) and Philippine (prodemocracy, anti-Marcos) orientations.[108] Reminiscent of Fred Ho's membership in the NOI, Habal's activism began with a nationality not "hers." Ethnic similarities attracted Habal to the United Mexican American Students organization at Long Beach State, as Filipino/as and Mexicans share a "similar Spanish colonial history," "the same Catholic background," and "a similar working class, immigrant culture."[109] Feeling "a need to center [her] political growth and development closer to Filipinos,"[110] Habal joined the Kalayaan (Filipino for "freedom") newspaper collective, one of the groups that would found the KDP at Santa Cruz, California in 1973.

Identities for Habal are positively conceived as ethnicities—albeit Mexican and Philippine ones inflected by Spanish colonialism—and negatively

---

107. Augusto Espiritu, "Journeys of Discovery and Difference: Transnational Politics and the Union of Democratic Filipinos," in Collet and Lien, *The Transnational Politics of Asian Americans*, 44.

108. Estella Habal, *San Francisco's International Hotel: Mobilizing the Filipino American Community in the Anti-Eviction Movement* (Philadelphia: Temple University Press, 2007), 71–72.

109. Estella Habal, "How I Became a Revolutionary," in Ho et al., *Legacy to Liberation*, 198–99.

110. Ibid., 201.

conceived against racial assimilation. Many American-born Filipina/os grew up speaking only English only to "find out that assimilation was meant for white immigrants, not racial minorities, even if they had no accents."[111] Abandoning the middle-class aspirations of their parents, student activists found inspiration in the 1930s labor struggles of the immigrant *manong* (Ilocano for "elder brother" or "uncle") and their contemporary struggles in Little Manilas. "We rebelled by venerating the elderly 'bachelors,'" Habal explains, "rejecting the conservatism of our parents and favoring the radicalism—and the broken English—of the manongs."[112] *Manong* carried connotations of "family" especially for those Filipino/a student activists who interacted with I-Hotel residents as fictive kin.[113]

Asian American activists took on the responsibility of preserving a Manilatown whose last infrastructural remnant was the I-Hotel at the edge of Chinatown, San Francisco. The I-Hotel was an alternative household for elderly Filipino and Chinese bachelors, working-class residents who conversed, ate, and relaxed in the communal facilities (kitchen, recreation room, etc.) or at nearby hangouts (restaurants, barbershops, etc.). Carl Rezal, a Filipino resident, felt that the I-Hotel "is just like a home. . . . The Oriental [customs] of the Filipino and the Chinese are not so much different."[114] The fictive and panethnic family's needs assuredly are, yet are more than, the needs of the biological body and of everyday intercourse. Such needs are in their social meaning necessities without which no household can survive, but in their political sense demands without which "the poor" cannot come into existence as "the people."

I-Hotel residents spoke the language of the Arendtian social in making public their concerns of bare life and everyday living. A pamphlet to a similar effect connected Asian Americans "shoved into lousy, inadequate housing" to the general "right to low-rent, decent housing," which "all people can support!"[115] This appeal to a common sense of common needs is an extension

---

111. Habal, *San Francisco's International Hotel*, 26–27. Habal points to the limits between the often-drawn analogy between white and nonwhite immigrants.

112. Ibid., 30.

113. This household had its share of intergenerational bonding as well as problematic sexual dynamics between activists and residents. See Beverly Kordziel, "To Be Part of the People: The International Hotel Collective," in Louie and Omatsu, *Asian Americans: The Movement and the Moment*, 246; see also Habal, *San Francisco's International Hotel*, 62–63.

114. Transcript of interview with Carl Rezal, Him Mark Lai Research Files (Box 69, folder 27, coll. AAS ARC 2010/1), Ethnic Studies Library, University of California, Berkeley.

115. The Committee to Fight for the International Hotel, "Tell the City and the Four Seas Decent Housing is a Right!" Him Mark Lai Research Files (Box 69, folder 27, coll. AAS ARC 2010/1), Ethnic Studies Library, University of California, Berkeley.

of political contest into the supposedly private, yet actually social realm of ownership. The counter-hegemonic discourse at the I-Hotel, unlike the Marxist discourse of Fred Ho, does not position black liberation as the empty signifier. Instead, the demand for low-income housing was the basic unit for the constitution of a popular front or a counter-hegemonic bloc.[116] The International Hotel Tenant Association's own demand was the general equivalent for the Asian American chain of equivalence between activists, residents, and groups acting-in-common.

Conflicts of housing demands versus property rights, social needs versus corporate profits were long-standing at the I-Hotel. In 1968, the owners of the hotel handed out the first eviction notice, only to have their plans for building a parking lot blocked by the efforts of the United Filipino Association. In 1977, new owners staged a state-enforced eviction over the nonviolent protest of thousands. By this time, an anti-eviction meta-coalition had formed around three relatively discrete coalitions: (1) an informal alliance of the IHTA and the KDP, (2) the Support Committee (led by the IWK), and (3) the Workers Committee (affiliated with the WMS).[117] However, the KDP-IHTA coalition disagreed with the Support Committee and especially the Workers Committee over the strategy and meaning of the campaign. In contrast to the Chinese American Maoists, who attacked their imperialist enemies, the IHTA and KDP struggled with corporate adversaries and searched for official allies.

A commonplace from Marxist anti-eviction literatures is that capitalists allied with local government are assaulting the people allied with local activists. An IWK newspaper found the "basic conflict between the interests of the people and those of big business" at the I-Hotel,[118] while the IWK-led Support Committee denounced capitalist machinations to "destroy and disperse these historic centers of resistance against national oppression."[119] Steve Yip of the WMS also put into spatial perspective this "fight to defend and extend a physical and political space" against "the real enemy" of "the power structure and

---

116. Laclau, *On Populist Reason*, 73.
117. Habal, *San Francisco's International Hotel*, 124–25. The WMS had merged with the Revolutionary Communist Party by 1975; the IWK would go on to merge with the August 29th Movement in 1978.
118. "I-Hotel Struggle Rallies Mass Support," *Getting Together*, Nov. 1–15, 1974, 3, Him Mark Lai Research Files (Box 69, folder 25, coll. AAS ARC 2010/1), Ethnic Studies Library, University of California, Berkeley.
119. International Hotel Support Committee, cited in Habal, *San Francisco's International Hotel*, 127.

their police,"[120] much like a WMS spokeswoman drew attention to the "fight to defend those progressive organizations located in the [I-Hotel] building against political repression."[121] The unfortunate reality of Maoist in-fighting aside,[122] the Support and Workers Committees agreed on the national and class-based character of the Asian American claim to the I-Hotel. Neither committee would enter a space of legitimated disagreement with their common enemies.

Acting on a different judgment, the KDP and IHTA sought potential friendships across the Marxist line of enmity. According to Habal, the IHTA and KDP disagreed with the Support Committee over the very meaning of the struggle: "We emphasized the anti-eviction movement as a struggle for housing as a human right over the racial or national components of the conflict." Habal, in this vein, criticizes the Workers Committee for posturing as the vanguard of the movement and acting without regard to IHTA wishes.[123] The KDP and IHTA—appealing to humanity, human rights, and other signs of universality—invited left-liberal officials into an alliance against corporate adversaries.[124] Their strategy presupposed that anti- and pro-eviction forces share a space of at least potential agreement. In contrast, the antistatist "revolutionary way" of the Marxists "relies on the masses of people, not the courts and politicians."[125] However, to the extent they accepted or did not challenge the leadership of the IHTA and KDP, the Support Committee and the Workers Committee participated in a precarious sublimation of antagonism. The IHTA and KDP engaged with the existing liberal democratic terrain, whereas the Support and Workers Committees withdrew from it.[126]

Neither agonistic engagements nor antagonistic withdrawals could stop city police from evicting the I-Hotel from August 3 to 4, 1977, over the civil

---

120. Yip, "Serve the People—Yesterday and Today," 21.
121. "4SEAS & CITY—Thick as Thieves," *Wei Min* 4, no. 3 (1975), 2, Him Mark Lai Research Files (Box 69, folder 27, coll. AAS ARC 2010/1), Ethnic Studies Library, University of California, Berkeley.
122. Wei, *The Asian American Movement*, 227–28.
123. Habal, *San Francisco's International Hotel*, 127.
124. The KDP-IHTA alliance sought out allies in Mayor George Moscone, who in 1976 proposed to buy the I-Hotel with federal community development funds, and Sheriff Richard Hongisto, who that same year showed passive resistance to enforcing an eviction order. Ibid., 178.
125. "I-Hotel: A Banner of Revolutionary Struggle," *Getting Together*, August 1977, 11, Him Mark Lai Research Files (Box 69, folder 26, coll. AAS ARC 2010/1), Ethnic Studies Library, University of California, Berkeley.
126. Mouffe, *Agonistics*, 65, 75.

disobedience of thousands. However, the discursive chain of equivalence held even as the bodily chain of protest around the hotel disintegrated. When the KDP, IHTA, and Support Committee told the protestors to disperse after several had been injured in skirmishes with police, the Workers Committee simply walked away rather than fighting back, despite never having agreed to nonviolent tactics in principle.[127] Only after the eviction had become a fait accompli did the Workers Committee threaten that "the people will not hesitate to take matters into their own hands" if the I-Hotel were not reopened.[128] Only after police violence had crushed popular power did movement militancy devolve into impotent posturing. In Maoist terms, nonantagonistic contradictions among the people increased once antagonistic confrontations with enemies could no longer be won.[129]

While the I-Hotel campaign failed to achieve its strategic objectives, it successfully navigated the terrain of 1970s Asian American counter-hegemony. A complex series of negotiations brought students and residents, socialists and nationalists, Chinese and Filipina/os into a popular front; theirs was an Asian American front that an assembled multitude of gays and lesbians, "people picketing in their wheel chairs," "people of all colors," musicians, and "even a protestor in . . . clown makeup" could stand with as the eviction drew near.[130] Each coalition's particular demands strained, but did not break the chain of equivalence constructed around the demand for low-income housing—one that could link diverse struggles across the United States and its borders.[131] The us/them frontier thusly drawn is the least strictly nonwhite/white of all the frontiers that I have drawn out of selected racial empowerment movements.

Disagreement over "their" and hence "our" identity at the late 1970s I-Hotel returned to the conflict at the late 1960s origins of the Asian American

---

127. Habal, *San Francisco's International Hotel*, 149.

128. Workers Committee to Fight for the I-Hotel & Victory Bldg., "Fight Demolition! Fight to Reopen International Hotel," Him Mark Lai Research Files (Box 69, folder 27, coll. AAS ARC 2010/1), Ethnic Studies Library, University of California, Berkeley.

129. Mao says that the friend/enemy contradiction is necessarily "antagonistic," whereas contradictions amongst the people are usually "nonantagonistic." Mao Tsetung, *Five Essays on Philosophy* (Peking: Foreign Languages, 1977), 80–81.

130. "Thousands Gathered to Protest Posting of Eviction Notices," *East/West*, June 15, 1977, 1, Him Mark Lai Research Files (Box 69, folder 26, coll. AAS ARC 2010/1), Ethnic Studies Library, University of California, Berkeley.

131. For example, black, white, and Latino residents went on rent-strike in Co-Op City, a retired workers housing project in the Bronx, to stop rent increases. "I-Hotel Tenants Want to Return, Housing Struggle Continues," *The New Voice* 6, no. 18 (1977): 3, Him Mark Lai Research Files (Box 69, folder 26, coll. AAS ARC 2010/1), Ethnic Studies Library, UC Berkeley.

movement. As Yen Le Espiritu shows, panethnicity originated as the critical alternative to racial lumping for Asian American student activists.[132] All activists repudiated the ethnic splitting practiced by, say, Japanese who distanced themselves from Chinese in the era of Asiatic exclusion or Chinese who dissociated themselves from Japanese during World War II. The rub was that Filipino/a students claimed they were brown to contest the "yellow power" banner favored by Chinese and Japanese students, who eventually accepted the term "Asian American."[133] This compromise shows that Chinese and Japanese hegemony over the Asian American student movement was just as incomplete as the KDP and IHTA hegemony over the I-Hotel popular front. Constitutive disagreement in both cases guarantees that Asian America cannot be fixed to determinate meanings or closed to interpretive conflicts. Constitutive agreement would have undermined panethnic struggles more effectively than model minoritization already has.

Conclusion: Racial Power Movement Contributions to U.S. Multiculturalism

This chapter has investigated how judgment constituted racial movement publics for Malcolm X, Alcatraz occupiers, and I-Hotel campaigners. In each case, an exemplary individual or set of individuals articulated a particular nonwhite/white conflict in the general form of a counter-public/official public distinction. Their judgments turned inward to transnational, pantribal, or panethnic communities as an appeal to their ethical, aesthetic, or economic senses. Their judgments turned outward toward the U.S. public in the guise of demands for self-determination, institutional spaces, and state actions. The very act of making concrete demands opened agonistic spaces between hitherto antagonists. I now contend that the selective appropriation of racial power demands has contributed to a common sense of U.S. multiculturalism.

Racial power movements aroused passionate reactions not only within black, Amerindian, and Asian American communities. They also provoke a sense of crisis among intellectuals aligned with the civil rights movement, who had to reexamine their criteria for evaluating social movements; ironically, it was often their harshest critics who avoided mischaracterizing these

---

132. Yen Le Espiritu, *Asian American Panethnicity: Bridging Institutions and Identities* (Philadelphia: Temple University Press, 1992), 32, 20–22.

133. "Asian America" itself was the empty signifier in this case.

movements as "merely symbolic," "single-issue," and the like.[134] In 1973, for example, C. Vann Woodward characterized the Black Panther Party as "[combining] a black vs. white race war of nationalism, black solidarity of all classes, with a 'Marxist-Leninist' class war in coalition with white revolutionaries."[135] Judgments of this sort are ostensibly about strategy and ideology. Yet its fundamental charge is that black power divides peoples who should be united. For Woodward, a progressive historian hopeful about white and black populist alliances, the people who belong together are fellow Americans.

Multicultural accounts of racial power excelled at addressing "progressive" anxieties over racial division. It can be argued, for example, that racial power movements helped to unite the American nation if both movements and nation are conceived as culturally plural. In the 1990s, William Wei located the Asian American movement "among the last of the 'ethnic-consciousness movements' . . . for racial equality, social justice, and political empowerment in a culturally pluralist America."[136] Around the same time, Troy Johnson and colleagues claimed that, "along with other ethnic group movements, the [red power movement] contributed to the debate over multiculturalism within the US national community."[137] These contemporary discourses are at some remove from the movement discourses that they remember in terms of "ethnic group" and "culturally pluralist America." They forget that racial power movements aspired to forge international, anticolonial, and transnational connections.

This terminological distance might be measured as a moderate concession to the 1970s and 1980s new right reaction against the 1960s and 1970s new left radicalism. It also points to the institutionalization of 1950s to 1970s racial conflicts as ethnic divisions of the U.S. polity. Here we pick up the thread of Chapter 2 in which the legitimation of the U.S. nation-state after the 1950s and 1960s civil rights movement partially turns on black "inclusion." Amid the 1960s to 1970s racial power movements, and continuing

---

134. On the etymological connections between crisis, criticism, and criteria, see Jane Gordon and Lewis Gordon, *Of Divine Warning: Reading Disaster in the Modern Age* (Boulder, CO: Paradigm, 2009), 19; on mischaracterizations of new social movements, see Day, *Gramsci Is Dead*, 69.

135. Woodward, *The Strange Career of Jim Crow*, 205. I cite from the chapter added to the third edition (1973) of Woodward. A more sympathetic account of black power is Victor Wolfenstein, "Race, Racism and Racial Liberation," *Western Political Quarterly* 30, no. 2 (1977): 175–82.

136. Wei, *The Asian American Movement*, 1.

137. Johnson et al., "American Indian Activism and Transformation," 38–39.

Cold War competition over the third world, U.S. officials considered how more general nonwhite "inclusions" could be effected. The idea was that blacks, Asians, and Amerindians could be incorporated under the rubrics of ethnic origins, cultural values, and interest groups—mainstream terms that substituted for movement keywords like racial enmity, colonial oppression, and class exploitation. This rearticulation hastened the contemporaneous decline of Anglo-conformist "Americanization."[138]

I intend to demonstrate that U.S. multiculturalism is—in logic, if not in fact—a counter-counter-hegemonic response to racial power. The crux of my claim is how the "counter" of counter-hegemonies are oriented on terrains of hegemonic struggle. Recall that the civil rights movement arose out of black counter-publics to demand national membership; its performances of racial desegregation re-founded the official public, that is, the republic as a whole.[139] The counter-hegemonic projects of racial power movements related ambivalently to the post–civil rights era hegemony. On the one hand, "we" addressed judgments to "our" public as if "their" public were fundamentally extrinsic to "our" public constitution. On the other hand, "we" addressed demands to "their" public as if creating space for "our" public within "their" public could transform the social whole. While the first moment is a hegemonic bid vis-à-vis a subaltern public, the second is a counter-hegemonic bid vis-à-vis the official public.

Whereas the post–civil rights era U.S. public included blackness on legal-constitutional grounds, racial power counter-publics excluded whiteness on commonsensical grounds. These differences between civil rights re-foundation and racial power counter-hegemony have existential sources. Civil rights activists were agonistically-with those whose violence and laws they contested, whereas racial power activists were antagonistically-against those whose "ways of life" and sensibilities they opposed. Yet the agonism/antagonism distinction is not an unbridgeable divide, for each articulation of a concrete demand is a potential bridge from a movement counter-public to the U.S. public. Institutional demands presuppose that contestants can enter a shared strategic and communicative space: the social realm of institutions

---

138. On the decline of Anglo-conformism, see King, *Making Americans*, chaps. 9–10.

139. As that which shifted U.S. racial formation from domination to hegemony, the civil rights movement could not have been a counter-hegemonic project. Omi and Winant, *Racial Formation in the United States*, 130–32; see also Winant, *Racial Conditions*, 24–29.

is an "objective" common ground and the political realm of speech is an intersubjective one.[140]

Negotiated in that space were the terms of incorporating counter-public projects into the official public order. Consider how officials handled black power demands for community separation, red power demands for centers on Alcatraz Island, and Asian American demands to stop the I-Hotel eviction. None of these demands were specifically satisfied, although some of them were incorporated in rearticulated forms.[141] As a presidential candidate, Richard Nixon endorsed "black power" proposals that would build up "the power that comes from participation in the political and economic processes of society."[142] While Bay Area Indians occupied Alcatraz Island, President Nixon promised to enact "self-determination" policies that would cede control over service programs to Amerindian governments.[143] Decades after the demolition of the original, San Francisco rebuilt the I-Hotel at a new site to partially meet the need—in the depoliticized sense of necessity—for affordable housing.[144]

These concessions did not eventuate in common understandings so much as they shifted the strategic locus of struggle. They set largely distributive terms of incorporating racial oppositions, actual or potential, into the social nation; put another way, they confined legitimated black, Amerindian, and Asian oppositions to the terrain of the U.S. welfare state. Legal-bureaucratic canalization, in turn, justified in advance the repression of racial conflicts remaining on the terrain of contentious politics, as when the state removed Alcatraz occupiers or criminalized black radicals.[145] Repressive domination supplemented hegemonic appropriation to signal the limits of what the state would accept as legitimate racial contest. The post–civil rights era U.S. public could accommodate some degree of racially inflected agonism, yet could not bear the full brunt of racial power antagonism.

---

140. Cf. Arendt, *The Human Condition*, 182–83.

141. Omi and Winant, *Racial Formation in the United States*, 187.

142. Richard Nixon, cited in Robert Allen, *Black Awakening in Capitalist America: An Analytic History* (Trenton, NJ: Africa World, 1992), 227–28.

143. Richard Nixon, "Message to Congress on Indian Affairs (July 8, 1970)," in *Red Power: The American Indians' Fight for Freedom*, 2nd ed., ed. Alvin Josephy, Joane Nagel, and Troy Johnson (Lincoln: University of Nebraska Press, 1999), 106–7.

144. After its demolition in 1979, the I-Hotel was rebuilt in 2005 with city and federal funds. A Chinatown site was selected because Manilatown no longer existed.

145. Dawson, *Black Visions*, 118. The FBI's Counter Intelligence Program (COINTELPRO) investigated and infiltrated all racial power movements as well as the civil rights movement.

Liberal democratic capacities for absorbing radical democratic mass mobilizations of the 1960s and 1970s had been built up throughout the 1950s to 1960s. The state in the 1950s and 1960s legitimated black/white division in electoral mechanisms, civil service, and urban development. This legitimation occurred in the register of legally regulated, interest-group pluralism. But in order to counter the (late) civil rights movement and racial power politicizations of everyday life, semi-official legitimation had to move into the register of normatively guided, cultural pluralism. Nonwhite "ethnic" divisions were soon legitimated in campus programs, museums, school curricula, audiovisual mass media, and arts centers. Ethnically based thinking flourished as traditional intellectuals disembarked the 1960s and 1970s "movement train" which, in their judgment, had traveled too far left. Sociologists, for instance, turned to cultural pluralism ("the salad bowl") as the ideal of ethnic assimilation ("the melting pot") grew increasingly unattractive.[146]

Pluralist U.S. nationalism is a resolution of conflicts over what counts as legitimate racial conflict and the terms of nonwhite incorporation. It replaces the many constitutions of racial counter-publics, which cut various peoples across official public boundaries, with the many populations of the American people, which the nation-state seeks to absorb. David Hollinger, then, is basically accurate in his quasi-Gramscian description of various sociohistorical blocs configured into an official "ethno-racial pentagon" of black, white, Asian, Hispanic, and Amerindian.[147] White, according to this racial geometry, is just another interest and/or cultural group—after all, the ethno-racial pentagon includes nonwhite groups excluded prior to the 1950s and 1960s reforms in U.S. immigration, naturalization, and civil rights law. An updated pluralism subtracts rather than sublimates nonwhite/white division to smooth over tenuous equations of, say, white Americans with American Indians.

Multiculturalism after the 1960s and 1970s resembles the constituted politics of racial power movements minus their constitutive nonwhite/white antagonisms. A nation-statist "we" absorbs the ethnic content from racial "us/them" divisions, substituting the conjunctive pluralism of "we are the one who are the many" for the disjunctive unity of "we are the ones who are not them." In order to cast them as normatively positive contributors to "a

---

146. Omi and Winant, *Racial Formation in the United States*, 42, 36; see also chap. 7.

147. David Hollinger, *Postethnic America: Beyond Multiculturalism*, rev. ed. (New York: Basic, 2000), chap. 2. These five categories—with Pacific Islander attached to Asian and Alaskan Native attached to American Indian—appeared on Office of Management and Budget directive no. 15 in 1977.

culturally pluralist America" (per Wei) or "the US national community" (per Johnson et al.), multiculturalists must confine racial power movements to the terrain of phenomenological positivity. This doubly positive form of remembrance depoliticizes movement and nation alike—yet this forgetting of antagonism and "negativity" has given rise to a conflict with those who remember otherwise. Jane and Lewis Gordon, for two, argue that our remembrance of antiracist activists of previous eras as strictly moral exemplars wages a "moralistic war on the political."[148] Among the potential casualties of this war, I argue in the next chapter, is the Great Transformation itself.

Multiculturalism emerged as a grassroots educational movement in the heyday of racial power, but it has since been rearticulated as a policy rubric for the U.S. academy and multinational corporations.[149] It is this (semi-)official variant of multiculturalism that has acquired an air of common sense. Arendt in this context would distinguish between common sense as a prospective site of critical reflection and common sense as a retrospective source of common understanding. For Arendt, proper judgments appeal to the former, whereas everyday prejudices (pre-judgments) appeal to the latter.[150] I have been characterizing multiculturalism as a commonplace of the kind that "we can toss out in conversation without any lengthy explanations."[151] When "lengthy explanations" are demanded, cultural pluralism can become a site of critical appeal again, as it was in its role as the opponent to scientific racism. Today's multiculturalist can refuse to tolerate white authoritarian nationalists who make (delusional) claims of "white genocide." They can also more prejudicially exclude "barbarians" beyond the pale of "civilization" (e.g., "Islamic fundamentalists").[152]

If one objects that I have been attacking cultural pluralism in thinly veiled normative terms, I would ask to what abstract norms or to which common senses this objection appeals. The historical complication is that multiculturalism might not have won the day had racial power never made demands on

---

148. Gordon and Gordon, *Of Divine Warning*, 101. Gordon and Gordon are discussing the parallel case of postapartheid South Africa.

149. Jodi Melamed, "The Spirit of Neoliberalism: From Racial Liberalism to Neoliberal Multiculturalism," *Social Text* 24, no. 4 (2006): 15; Hardt and Negri, *Empire*, 150–54.

150. Cf. Hans-Georg Gadamer, *Reason in the Age of Science*, trans. Frederick Lawrence (Cambridge, MA: MIT Press, 1983), 82.

151. Hannah Arendt, *The Promise of Politics*, ed. Jerome Kohn (New York: Schocken, 2005), 99.

152. Wendy Brown, *Regulating Aversion: Tolerance in the Age of Identity and Empire* (Princeton, NJ: Princeton University Press, 2006), 182.

the official public. Nor can the "integrationist" civil rights movement be so brightly remembered except against the background of "segregationist" racial power movements (to use labels shared by neoliberals and neoconservatives). So I praise racial power activists for their courage, resolve, and commitment in spite of their less-than-triumphant hegemonic bids. I praise racial power activists for their transformations of ethics, aesthetics, and economics into sites of critical judgment, despite my reservations about their sometimes prejudicial gender, sexuality, and nationalist politics.[153] Underdogs are not always right and not frequently triumphant. The underdog is simply the overman's worst enemy.

---

153. See Beltrán, *The Trouble with Unity*, chap. 2.

6

A Reaffirmation of Extraordinary Racial Politics

> All wars are fought twice, the first time on the battlefield, the second time in memory.
> —VIET THANH NYUGEN, "Remembering War, Dreaming Peace"

> Considerations like these are not at all meant to offer solutions or give advice. At best, they might encourage sustained and closer reflection on the nature and the intrinsic potentialities of action, which never before has revealed its greatness and its dangers so openly.
> —HANNAH ARENDT, *Between Past and Future*

Anti-establishment rage on the new right is a reaction not so much to racial enmity on the new left, but rather to the systematic containment and management of it. This is but one of the many racial ironies of our present. Racial presence has been felt by a few in the upper echelons of the arts, sciences, and politics, even as racial justice for many in education, economics, and health continues to be a distant prospect.[1] Latin American, Middle Eastern, and Asian migration could destabilize white/nonwhite and white/black imaginaries, yet both binaries are entrenched in U.S. institutions and ideologies.[2] Postcolonial aspirations are undermined by settler colonialisms resurgent, while movements for social justice are dealing with crises of mass deportation and incarceration. The white populism of the Trump presidency, as the symbolic negation of the multicultural liberalism of the Obama presidency, consummates this series of contradictions.

---

1. Cristina Beltrán, "Racial Presence versus Racial Justice: The Affective Power of an Aesthetic Condition," *Du Bois Review* 11, no. 1 (2014): 137–58.

2. Alcoff, *The Future of Whiteness*, 1–38; Bonilla-Silva, *Racism without Racists*, chap. 8; Haney López, *White by Law*, chap. 8.

In other words, the 1950s to 1970s Great Transformation initiated U.S. racial trajectories that have lost speed, but stayed in motion. Thereafter, nonwhite movement activists dug into the trenches of civil society, where Derrick Bell advised blacks to struggle against white reactionaries without any expectations of victory.[3] Combining pessimism of the intellect with optimism of the will, as Gramscians like to say, combatants continued to extend egalitarian contests into more and more domains of quotidian life (e.g., sexuality, digital media, conversation, visible embodiment).[4] Simultaneously, movement activists sometimes decided to enter institutionalized U.S. politics or the terrain of the racial state.[5]

The 1970s to 1980s Great Backlash, if I may, has lost less speed than the Great Transformation of the 1950s to the 1970s. In addition to securing rollbacks in the racial state, this trajectory is today winning a "culture war" against all vestiges of "political correctness."[6] The hegemony of color-blind multiculturalism, however, had already been eroding under the leftist pressure of No Dakota Access Pipeline (NoDAPL) and Black Lives Matter as well as the rightist pressure of the "Alt-Right" and Tea Party. Yet earlier, the Obama presidency brought U.S. politics into a "most racial" rather than a "post-racial" era—an era that renormalized explicit as opposed to "dog-whistle" appeals to white resentments.[7]

For its part, the academic left is more engaged than ever with the intersectional, feminist of color, and queer theorists among its ranks.[8] My worry, though, is that even the most critical new left thinkers are farther than ever from imagining how an event of U.S. public constitution could occur, much less qualify as progressive. This failure is all the direr if the fascist right or the communist left will be the only forces drawing from the poetry and

---

3. Derrick Bell, *Faces at the Bottom of the Well: The Permanence of Racism* (New York: Basic, 1992), chap. 5; cf. Ta-Nehisi Coates, *Between the World and Me* (New York: Random House, 2015).

4. Laclau and Mouffe, *Hegemony and Socialist Strategy*, 159–71.

5. Omi and Winant, *Racial Formation in the United States*, 175–76.

6. For a different viewpoint, see Morris Fiorina, Samuel Abrams, and Jeremy Pope, *Culture War? The Myth of a Polarized America*, 3rd ed. (Boston: Longman, 2011).

7. On the Obama presidency, see Michael Tesler, *Post-Racial or Most-Racial? Race and Politics in the Obama Era* (Chicago: University of Chicago Press, 2016). On dog-whistle politics, see Ian Haney López, *Dog Whistle Politics: How Coded Racial Appeals Have Reinvented Racism & Wrecked the Middle Class* (Oxford, UK: Oxford University Press, 2014).

8. See, e.g., Laurie Balfour, Falguni Sheth, Heath Fogg Davis, Shatema Threadcraft, and Jemima Repo, "Critical Exchange: Bodies in Politics," *Contemporary Political Theory* 15, no. 1 (2016): 80–118. On the limits of intersectionality, see Jakeet Singh, "Religious Agency and the Limits of Intersectionality," *Hypatia* 30, no. 4 (2015): 657–74.

promise of extraordinary politics. Radical democrats must recapture the terrain of constitutive power, which no bloc is effectively inhabiting, lest authoritarian nationalists find their way there. The post–civil rights era is over, and Trumpism is its tragic end.

As our everyday politics grow all the more farcical, our theories of everyday politics need to recover their extraordinary potential. These are the ultimate, dare I say comic, stakes of this chapter. In the first section, I recollect our four events back into a common framework, reemphasizing that the common denominator of all extraordinary racial politics is existential. In the second section, I consider the risks and rewards of tapping into the extraordinary dimension latent within ordinary U.S. racial politics. My conclusion is that an affirmation of extraordinary racial politics is an affirmation of the political, as there is no politics—no matter how ordinary—without a constitutive potential.

Section I: Recollecting Instances of Extraordinary Racial Politics

These final recollections return to the Arendtian triad of activity, narrative, and concept. Arendt argues that stories, by themselves, cannot preserve actions in public memory; it takes "a framework of conceptual notions" to save "the stories which grow out of what men do and endure" from "[sinking] back into the futility inherent in the living word and the living deed."[9] Conceptualization, on this view, is no less memory-work than storytelling. This book has conceptualized southeastern Indian removal, the Japanese internment, the civil rights movement, and racial power movements within the framework of extraordinary racial politics. It has shown that reading European political theories through U.S. racial formations renders both "simultaneously recognizable and wholly new," as Jane Gordon describes the process of creolization.[10] In short, this book has condensed narratives within a conceptual frame as much as it has used narratives to stretch that conceptual frame.

Creolization has also occurred at the level of distinctive theoretical perspectives—where political theories of why politics exists become critical investigations of how domination works,[11] where critical theories of race are

---

9. Arendt, *On Revolution*, 212.
10. Gordon, *Creolizing Rousseau*, 159–60.
11. On the reason-for-being of politics, see Arendt, *Between Past and Future*, 145, 149; on critical investigations, see Young, *Justice and the Politics of Difference*, 5–6.

philosophies of existence. My purpose has not been to abstractly theorize such conjunctures, but to narrate the diverse experiences that make them meaningful.[12] The previous four chapters set the concept of extraordinary racial politics into motion, traced the extraordinary into diverse events. Our events can now be recollected into the original framework, which from the outset implicitly contained a wealth of historically situated experiences.[13] This is our task of remembrance.

Chapter 1 worked the concepts of racial formation and public constitution up into the concept of extraordinary racial politics. This work was feasible because certain ethnic studies scholars (Charles Mills as well as Michael Omi and Howard Winant) and certain political theorists (Carl Schmitt and Hannah Arendt) make analogous distinctions of extraordinary politics/ordinary politics. I balanced tendencies that, taken alone, are problematic: the tendency of ethnic studies to subsume extraordinary moments to everyday processes, and the tendency of political theory to disconnect extraordinary events from everyday orders. Extraordinary racial politics was then unpacked in terms of (1) its power to suspend racial order, (2) its power to initiate racial transformations, and (3) its power to reinstate racial order. Figure 6.1 illustrates that the second power—rooted in our capacity to achieve the new—is at the "center" of extraordinary racial politics. It also shows that constitutive racial events are part of, yet distinguishable from, constituted racial trajectories.

Chapter 1 anticipated how subsequent chapters would divide into Arendtian and Schmittian narratives. I classified the civil rights movement as a near-paradigmatic case of Arendtian action, while characterizing racial power movements as anomalous cases of Arendtian action that bore traces of friendship and enmity. I classified the Japanese internment as a near-paradigmatic case of Schmittian decision, while characterizing southeastern Indian removals as anomalous cases of Schmittian decisions that lacked friend/enemy structures. Chapters 2 through 5 maintained a (roughly) chronological order of events. The current task of remembrance, however, is better served by a conceptual ordering. What follows recollects the Arendtian Chapters 2 and 5 before the Schmittian Chapters 4 and 3, revisiting paradigmatic before anomalous cases.

---

12. On politics as a condition of meaningful experience, see Dana Villa, *Arendt and Heidegger: The Fate of the Political* (Princeton, NJ: Princeton University Press, 1996), chap. 3; see also McCormick, *Carl Schmitt's Critique of Liberalism*, chap. 2.

13. This movement is in broad strokes "dialectical," although the events are not dialectically connected.

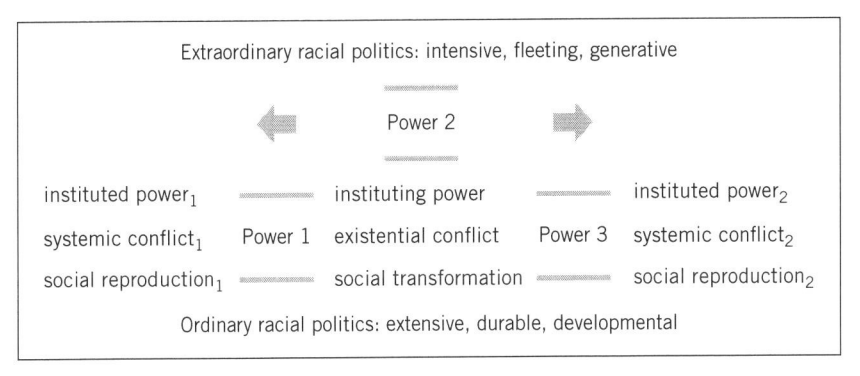

```
┌─────────────────────────────────────────────────────────────────────┐
│         Extraordinary racial politics: intensive, fleeting, generative         │
│                            ─────────                                │
│                    ⇐      Power 2      ⇒                            │
│                            ─────────                                │
│  instituted power₁   ─────  instituting power  ─────  instituted power₂ │
│  systemic conflict₁  Power 1  existential conflict  Power 3  systemic conflict₂ │
│  social reproduction₁ ───── social transformation ───── social reproduction₂ │
│         Ordinary racial politics: extensive, durable, developmental            │
└─────────────────────────────────────────────────────────────────────┘
```

Figure 6.1 Extraordinary and Ordinary Racial Politics

To begin with moments of public freedom: the more it qualified as a biographical and historical beginning, the more an event came to constitute the Arendtian public. The actors of Chapters 2 and 5 made contentious claims (e.g., for social rights) and initiated new processes (e.g., of multicultural production).[14] They worked outside or against the terrain of institutionalized politics, either because the state directed repression and hostility toward them, as with racial power movements, or because the state presented limited opportunity structures, as with the civil rights movement. Their freedoms were largely self-organized within the trenches and fortifications of civil society. What U.S. governments of all kinds could provide, at best, was material support and legal authority.

Chapter 2, "Racial Re-foundations and the Rise of the Nation-State," presented the civil rights movement as our exemplum of Arendtian action. I argued that the 1950s to 1960s movement rearticulated black membership in terms of social contest and, as a consequence, rearticulated U.S. citizenship in national-state terms. Put another way, the U.S. constitution was so founded on whites-only citizenship that it took an extraordinary politics of re-foundation to disestablish it. To affirm the U.S. civil rights movement is not to dream of a nation-state without black and white division, to condemn black politics that tactically and strategically differ from it, or to memorialize civil rights leaders as objects of nationalist veneration.[15] To affirm that

---

14. Cf. John Guidry and Mark Sawyer, "Contentious Pluralism: The Public Sphere and Democracy," *Perspectives on Politics* 1, no. 2 (2003): 273–89.

15. On the condemnation, see Juliet Hooker, "The Paradoxes of U.S. Black Politics: From Democratic Sacrifice to Democratic Repair," *Political Theory* 44, no. 4 (2016): 456–57; on the memorialization, see Bell, *Silent Covenants*, 198.

movement is to remember its radical enactment of participation, its social connotation of equality, and its revolutionary achievement of re-foundation.

Chapter 5, "Racial Counter-Publics and the Power of Judgment," picked up where Chapter 2 left off—namely, in the 1960s to 1970s territory of Arendtian contests. I argued that racial power activists, who had to judge without given norms or secure names, called on common senses to articulate demands and identities. By this time, the racial state had selectively incorporated civil rights movement demands into a new ordinary politics with new legal norms. Judgments of white/nonwhite antagonism were key operators of extraordinary counter-public challenges to this still-fragile public order. Even when initiating socialist and transnational turns, however, racial power often extended the radical democratic trajectories of the U.S. re-foundation. To affirm these shared trajectories is to remember that both civil rights and racial power movements meant public freedom.

As for their differences, the civil rights movement fit well into Arendt's conjunctive public realm, while racial power movements left behind remainders of Schmitt's disjunctive public identification. An agonistic movement that, as a matter of principle, repudiated antagonistic force is distinctive from antagonistic movements that, as a matter of strategy, effected agonistic "bracketings": the civil rights movement strove to legitimize racial conflict in the U.S. public, whereas racial power movements strove to bridge the official public and subaltern counter-publics. This difference in orientation corresponds to a difference in aims: the civil rights movement re-founded U.S. citizenship, while racial power movements judged nonwhite commonalities. Table 6.1 compares and contrasts these two citizen-driven varieties of extraordinary racial politics.

As far as their biographies went, the actors of Chapters 2 and 5 "had in common neither gifts nor convictions; neither profession nor milieu."[16] What the founder Thomas Jefferson, the re-founder Martin Luther King Jr., the Filipina activist Estella Habal, and the Shoshone-Bannock activist LaNada Boyer shared was courage, to call this virtue by its ancient name. Courage consisted in a risk of bodily security, in the attempt to "insert one's self into the world and begin a story of one's own."[17] While all were relatively indifferent to social status, each experience of freedom varied across social stratifications. Only Jefferson, a propertied white male, could fully partake of the

---

16. Hannah Arendt, *Men in Dark Times* (New York: Harcourt Brace, 1968), vii.
17. Arendt, *On Revolution*, 186.

TABLE 6.1 CITIZEN-DRIVEN EXTRAORDINARY RACIAL POLITICS

Event(s)	Mode of action	Aim of action
Civil rights movement	Agonistic conjuncture	Constitutional authority
Racial power movements	Antagonistic disjuncture	Community appeal
Shared stakes: freedom		Shared experience: courage

official public; King, Habal, and Boyer participated in counter-publics due to other-imposed exclusions and self-assumed commitments. Such luminaries in their respective communities—black religious, Filipina/o transnational, Amerindian urban—appeared "shadowy" to the gaze of white normativity.

If the stakes of citizen actions were public freedom, the stakes of state decisions were public order. Just as courageous and boundary-crossing actions constitute Arendtian publics, anxious and boundary-setting decisions constitute Schmittian publics. So the more fearful and cutting it was, the more Schmittian an event appeared. The officials in Chapters 4 and 3 decided what would count as order and how groups would (not) belong to it. They divided threatened from threatening populations in global crises of war, as with the Japanese internment, or domestic from domesticated populations in continental crises of expansion, as with southeastern Indian removals. They assessed the disorderliness of racial groupings (e.g., Nisei or Issei, Cherokee or Seminole) on spatial criteria (e.g., West or East Coast, east or west of the Mississippi), assuming "responsibility regarding danger and, in this sense, responsibility for protecting the subjects [i.e., full members] of the state."[18]

Chapter 4, "Racial States of Exception and the Decision on Enmity," investigated our paradigm case of Schmittian decision. I argued that Japanese incarcerations and resettlements consisted in the state fabricating and resolving an emergency situation. As for its consequences, the racial state set exceptional norms for wartime and postwar Asian integration. Civil libertarians and critical theorists alike should remember how this event conjoined "external" war and "internal" security, sovereign decisions and social projects. The internment is not fundamentally—to stylize a few genres of popular remembrance—a lesson in how not to treat racial minorities, a *sui generis* wartime mistake, or an inevitable culmination of anti-Asiatic exclusion.[19] The moral of my story, espe-

---

18. Carl Schmitt, *The Leviathan in the State Theory of Thomas Hobbes: Meaning and Failure of a Political Symbol*, trans. George Schwab and Erna Hilfstein (Westport, CT: Greenwood, 1996), 72; see also Thomas Hobbes, *Leviathan* (Cambridge: Cambridge University Press, 1996), chap. 21.

19. A parallel critique of "eternal anti-Semitism" is Arendt, *Origins of Totalitarianism*, 7–8.

cially as it relates to the adjudication of *courte durée* and *longue durée* explanations, is that extraordinary racial politics is both relatively unpredictable and retrospectively intelligible.

Chapter 3, "Racial Removal Contracts and the *Nomos* of the New World," anticipated Chapter 4's theme of Schmittian crises. Southeastern land appropriation, I contended, was an extraordinary response to a crisis of U.S. territorial expansion. The domestication of southeastern indigenous polities resolved land disputes between southern state and southeastern indigenous polities. Mid-nineteenth-century Indian removal has been remembered as a massive land-grab, a tragedy of indigenous suffering, and a travesty of federal-Indian diplomacy. Our remembrance centered on the racial state's solicitation of subaltern consent in the reconstitution of U.S. federal order. Even as we admit that Asian Americans have been implicated in white settler colonization,[20] we can see that southeastern Indian removal and Japanese internment shared the stakes of concrete spatial and racial order.

Beyond these stakes, Japanese American incarceration had the structure of Schmittian decisions, while southeastern Amerindian domestication left behind remainders of the Arendtian social. Sovereign decisions that identified friends/enemies are different than administrative decisions that identified guardian/wards: Japanese assimilation presupposed mutually exclusive Japanese and American nations had come into violent conflict, while Amerindian domestication presupposed that Amerindian polities had consented to their U.S. federal incorporation. This difference in assumptions corresponds to a difference in aims: Japanese internment generated and resolved a state of exception, while Indian removals appropriated and ordered indigenous land. Table 6.2 compares and contrasts these two state-centered varieties of extraordinary racial politics.

Whereas our Arendtian actors achieved public freedom, our Schmittian deciders established public order. Chapters 4 and 3 did not concern the personalities of General John DeWitt, War Relocation Authority Director Dillon Myer, Chief Justice John Marshall, or President Andrew Jackson.[21] These chapters recounted how officials exercised powers of their offices—usages of power that, due to their constitutive nature, could not be fully authorized.

---

20. Most literature on this topic is about Japanese settlement in Hawaii; see, e.g., Dean Itsuji Saranillio, "Why Asian Settler Colonialism Matters: A Thought Piece on Critiques, Debates, and Indigenous Difference," *Settler Colonial Studies* 3, no. 3–4 (2013): 280–94.

21. DeWitt's racism, Myer's banality, Marshall's cleverness, and Jackson's charisma would be equally irrelevant to Schmitt. The office of sovereignty is authorized by the representation of the people's unity. Kalyvas, *Democracy and the Politics of the Extraordinary*, 157–58.

TABLE 6.2 STATE-DRIVEN EXTRAORDINARY RACIAL POLITICS		
Event(s)	Structure of decision	Order to be decided
Japanese internment	Friend/enemy	U.S. national-state
Southeast Indian removals	Guardian/ward	U.S. federalism
Shared stakes: order		Shared experience: anxiety

Legal and bureaucratic racial projects could not mask impositions of either/or logics on multifaceted antagonisms; nor could such projects disguise uneasiness surrounding "disorderly" races. If activists experienced courage in the pursuit of freedom, officers experienced anxiety in the face of disorder.[22] Perhaps we might expect as much from DeWitt and Jackson, who had military experience. Yet Myer, the career bureaucrat, and Marshall, the learned judge, were just as eager to distinguish normal from exceptional situations.

Both courage and anxiety above are meant in the existential sense of self-constitution. The assumption is that extraordinary politics is oriented to life and death in the same way that ordinary politics is oriented to wants and needs. Our paradigm cases from Chapters 2 and 4 exemplify how power exposed physical lives to insecurity: the civil rights activist resolved to potentially die and yet not kill, while the Japanese American soldier decided to potentially kill and die. Our anomalous cases from Chapters 3 and 5 exemplify how strife could become more paradigmatically Arendtian or Schmittian: possibly the antagonist of the federal government, the Alcatraz activist who posed demands to the state approached civil rights movement agonism; possibly the ward of the federal government, the Seminole partisan who fought the U.S. army drew closer to the Nisei citizen-soldiers' experience of combat. Our recollection ends with the reminder that extraordinary politics means human lives and powers in common and at risk. This insight is, *in nuce*, what existential political theory has to offer critical race theory.

Section II: Revitalizing Conflict in Extraordinary Racial Politics

Extraordinary politics is the point at which trajectories coming out of the past take unpredictable, yet intelligible turns toward the future.[23] This point of contingency denies any trajectory an inevitable direction—be it toward

---

22. Cf. Søren Kierkegaard, *Fear and Trembling/Repetition*, trans. Howard Hong and Edna Hong (Princeton, NJ: Princeton University Press, 1983), 54–67.
23. Cf. Arendt, *Life of the Mind*, pt. 1, 207–10; Arendt, *Between Past and Future*, 10–14.

justice or injustice, equality or inequality. Hence our affirmation of extraordinary racial politics cannot simply devalue state crises and valorize mass mobilizations. Racist states of exception may give us pause, but we remember that emergency racial politics have also included Lincoln's Emancipation Proclamation.²⁴ Emancipatory subaltern movements may give us hope, yet we remember that racial mass mobilizations have included "Alt-Right" marches and anti-Abolitionist riots.²⁵

This section explores the potential risks and rewards of recovering (the concept of) extraordinary racial politics in the Trump-era United States. Although I appreciate anxieties toward extraordinary politics and racial politics, I affirm generative racial contests in our time and place of liberal democratic crisis. There are good reasons to affirm the conflict inherent in U.S. racial formation and to affirm the radical democratic potential of U.S. racial movements. Conversely, there is little to be said against extraordinary racial politics that could not be said against extraordinary politics of any kind. There is, furthermore, little to be said against extraordinary politics that could not be said against politics *tout court*.

This study has taken the extraordinary racial politics/ordinary racial politics distinction to be a special case of the extraordinary politics/ordinary politics distinction. Most critical race theorists could accept my proposal that politics explains race more than race explains politics.²⁶ Yet, as ethnic studies could be more precise and explicit on this question, I have explicitly defended the notion that politics, whether ordinary or extraordinary, is specified by powers-in-conflict.²⁷ As Michael Hanchard suggests, an attempt to specify "the racial" in terms of "the political" assumes that neither the former nor the latter can be everywhere and nowhere, always and never.²⁸

Modern public life, I have contended, includes both "the political" and "the social." As a special case of the political, extraordinary politics are conflicts with the power to create and transform selves and collectivities; as a

---

24. I do not claim that Lincoln intended to promote racial equality; I only mean that the act outdid the actor. See Bell, *Silent Covenants*, 52–56.
25. Olson, *The Abolition of White Democracy*, 31–32.
26. Ibid., xii; Sheth, *Toward a Political Philosophy of Race*, 22; Goldberg, *Racist Culture*, 87.
27. Cf. Wendy Brown, *Edgework: Critical Essays on Knowledge and Politics* (Princeton, NJ: Princeton University Press, 2005), 75–76.
28. Hanchard, *Party/Politics*, 9–10, 28–30; see also Michael Hanchard, *Orpheus and Power: The "Movimento Negro" of Rio de Janeiro and São Paulo, Brazil, 1945–1988* (Princeton, NJ: Princeton University Press, 1994), 16.

special case of the social, ordinary politics are conflicts that reproduce or even reform an existing order of power. I read along these lines Omi and Winant's claim that race is a "complex of social meanings constantly being transformed by political struggle."[29] This historical-sociological line of reasoning has been drawn into existential-phenomenological territory, where racial formation serves as a privileged route into the broader field of public constitution. Public constitution, in turn, is a privileged route into the broader field of politics—not all of which are extraordinary, but none of which are without an extraordinary potential.

Liberals, who have always been suspicious of public power and existential conflict, have recently become uncomfortable with racialized powers-in-conflict. Popularizing the term "racism" to attack Nazi eugenics and anti-Semitism,[30] postwar U.S. liberals sought to discard race and to recognize cultures (initially in religious terms). Color-blind and multicultural liberals continue in this tradition of problematizing racial struggle and race itself. Isn't postracialism the cure for racialized pathologies of indifference toward others and exclusionary solidarities? Isn't it better to come together around American ideals, interests, and identities, especially those not yet recognized because they are African American?

U.S. liberals tend to connect the achievement of liberal democratic citizenship to the withering away of race. The rub is that—on the most charitable view—liberalism is a deeply racialized formation, as tied to racial oppression as it is open to racial emancipation. On Goldberg's "liberal paradox," transatlantic commitments to liberty and equality coincide with the racist generation of identities and exclusions.[31] More specific to the United States are debates over whether U.S. liberalism is analytically distinct from U.S. racism or whether U.S. racism is actually constitutive of U.S. liberalism.[32] Whether racial justice is achievable under liberal democracy is an open question, but whether U.S. liberal democracy has facilitated racial injustice is not. My Schmittian cases are two pointed examples of how it has.

The crisis of liberal democracy is not that open discussion no longer legitimates elected governments, as it arguably was last century.[33] It is that

---

29. Omi and Winant, *Racial Formation in the United States*, 110.
30. McWhorter, *Racism and Sexual Oppression*, 231–33, 245–49.
31. Goldberg, *Racist Culture*, 6.
32. For the former position, see Smith, *Civic Ideals*; for the latter, see Olson, *The Abolition of White Democracy*.
33. Schmitt, *The Crisis of Parliamentary Democracy*, chap. 2.

neoliberalism, which replaces all vestiges of the public-oriented *homo politicus* with the market-rational *homo economicus*, is making *political* liberalism or liberal *democracy* increasingly untenable.[34] Trumpism is a *Herrenvolk* democratic resurgence (the nation is rooted in white "European folk") within a totalizing, authoritarian neoliberalism (competition and capital will organize all of life). White populism even more than color-blindness rejects the principle of legitimated conflict—a prime instance of which has been post–civil rights era racial conflict. In the post–civil rights era, the major threat to multiracial democracy was difference-blind liberalism; in the Trump era, the major threat is neoliberal white democracy.

The judgment that a nonwhite turn to "identity politics" is responsible for the resurgence of white identity politics, however, is deeply mistaken. The nostalgia for a nonidentitarian progressivism, like the nostalgia for a morally unified nation, is a longing for a "good old days" that never existed. For the informal U.S. constitution is infinitely closer to eliminating white dominance than eliminating racial division itself, howsoever far it remains from the former. Raceless or classless utopias, communist or nationalist utopias are all fantasies, in Iris Young's words, of "social wholeness, symmetry, a secure and solid [selfhood]."[35] Politics for utopians of all stripes is a problem of division and conflict to be solved by apolitical means.

However, as my Arendtian cases have shown, racial conflict can mean existential achievement for political actors themselves. Neither destinations nor "successes," Derrick Bell argues, can make long marches meaningful; meaning is rather what stands out from, yet remains immanent to, the struggle itself.[36] When asked why she risked her life in fighting for school desegregation in small town Mississippi, Behonor McDonald explained she "lives to harass white folk."[37] McDonald is antagonistic, yet less so than whites who equate black contestation with "violence."[38] Even the agonistic mega-*marchas* manifested what Beltrán calls "festive anger," an almost antagonistic passion that belies the depiction of Latino/a marchers as "nonthreatening."[39]

---

34. Wendy Brown, *Undoing the Demos: Neoliberalism's Stealth Revolution* (New York: Zone, 2015), chap. 1; cf. Jodi Dean, *Democracy and Other Neoliberal Fantasies: Communicative Capitalism and Left Politics* (Durham, NC: Duke University Press, 2009), 13–16.

35. Young, *Justice and the Politics of Difference*, 232.

36. Bell, *Faces from the Bottom of the Well*, 198.

37. Bell, *Silent Covenants*, 103.

38. See Gordon, *Fanon and the Crisis of European Man*, 77–79; see also Hooker, "The Paradoxes of U.S. Black Politics," 462–65.

39. Beltrán, *The Trouble with Unity*, 143.

What these political actors achieved was courage in the face of racial antagonisms still painfully alive.

We might expect radical democrats to recognize these and similar moments as exemplars of *agon* (struggle), then. Sadly, radical democrats often lack any theory of race or, when addressing race empirically, do not avail themselves of relevant ethnic studies. To draw on Linda Martín Alcoff, some even pre-judge visible identities as necessarily oppressive, illusory, and pathological.[40] I invite especially radical democrats of this persuasion to see that the accent of so-called identity politics is on politics, not identity. Radical democrats must affirm struggles to dismantle oppressive identifications and struggles to inaugurate emancipatory ones.

Perhaps radical democrats steer clear of "race struggle" due to its fascist connotations in the same way they steer clear of "class struggle" due to its communist connotations. After all, a standard line of critique is that agonistic valorizations of rhetoric, affect, and power will result in irrational violence.[41] A standard line of defense is to align radical democracy with constitutional liberalism, as in Mouffe's argument that European agonists want to revitalize liberal democracy.[42] This defense accepts much of the liberal polemic against fascism and communism, according to which both are aggressive, pseudo-democratic, and—in essence—totalitarian.[43] Indeed, in the context of mid-twentieth-century Europe, extraordinary politics was surely associated with extraordinary danger.

Outside of that context, and perhaps even within it, radical democrats should not reduce extraordinary politics to extraordinary peril. If we do, we will effectively accept the liberal democratic ("anti-populist") conflation of the NoDAPL with the "Alt-Right" movement, Sanders-like socialism with Trumpist neoliberalism. We will effectively ignore that ordinary politics means extraordinary danger for many nonwhites and that such politics conform to racist norms rather than deviate from race-neutral norms.[44] We will

---

40. Alcoff, *Visible Identities*, chaps. 2–3; see also Alcoff, *The Future of Whiteness*, chap. 3.

41. See, e.g., Peter Steinberger, "Rationalism in Politics," *American Political Science Review* 109, no. 4 (2015): 762.

42. Mouffe, *Agonistics*, 74–75, 119–20.

43. See, e.g., José Ortega y Gasset, *Revolt of the Masses* (New York: Norton, 1960); F. A. Hayek, *The Road to Serfdom: The Definitive Edition* (Chicago: University of Chicago Press, 2007).

44. Even nonracial norms may be racialized in application or effect. Haney López, *White by Law*, 87–88; Michelle Alexander, *The New Jim Crow: Mass Incarceration in the Age of Colorblindness*, rev. ed. (New York: New Press, 2012), chap. 3.

likely default to the liberal positions that ordinary politics is the solution to extraordinary politics and that nonracial politics is the solution to racial politics. I hold, on the contrary, that the best counter to the perils of extraordinary racial conflict is the promise of extraordinary racial conflict. Extraordinary racial politics is the very problem it is trying to solve.

An extraordinary racial politics of freedom and equality is our only hope for surpassing an extraordinary racial politics of law and order. If Trump is symptomatic of an all-around legitimation crisis for U.S. liberal democracy, the worst strategy for progressives would be to "double down" on the U.S. neoliberal constitution that gave rise to Trump. More hopeful is that the U.S. democratic constitution, which is usually submerged in subaltern social formations, appeared partially inside Bernie Sanders's presidential campaign. Progressivisms beyond Sanders may, as Walter Benjamin says, "bring about a real state of emergency" or, as Homi Bhabha says, allow for "a state of emergence."[45]

Movements led by millennials of color may achieve the critical alternative to Trumpism. My hope is grounded not on morality or epistemology, the superior virtue or privileged standpoint of this group. It is based on political and anthropological reasons—to wit, that extraordinary racial crisis is a privileged point of access into the informal U.S. constitution and that, to make an Arendtian association, the youth are "natural" beginners. In the beginning and in the end, the event of U.S. public constitution is generative of and generated by the process of U.S. racial formation. Ordinary racial politics draws vitality from the extraordinary dimension, while extraordinary racial politics is fulfilled in the ordinary dimension. The ordinary and the extraordinary stand and fall together.[46]

A reaffirmation of extraordinary racial politics in our time and place would be the revitalization of politics itself. Conversely, the desire to eliminate race in the here and now amounts to the desire to eliminate politics. The elimination of politics could improve our species,[47] but at the cost of courting great disasters. Thus conclude our reflections, which I hope have illuminated some contours of our dark times. Although every generation must find

---

45. Homi Bhabha, *The Location of Culture* (New York: Routledge, 1994), 41; Walter Benjamin, *Illuminations*, trans. Harry Zohn (New York: Schocken, 1968), 257.

46. Cf. Kalyvas, *Democracy and the Politics of the Extraordinary*, 199–205.

47. James Madison, "No. 51," in Hamilton et al., *The Federalist Papers*, 322; cf. Claude Lefort, *The Political Forms of Modern Society: Bureaucracy, Democracy, Totalitarianism* (Cambridge: Polity, 1986), 280.

its mission in relative opacity,[48] coming generations may find inspiration in the Great Transformation. We have done well to recollect the spirit of these new social movements. We would do even better to repeat it with a difference. My friends—for we are friends, even if we have no enemies—let us remember and repeat. Otherwise our cause will be lost twice.

---

48. Fanon, *Wretched of the Earth*, 145; cf. Enrique Dussel, *Twenty Theses on Politics*, trans. George Ciccariello-Maher (Durham, NC: Duke University Press, 2008), 101, 118.

Bibliography

Agamben, Giorgio. *Homo Sacer: Sovereign Power and Bare Life.* Translated by Daniel Heller-Roazen. Stanford, CA: Stanford University Press, 1998.

———. *State of Exception.* Translated by Kevin Attell. Chicago: University of Chicago Press, 2005.

Alcoff, Linda Martín. *The Future of Whiteness.* Cambridge: Polity, 2015.

———. *Visible Identities: Race, Gender and the Self.* Oxford, UK: Oxford University Press, 2006.

Alexander, Michelle. *The New Jim Crow: Mass Incarceration in the Age of Colorblindness.* Rev. ed. New York: New Press, 2012.

Allen, Danielle. "Invisible Citizens: Political Exclusion and Domination in Arendt and Ellison." In *Nomos XLVI: Political Exclusion and Domination,* edited by Stephen Macedo and Melissa Williams, 29–76. New York: New York University Press, 2005.

———. *Talking to Strangers: Anxieties of Citizenship since* Brown v. Board of Education. Chicago: University of Chicago Press, 2004.

Allen, Robert. *Black Awakening in Capitalist America: An Analytic History.* Trenton, NJ: Africa World, 1992.

Althusser, Louis. *Lenin and Philosophy and Other Essays.* Translated by Ben Brewster. New York: Monthly Review, 1971.

Arendt, Hannah. "Action and the Pursuit of Happiness." *Hannah Arendt Papers.* Manuscript Division of the Library of Congress. Accessed April 18, 2017. https://memory.loc.gov/cgi-bin/ampage?collId=mharendt&fileName=05/051010/051010page.db&recNum=0.

———. *Between Past and Future: Eight Exercises in Political Thought.* Rev. ed. New York: Penguin, 2006.

———. *Crises of the Republic.* New York: Harcourt Brace Jovanovich, 1972.

---. *The Human Condition*. 2nd ed. Chicago: University of Chicago Press, 1998.
---. *The Jewish Writings*. Edited by Jerome Kohn and Ronald Feldman. New York: Schocken, 2007.
---. *Lectures on Kant's Political Philosophy*. Edited by Ronald Beiner. Chicago: University of Chicago Press, 1982.
---. *The Life of the Mind*. New York: Harcourt Brace Jovanovich, 1978.
---. *Men in Dark Times*. New York: Harcourt Brace, 1968.
---. *On Revolution*. New York: Penguin, 1990.
---. *On Violence*. New York: Harcourt Brace, 1970.
---. *The Origins of Totalitarianism*. Rev. ed. San Diego, CA: Harvest, 1973.
---. *The Promise of Politics*. Edited by Jerome Kohn. New York: Schocken, 2005.
---. *Rahel Varnhagen: The Life of a Jewish Woman*. Rev. ed. New York: Harcourt Brace Jovanovich, 1974.
---. *Responsibility and Judgment*. Edited by Jerome Kohn. New York: Schocken, 2003.
Aristotle. *Aristotle: "The Politics" and "The Constitution of Athens."* Edited by Stephen Everson. Cambridge: Cambridge University Press, 1996.
Armitage, David, ed. *Theories of Empire, 1450–1800*. Aldershot, UK: Ashgate, 1998.
Azuma, Eiichiro. *Between Two Empires: Race, History, and Transnationalism in Japanese America*. Oxford, UK: Oxford University Press, 2004.
---. "Dancing with the Rising Sun: Strategic Alliances between Japanese Immigrants and Their 'Home' Government." In *The Transnational Politics of Asian Americans*, edited by Christian Collet and Pei-te Lien, 25–37. Philadelphia: Temple University Press, 2009.
Badiou, Alain. *Being and Event*. Translated by Oliver Feltham. London: Continuum, 2005.
Balfour, Lawrie, Falguni Sheth, Heath Fogg Davis, Shatema Threadcraft, and Jemima Repo. "Critical Exchange: Bodies in Politics." *Contemporary Political Theory* 15, no. 1 (2016): 80–118.
Bell, Derrick. *Faces at the Bottom of the Well: The Permanence of Racism*. New York: Basic, 1992.
---. *Silent Covenants: Brown v. Board of Education and the Unfulfilled Hopes of Racial Reform*. Oxford, UK: Oxford University Press, 2004.
Beltrán, Cristina. "Going Public: Hannah Arendt, Immigrant Action, and the Space of Appearance." *Political Theory* 37, no. 5 (2009): 595–622.
---. "Racial Presence versus Racial Justice: The Affective Power of an Aesthetic Condition." *Du Bois Review* 11, no. 1 (2014): 137–58.
---. *The Trouble with Unity: Latino Politics and the Creation of Identity*. Oxford, UK: Oxford University Press, 2010.
Bendersky, Joseph. *Carl Schmitt: Theorist for the Reich*. Princeton, NJ: Princeton University Press, 1983.
Benedict, Ruth. *Patterns of Culture*. Boston: Houghton Mifflin, 1959.
Benhabib, Seyla. *The Reluctant Modernism of Hannah Arendt*. New ed. Lanham, MD: Rowman and Littlefield, 2003.
Benjamin, Walter. *Illuminations*. Translated by Harry Zohn. New York: Schocken, 1968.
Bennett, Claudette. "Racial Categories Used in the Decennial Censuses, 1790 to the Present." *Government Information Quarterly* 17, no. 2 (2000): 161–80.

Bhabha, Homi. *The Location of Culture*. New York: Routledge, 1994.
Boas, Franz. *The Mind of Primitive Man*. New York: Macmillan, 1911.
Bonilla-Silva, Eduardo. *Racism without Racists: Color-Blind Racism and the Persistence of Racial Inequality in the United States*. 2nd ed. Lanham, MD: Rowman and Littlefield, 2006.
Boyer, LaNada. "Growing Up in E'da How—One Idaho Girlhood." In *The Schooling of Native America*, edited by Thomas Thompson, 29–42. Washington, DC: American Association of Colleges for Teacher Education, 1978.
———. "Reflections of Alcatraz." In *American Indian Activism: Alcatraz to the Longest Walk*, edited by Troy Johnson, Joane Nagel, and Duane Champagne, 88–103. Urbana: University of Illinois Press, 1997.
Brief of Amicus Curiae Fred Korematsu in Support of Petitioners. *Rasul v. Bush*. 542 U.S. 466 (2003).
Brief of Amicus Curiae Fred Korematsu, the Bar Association of San Francisco, the Asian Law Caucus, the Asian American Bar Association of the Greater Bay Area, Asian Pacific Islander Legal Outreach, and the Japanese American Citizens League in Support of Respondents. *Rumsfeld v. Padilla*. 542 U.S. 426 (2003).
Brodkin, Karen. *How Jews Became White Folks and What That Says about Race in America*. New Brunswick, NJ: Rutgers University Press, 1998.
Brown, Wendy. *Edgework: Critical Essays on Knowledge and Politics*. Princeton, NJ: Princeton University Press, 2005.
———. *Regulating Aversion: Tolerance in the Age of Identity and Empire*. Princeton, NJ: Princeton University Press, 2006.
———. *States of Injury: Power and Freedom in Late Modernity*. Princeton, NJ: Princeton University Press, 1995.
———. *Undoing the Demos: Neoliberalism's Stealth Revolution*. New York: Zone, 2015.
Brown v. Board of Education. 347 U.S. 483 (1954).
Bruyneel, Kevin. *The Third Space of Sovereignty: The Postcolonial Politics of U.S.-Indigenous Relations*. Minneapolis: University of Minnesota Press, 2007.
Carmichael, Stokely, and Charles Hamilton. *Black Power: The Politics of Liberation in America*. New York: Random House, 1967.
Cash, W. J. *The Mind of the South*. New York: Alfred A. Knopf, 1941.
Cass, Lewis. "Removal of the Indians." *North American Review* 30 (1830): 62–121.
Champagne, Duane. *Social Order and Political Change: Constitutional Governments among the Cherokee, the Choctaw, the Chickasaw, and the Creek*. Stanford, CA: Stanford University Press, 1992.
Chan, Sucheng. *Asian Americans: An Interpretive History*. Boston: Twayne, 1991.
Chang, Robert. "Toward an Asian American Legal Scholarship: Critical Race Theory, Post-Structuralism, and Narrative Space." *California Law Review* 81, no. 5 (1993): 1241–1323.
Cherokee Nation v. Georgia. 30 U.S. 1 (1831).
Chinese Exclusion Repeal Act of 1943. 57 Stat. 600 (1943).
Chuh, Kandice. *Imagine Otherwise: On Asian Americanist Critique*. Durham, NC: Duke University Press, 2003.
Civil Rights Congress. *We Charge Genocide: The Historic Petition to the United Nations for Relief from a Crime of the United States Government against the Negro People*. New York: Civil Rights Congress, 1951.

"Civilizing the White Man." *American Indian* 1, no. 4 (1970): 2.

Clinton, Robert, Carole Goldberg, and Rebecca Tsosie. *American Indian Law: Native Nations and the Federal System*. 4th ed. Newark, NJ: LexisNexis, 2003.

Coates, Ta-Nehisi. *Between the World and Me*. New York: Random House, 2015.

Collet, Christian, and Pei-Te Lien, eds. *The Transnational Politics of Asian Americans*. Philadelphia: Temple University Press, 2009.

Commission on Wartime Relocation and Internment of Civilians. *Personal Justice Denied: Report of the Commission on Wartime Relocation and Internment of Civilians*. Washington, DC: Government Printing Office, 1982.

Constitution of the Cherokee Nation. July 24, 1827, New Town Echota. *Tennessee Documentary History, 1796–1850*. Accessed April 18, 2017. http://diglib.lib.utk.edu/cgi/t/text/text-idx?c=tdh;cc=tdh;sid=70c00e216e581ff6c26c8d8237ad1425;q1=cherokee%20nation;rgn=main;view=text;idno=tl217.

Cornell, Stephen. *The Return of the Native: American Indian Political Resurgence*. Oxford, UK: Oxford University Press, 1988.

Cotterill, R. S. *The Southern Indians: The Story of the Civilized Tribes before Removal*. Norman: University of Oklahoma Press, 1954.

Coulthard, Glen. *Red Skins, White Masks: Rejecting the Colonial Politics of Recognition*. Minneapolis: University of Minnesota Press, 2014.

Dahl, Adam. "Nullifying Settler Democracy: William Apess and the Paradox of Settler Sovereignty." *Polity* 48, no. 2 (2016): 279–304.

Daniels, Roger. *Asian America: Chinese and Japanese in the United States since 1850*. Seattle: University of Washington Press, 1988.

———. *Concentration Camps: North America; Japanese in the United States and Canada during World War II*. Rev. ed. Malabar, FL: Krieger, 1993.

———. *The Decision to Relocate the Japanese Americans*. Reprint ed. Malabar, FL: Krieger, 1986.

———. *Prisoners without Trial: Japanese Americans in World War II*. New York: Hill and Wang, 1993.

Dawson, Michael. *Black Visions: The Roots of Contemporary African-American Political Ideologies*. Chicago: University of Chicago Press, 2001.

Day, Richard. *Gramsci Is Dead: Anarchist Currents in the Newest Social Movements*. London: Pluto, 2005.

De Genova, Nicolas. *Working the Boundaries: Race, Space, and "Illegality" in Mexican Chicago*. Durham, NC: Duke University Press, 2005.

Dean, Jodi. *Democracy and Other Neoliberal Fantasies: Communicative Capitalism and Left Politics*. Durham, NC: Duke University Press, 2009.

Del Sol, Liz. "Finding Our Common Interests: Personal Reflections about the Asian Movement." In *Asian Americans: The Movement and the Moment*, edited by Steve Louie and Glenn Omatsu, 138–47. Los Angeles: UCLA Asian American Studies Center, 2000.

Delgado, Richard, and Jean Stefancic. *Critical Race Theory: An Introduction*. New York: New York University Press, 2001.

Deloria Jr., Vine. *Custer Died for Your Sins: An Indian Manifesto*. Rev. ed. New York: Macmillan, 1988.

Department of the Interior. "History of Interior." *U.S. Department of the Interior*. Accessed May 1, 2017. http://www.doi.gov/whoweare/history.cfm.

DeWitt, John. *Japanese Evacuation from the West Coast, 1942: Final Report.* Washington, DC: Government Printing Office, 1943.
Disch, Lisa. "More Truth Than Fact: Storytelling as Critical Understanding in the Writings of Hannah Arendt." *Political Theory* 21, no. 4 (1993): 665–94.
Dovi, Suzanne. "Preferable Descriptive Representatives: Will Just Any Woman, Black, or Latino Do?" *American Political Science Review* 96, no. 4 (2002): 745–54.
Dower, John. *War without Mercy: Race and Power in the Pacific War.* New York: Pantheon, 1986.
Drinnon, Richard. *Keeper of Concentration Camps: Dillon S. Myer and American Racism.* Berkeley: University of California Press, 1987.
Du Bois, W.E.B. *Black Reconstruction in America.* New York: Atheneum, 1992.
———. *The Souls of Black Folk.* New York: Dover, 1994.
Dussel, Enrique. *Twenty Theses on Politics.* Translated by George Ciccariello-Maher. Durham, NC: Duke University Press, 2008.
Duus, Masayo Umezawa. *Unlikely Liberators: The Men of the 100th and 442nd.* Translated by Peter Duus. Honolulu: University of Hawaii Press, 1987.
Elazar, Daniel. *American Federalism: A View from the States.* 3rd ed. New York: Harper and Row, 1984.
———. "Civil War and the Preservation of American Federalism." *Publius* 1, no. 1 (1971): 39–58.
Erlenbusch, Verena. "The Place of Sovereignty: Mapping Power with Agamben, Butler, and Foucault." *Critical Horizons* 14, no. 1 (2013): 44–69.
Espiritu, Augusto. "Journeys of Discovery and Difference: Transnational Politics and the Union of Democratic Filipinos." In *The Transnational Politics of Asian Americans*, edited by Christian Collet and Pei-te Lien, 38–55. Philadelphia: Temple University Press, 2009.
Espiritu, Yen Le. *Asian American Panethnicity: Bridging Institutions and Identities.* Philadelphia: Temple University Press, 1992.
Ex Parte Endo. 323 U.S. 283 (1944).
Executive Order 9066 of February 19, 1942, Authorizing the Secretary of War to Prescribe Military Areas. *Our Documents.* Accessed April 21, 2017. https://www.ourdocuments.gov/doc.php?doc=74&page=transcript.
Fanon, Frantz. *Black Skins, White Masks.* Translated by Richard Philcox. New York: Grove, 2008.
———. *A Dying Colonialism.* Translated by Haakon Chevalier. New York: Grove, 1965.
———. *The Wretched of the Earth.* Translated by Richard Philcox. New York: Grove, 2004.
Farrand, Max, ed. *Records of the Federal Convention of 1787.* 4 vols. Rev. ed. New Haven, CT: Yale University Press, 1966.
Ferguson, Edwin, and Philip Glick. *Legal and Constitutional Phases of the WRA Program.* Washington, DC: Government Printing Office, 1946.
Fiorina, Morris, Samuel Abrams, and Jeremy Pope. *Culture War? The Myth of a Polarized America.* 3rd ed. Boston: Longman, 2011.
Fisher v. University of Texas. 579 U.S. ___ (2016).
Fong, Edmund. "Beyond the Racial Exceptionalism of the Japanese Internment." *Politics, Groups, and Identities* 1, no. 2 (2013): 239–43.

Foreman, Grant. *Indian Removal: The Emigration of the Five Civilized Tribes of Indians.* Rev. ed. Norman: University of Oklahoma Press, 1953.

Fortunate Eagle, Adam (Nordwall). "Urban Indians and the Occupation of Alcatraz Island." In *American Indian Activism: Alcatraz to the Longest Walk*, edited by Troy Johnson, Joane Nagel, and Duane Champagne, 52–73. Urbana: University of Illinois Press, 1997.

Fortunate Eagle, Adam, with Tim Findley. *Heart of the Rock: The Indian Invasion of Alcatraz.* Norman: University of Oklahoma Press, 2002.

Foucault, Michel. *The History of Sexuality: An Introduction.* Vol. I. Translated by Robert Hurley. New York: Vintage, 1990.

———. *"Society Must Be Defended": Lectures at the Collège de France, 1975–76.* Translated by David Macey. New York: Picador, 2003.

Frank, Jason. *Constituent Moments: Enacting the People in Postrevolutionary America.* Durham, NC: Duke University Press, 2010.

Fraser, Nancy. *Justice Interruptus: Critical Reflections on the "Postsocialist" Condition.* New York: Routledge, 1997.

Freud, Sigmund. *The Interpretation of Dreams.* Translated by James Strachey. New York: Avon, 1998.

Gadamer, Hans-Georg. *Reason in the Age of Science.* Translated by Frederick Lawrence. Cambridge, MA: MIT Press, 1983.

Gallie, W. B. "Essentially Contested Concepts." *Proceedings of the Aristotelian Society* 56 (1955–1956): 167–98.

Gilmore, Ruth Wilson. *Golden Gulag: Prisons, Surplus, Crisis, and Opposition in Globalizing California.* Berkeley: University of California Press, 2007.

Gilroy, Paul. *Against Race: Imagining Political Culture beyond the Color Line.* Cambridge, MA: Harvard University Press, 2000.

Gines, Kathryn. *Hannah Arendt and the Negro Question.* Bloomington: Indiana University Press, 2014.

Glenn, Evelyn Nakano. *Unequal Freedom: How Race and Gender Shaped American Citizenship and Labor.* Cambridge, MA: Harvard University Press, 2002.

Goldberg, David Theo. *The Racial State.* Oxford, UK: Blackwell, 2002.

———. *Racist Culture: Philosophy and the Politics of Meaning.* Oxford, UK: Blackwell, 1993.

Gonzales, Alfonso. *Reform without Justice: Latino Migrant Politics and the Homeland Security State.* Oxford, UK: Oxford University Press, 2014.

Gordon, Jane. *Creolizing Political Theory: Reading Rousseau through Fanon.* New York: Fordham University Press, 2014.

———. *Why They Couldn't Wait: A Critique of Black-Jewish Conflict over Community Control in Ocean Hill-Brownsville (1967–1971).* New York: Routledge, 2001.

Gordon, Jane, and Lewis Gordon. *Of Divine Warning: Reading Disaster in the Modern Age.* Boulder, CO: Paradigm, 2009.

Gordon, Lewis. *Fanon and the Crisis of European Man: An Essay on Philosophy and the Human Sciences.* New York: Routledge, 1995.

Gossett, Thomas. *Race: The History of an Idea in America.* New ed. Oxford, UK: Oxford University Press, 1997.

Graham, Hugh Davis. *The Civil Rights Era: Origins and Developments of National Policy, 1960–1972*. Oxford, UK: Oxford University Press, 1990.
Gramsci, Antonio. *Selections from the Prison Notebooks*. Translated by Quintin Hoare and Geoffrey Nowell Smith. New York: International, 1971.
Gratz v. Bollinger. 539 U.S. 244 (2003).
Green, Michael, and Theda Perdue. *The Columbia Guide to American Indians of the Southeast*. New York: Columbia University Press, 2001.
Grutter v. Bollinger. 539 U.S. 306 (2003).
Guardiola-Rivera, Oscar. *What If Latin America Ruled the World? How the South Will Take the North through the 21st Century*. New York: Bloomsbury, 2010.
Guidry, John, and Mark Sawyer. "Contentious Pluralism: The Public Sphere and Democracy." *Perspectives on Politics* 1, no. 2 (2003): 273–89.
Habal, Estella. "How I Became a Revolutionary." In *Legacy to Liberation: Politics and Culture of Revolutionary Asian Pacific America*, edited by Fred Ho, Carolyn Antonio, Diane Fujino, and Steve Yip, 197–210. Edinburgh, UK: AK, 2000.
———. *San Francisco's International Hotel: Mobilizing the Filipino American Community in the Anti-Eviction Movement*. Philadelphia: Temple University Press, 2007.
Hagan, William. *American Indians*. 3rd ed. Chicago: University of Chicago Press, 1993.
Hall, Stuart. *Race: The Floating Signifier*, DVD. Directed by Sut Jally. Northampton, MA: Media Education Foundation, 1997.
Hamilton, Alexander, John Jay, and James Madison. *The Federalist Papers*. Edited by Clinton Rossiter. New York: Signet, 1999.
Hanchard, Michael. *Orpheus and Power: The "Movimento Negro" of Rio de Janeiro and São Paulo, Brazil, 1945–1988*. Princeton, NJ: Princeton University Press, 1994.
———. *Party/Politics: Horizons in Black Political Thought*. Oxford, UK: Oxford University Press, 2006.
Hancock, Ange-Marie. *Solidarity Politics for Millennials: A Guide to Ending the Oppression Olympics*. New York: Palgrave Macmillan, 2011.
Haney López, Ian. *Dog Whistle Politics: How Coded Racial Appeals Have Reinvented Racism & Wrecked the Middle Class*. Oxford, UK: Oxford University Press, 2014.
———. *Racism on Trial: The Chicano Fight for Justice*. Cambridge, MA: Harvard University Press, 2003.
———. *White by Law: The Legal Construction of Race*. Rev. ed. New York: New York University Press, 2006.
Hannaford, Ivan. *Race: The History of an Idea in the West*. Baltimore, MD: Johns Hopkins University Press, 1996.
Harding, Vincent. *There Is a River: The Black Struggle for Freedom in America*. New York: Harcourt Brace Jovanovich, 1981.
Hardt, Michael, and Antonio Negri. *Empire*. Cambridge, MA: Harvard University Press, 2000.
Harris, Cheryl. "Whiteness as Property." In *Critical Race Theory: The Key Writings That Formed the Movement*, edited by Kimberlé Crenshaw, Neil Gotanda, Gary Peller, and Kendall Thomas, 276–91. New York: New Press, 1995.
Hauptmann, Emily. "A Local History of 'the Political.'" *Political Theory* 32, no. 1 (2009): 34–60.

Hayashi, Brian Masaru. *Democratizing the Enemy: The Japanese American Internment.* Princeton, NJ: Princeton University Press, 2004.
Hayek, F. A. *The Road to Serfdom: The Definitive Edition.* Chicago: University of Chicago Press, 2007.
Hegel, G.W.F. *Phenomenology of the Spirit.* Translated by A. V. Miller. Oxford, UK: Oxford University Press, 1977.
Heiner, Brady. "Foucault and the Black Panthers." *City* 11, no. 3 (2007): 313–56.
Him Mark Lai Research Files (collection AAS ARC 2010/1). Ethnic Studies Library. University of California, Berkeley.
Hirabayashi, Lane. "Incarceration." In *Keywords for Asian American Studies*, edited by Cathy Schlund-Vials, Linda Trinh Võ, and K. Scott Wong, 133–38. New York: New York University Press, 2015.
Hirabayashi v. United States. 320 U.S. 81 (1943).
Ho, Fred. "Fists for Revolution: The Revolutionary History of I Wor Kuen/League of Revolutionary Struggle." In *Legacy to Liberation: Politics and Culture of Revolutionary Asian Pacific America*, edited by Fred Ho, Carolyn Antonio, Diane Fujino, and Steve Yip, 3–14. Edinburgh, UK: AK, 2000.
———. *Wicked Theory, Naked Practice: A Fred Ho Reader.* Edited by Diane Fujino. Minneapolis: University of Minnesota Press, 2009.
Ho, Fred, Carolyn Antonio, Diane Fujino, and Steve Yip, eds. *Legacy to Liberation: Politics and Culture of Revolutionary Asian Pacific America.* Edinburgh, UK: AK, 2000.
Hobbes, Thomas. *Leviathan.* Cambridge: Cambridge University Press, 1996.
Hollinger, David. *Postethnic America: Beyond Multiculturalism.* Rev. ed. New York: Basic, 2000.
Honig, Bonnie. *Democracy and the Foreigner.* Princeton, NJ: Princeton University Press, 2001.
———. *Emergency Politics: Paradox, Law, Democracy.* Princeton, NJ: Princeton University Press, 2009.
———. *Political Theory and the Displacement of Politics.* Ithaca, NY: Cornell University Press, 1993.
Hooker, Juliet. "The Paradoxes of U.S. Black Politics: From Democratic Sacrifice to Democratic Repair." *Political Theory* 44, no. 4 (2016): 448–69.
———. *Race and the Politics of Solidarity.* Oxford, UK: Oxford University Press, 2009.
Horsman, Reginald. *Race and Manifest Destiny: The Origins of American Racial Anglo-Saxonism.* Cambridge, MA: Harvard University Press, 1981.
"How to Tell Your Friends from the Japs." *Time*, December 22, 1941.
Hudson, Charles. *The Southeastern Indians.* Knoxville: University of Tennessee Press, 1976.
Ignatiev, Noel. *How the Irish Became White.* New York: Routledge, 1995.
Indian Removal Act of 1830. 4 Stat. 411 (1830).
Jackson, Andrew. "Farewell Address, March 4, 1837." *American Presidency Project.* University of California, Santa Barbara. Accessed April 18, 2017. http://www.presidency.ucsb.edu/ws/?pid=67087.
James, C.L.R. *The Black Jacobins: Toussaint L'Ouverture and the San Domingo Revolution.* Rev. ed. New York: Vintage, 1989.

Japanese American Research Project (Collection 2010). Department of Special Collections, Young Research Library. University of California, Los Angeles.

Jefferson, Thomas. *Notes on the State of Virginia*. Chapel Hill: University of North Carolina Press, 1955.

Johnson, Troy. *The Occupation of Alcatraz Island: Indian Self-Determination and the Rise of Indian Activism*. Urbana: University of Illinois Press, 1996.

Johnson, Troy, Joane Nagel, and Duane Champagne, eds. *American Indian Activism: Alcatraz to the Longest Walk*. Urbana: University of Illinois Press, 1997.

Johnson v. McIntosh. 21 U.S. 543 (1823).

Jordan, Winthrop. *White over Black: American Attitudes toward the Negro, 1550–1812*. Chapel Hill: University of North Carolina Press, 1968.

Josephy, Alvin, Joane Nagel, and Troy Johnson, eds. *Red Power: The American Indians' Fight for Freedom*. 2nd ed. Lincoln: University of Nebraska Press, 1999.

Jurkevics, Anna. "Hannah Arendt Reads Carl Schmitt's *The Nomos of the Earth*: A Dialogue on Law and Geopolitics from the Margins." *European Journal of Political Theory* 16, no. 3 (2017): 345–66.

Kalyvas, Andreas. *Democracy and the Politics of the Extraordinary: Max Weber, Carl Schmitt, and Hannah Arendt*. Cambridge: Cambridge University Press, 2008.

Kant, Immanuel. *Critique of Judgment*. Translated by Werner Pluhar. Indianapolis: Hackett, 1987.

Kateb, George. *Hannah Arendt: Politics, Conscience, Evil*. Oxford, UK: Martin Robinson, 1984.

Kelley, Robin. *Freedom Dreams: The Black Radical Imagination*. Boston: Beacon, 2002.

Kierkegaard, Søren. *Fear and Trembling/Repetition*. Translated by Howard Hong and Edna Hong. Princeton, NJ: Princeton University Press, 1983.

Kilian, Norbert. "New Wines in Old Skins? American Definitions of Empire and the Emergence of a New Concept." In *Theories of Empire, 1450–1800*, edited by David Armitage, 307–24. Aldershot, UK: Ashgate, 1998.

Kim, Claire. *Bitter Fruit: The Politics of Black-Korean Conflict in New York City*. New Haven, CT: Yale University Press, 2000.

———. "The Racial Triangulation of Asian Americans." *Politics and Society* 27, no. 1 (1999): 105–38.

———. "Unyielding Positions: A Critique of the 'Race' Debate." *Ethnicities* 4, no. 3 (2004): 337–55.

Kim, Thomas. *The Racial Logic of Politics: Asian Americans and Party Competition*. Philadelphia: Temple University Press, 2007.

King, Desmond. *Making Americans: Immigration, Race, and the Origins of the Diverse Democracy*. Cambridge, MA: Harvard University Press, 2000.

King, Desmond, and Rogers Smith. "Racial Orders in American Political Development." *American Political Science Review* 99, no. 1 (2005): 75–92.

———. "'Without Regard for Race': Critical Ideational Development in Modern American Politics." *Journal of Politics* 76, no. 4 (2014): 958–71.

King Jr., Martin Luther. *Why We Can't Wait*. New York: Penguin, 1964.

Klein, Steven. "'Fit to Enter the World': Hannah Arendt on Politics, Economics, and the Welfare State." *American Political Science Review* 108, no. 4 (2014): 856–69.

Kordziel, Beverly. "To Be Part of the People: The International Hotel Collective." In *Asian Americans: The Movement and the Moment*, edited by Steve Louie and Glenn Omatsu, 240–47. Los Angeles: UCLA Asian American Studies Center, 2000.

Korematsu v. United States. 323 U.S. 214 (1944).

Laclau, Ernesto. *On Populist Reason*. London: Verso, 2005.

Laclau, Ernesto, and Chantal Mouffe. *Hegemony and Socialist Strategy: Towards a Radical Democratic Politics*. Rev. ed. London: Verso, 2001.

Le Bon, Gustave. *The Crowd: A Study of the Popular Mind*. London: T. Fischer Unwin, 1903.

Lea, Homer. *The Valor of Ignorance*. New York: Harper and Brothers, 1909.

Lee, Erika. *The Making of Asian America: A History*. New York: Simon and Schuster, 2015.

Lee, Fred. "Fantasies of Asian American Kinship Disrupted: Identification and Disidentification in Michael Kang's *The Motel*." *Critical Philosophy of Race* 4, no. 1 (2016): 6–29.

———. "The Japanese Internment and the Racial State of Exception." *Theory & Event* 10, no. 1 (2007). Accessed April 18, 2017. https://muse.jhu.edu/article/213866.

———. "Post-Naturalistic Racialization in the 'Post-Racial' United States: The Shifting rather than Declining Significance of Race." *Theory & Event* 20, no. 3 (2017): 653–78.

———. "Reconsidering the Jefferson-Hemings Relationship: Nationalist Historiography without Nationalist Heroes, Racial Sexuality without Racial Significance." *Political Research Quarterly* 66, no. 3 (2013): 500–515.

Lee, Robert. *Orientals: Asian Americans in Popular Culture*. Philadelphia: Temple University Press, 1999.

Lefort, Claude. *Democracy and Political Theory*. Translated by David Macey. Cambridge: Polity, 1988.

———. *The Political Forms of Modern Society: Bureaucracy, Democracy, Totalitarianism*. Cambridge: Polity, 1986.

Locke, Jill. "Little Rock's Social Question: Reading Arendt on School Desegregation and Social Climbing." *Political Theory* 41, no. 4 (2013): 533–61.

Locke, John. *Two Treatises of Government*. Cambridge: Cambridge University Press, 1988.

Louie, Steve, and Glenn Omatsu, eds. *Asian Americans: The Movement and the Moment*. Los Angeles: UCLA Asian American Studies Center, 2000.

Lowe, Lisa. *Immigrant Acts: On Asian American Cultural Politics*. Durham, NC: Duke University Press, 1996.

———. *The Intimacies of Four Continents*. Durham, NC: Duke University Press, 2015.

Lupton, Julia. "Shylock between Exception and Emancipation: Shakespeare, Schmitt, Arendt." *Journal for Cultural and Religious Theory* 8, no. 3 (2007): 42–53.

Machiavelli, Niccolò. *Discourses on Livy*. Translated by Harvey Mansfield and Nathan Tarcov. Chicago: University of Chicago Press, 1996.

Maeda, Daryl. *Chains of Babylon: The Rise of Asian America*. Minneapolis: University of Minnesota Press, 2009.

Magliocca, Gerard. *Andrew Jackson and the Constitution: The Rise and Fall of Generational Regimes*. Lawrence: University of Kansas Press, 2007.

Mahmood, Saba. *Politics of Piety: The Islamic Revival and the Feminist Subject.* Princeton, NJ: Princeton University Press, 2004.

Malkin, Michelle. *In Defense of Internment: The Case for "Racial Profiling" in World War II and the War on Terror.* Washington, DC: Regnery, 2004.

Manzanar War Relocation Center Records (Collection 122). Department of Special Collections, Young Research Library. University of California, Los Angeles.

Mao Tsetung. *Five Essays on Philosophy.* Peking: Foreign Languages, 1977.

Mao Zedong. "A New Storm Against Imperialism." *Peking Review,* April 19, 1968.

Marable, Manning. *Malcolm X: A Life of Reinvention.* New York: Penguin, 2011.

———. *Race, Reform, and Rebellion: The Second Reconstruction and Beyond in Black America, 1945–2006.* 3rd ed. Jackson: University of Mississippi Press, 2007.

Markell, Patchen. *Bound by Recognition.* Princeton, NJ: Princeton University Press, 2003.

———. "The Rule of the People: Arendt, *Archê,* and Democracy." *American Political Science Review* 100, no. 1 (2006): 1–14.

Marshall, T. H. *Class, Citizenship, and Social Development.* Westport, CT: Greenwood, 1973.

Marx, Anthony. *Making Race and Nation: A Comparison of South Africa, the United States, and Brazil.* Cambridge: Cambridge University Press, 1998.

Marx, Karl. *Capital: A Critique of Political Economy.* Vol. I. Translated by Ben Fowkes. New York: Penguin, 1976.

———. "On the Jewish Question." In *The Marx-Engels Reader,* edited by Robert Tucker, 26–52. New York: Norton, 1978.

Matthewson, Tim. "Jefferson and the Non-Recognition of Haiti." *Proceedings of the American Philosophical Society* 140, no. 1 (1996): 22–48.

Mbembe, Achille. "Necropolitics." *Public Culture* 15, no. 1 (2003): 11–40.

McAdam, Doug. *Political Process and the Development of Black Insurgency, 1930–1970.* Chicago: University of Chicago Press, 1982.

McCarthy, Thomas. *Race, Empire, and the Idea of Human Development.* Cambridge: Cambridge University Press, 2009.

McClure, Kirstie. "The Odor of Judgment: Exemplarity, Propriety, and Politics in the Company of Hannah Arendt." In *Hannah Arendt and the Meaning of Politics,* edited by Craig Calhoun and John McGowan, 53–84. Minneapolis: University of Minnesota Press, 1997.

———. "On the Subject of Rights: Pluralism, Plurality and Political Identity." In *Dimensions of Radical Democracy: Pluralism, Citizenship, Community,* edited by Chantal Mouffe, 108–27. London: Verso, 1992.

———. "The Social Question, Again." *Graduate Faculty Philosophy Journal* 28, no. 1 (2007): 85–113.

McCormick, John. *Carl Schmitt's Critique of Liberalism: Against Politics as Technology.* Cambridge: Cambridge University Press, 1997.

McWhorter, Ladelle. *Racism and Sexual Oppression in Anglo-America: A Genealogy.* Bloomington: Indiana University Press, 2009.

McWilliams, Carey. *Prejudice: Japanese Americans, Symbols of Racial Intolerance.* Boston: Little, Brown, 1944.

Melamed, Jodi. "The Spirit of Neoliberalism: From Racial Liberalism to Neoliberal Multiculturalism." *Social Text* 24, no. 4 (2006): 1–24.

Melendez, Miguel. *We Took to the Streets: Fighting for Latino Rights with the Young Lords*. New Brunswick. NJ: Rutgers University Press, 2003.

Mills, Charles. *From Race to Class: Essays in White Marxism and Black Radicalism*. Lanham, MD: Rowman and Littlefield, 2003.

———. *The Racial Contract*. Ithaca, NY: Cornell University Press, 1997.

Mills, Charles, and Carole Pateman. *Contract and Domination*. Cambridge: Polity, 2007.

"Mimic." Cartoon. *Washington Post*, July 1, 1942.

"Monroe Doctrine." *Annals of Congress*, 18th Cong., 1st sess., 11–24.

Morgan, Edmund. *American Slavery, American Freedom: The Ordeal of Colonial Virginia*. New York: Norton, 1975.

———. "Slavery and Freedom: The American Paradox." *Journal of American History* 59, no. 1 (1972): 5–29.

Morris, Aldon. *The Origins of the Civil Rights Movement: Black Communities Organizing for Change*. New York: Free Press, 1984.

Moruzzi, Norma Claire. *Speaking through the Mask: Hannah Arendt and the Politics of Social Identity*. Ithaca, NY: Cornell University Press, 2000.

Mott, Wesley. "The Rhetoric of Martin Luther King Jr.: Letter from Birmingham Jail." *Pylon* 36, no. 4 (1975): 411–21.

Mouffe, Chantal. *Agonistics: Thinking the World Politically*. London: Verso, 2013.

———. "Carl Schmitt and the Paradox of Liberal Democracy." In *The Challenge of Carl Schmitt*, edited by Chantal Mouffe, 38–53. London: Verso, 1999.

———. *The Democratic Paradox*. London: Verso, 2000.

———. *On the Political*. London: Routledge, 2005.

———. *The Return of the Political*. Rev. ed. London: Verso, 2005.

Muñoz, Carlos. *Youth, Identity, Power: The Chicano Movement*. Rev. ed. London: Verso, 2007.

Muñoz, José Esteban. *Disidentifications: Queers of Color and the Performance of Politics*. Minneapolis: University of Minnesota Press, 1999.

Nagel, Joane. *American Indian Ethnic Renewal: Red Power and the Resurgence of Identity and Culture*. Oxford, UK: Oxford University Press, 1996.

Nakanishi, Don. "Foreword." In *The Transnational Politics of Asian Americans*, edited by Christian Collet and Pei-te Lien, ix–xiv. Philadelphia: Temple University Press, 2009.

"National 'Indian' Park Planned for Alcatraz, Indians Angry." *American Indian* 1, no. 5 (1970): 1–2.

Naturalization Act of 1790. 1 Stat. 103 (1790).

Naturalization Act of 1870. 16 Stat. 254 (1870).

Ngai, Mae. *Impossible Subjects: Illegal Aliens and the Making of Modern America*. Princeton, NJ: Princeton University Press, 2004.

Nichols, Robert. "Indigeneity and the Settler Contract Today." *Philosophy and Social Criticism* 39, no. 2 (2013): 165–86.

Nobles, Melissa. *Shades of Citizenship: Race and the Census in Modern Politics*. Stanford, CA: Stanford University Press, 2000.

Norton, Anne. *Alternative Americas: A Reading of Antebellum Political Culture*. Chicago: University of Chicago Press, 1986.

Nyugen, Viet Thanh. "Remembering War, Dreaming Peace: On Cosmopolitanism, Compassion, and Literature." *Japanese Journal of American Studies* 20 (2009): 149-74.
O'Brien, Robert. *The College Nisei*. Palo Alto, CA: Pacific, 1949.
Ojakangas, Mika. *A Philosophy of Concrete Life: Carl Schmitt and the Political Thought of Late Modernity*. 2nd ed. Bern, CH: Peter Lang, 2006.
Okihiro, Gary. *Cane Fires: The Anti-Japanese Movement in Hawaii, 1865-1945*. Philadelphia: Temple University Press, 1991.
———. *The Columbia Guide to Asian American History*. New York: Columbia University Press, 2001.
———. *Margins and Mainstreams: Asians in American History and Culture*. Seattle: University of Washington Press, 1994.
———. "Religion and Resistance in America's Concentration Camps." *Phylon* 45, no. 3 (1984): 220-33.
———. *Storied Lives: Japanese American Students and World War II*. Seattle: University of Washington Press, 1999.
———. "Tule Lake under Martial Law: A Study in Japanese Resistance." *Journal of Ethnic Studies* 5, no. 3 (1977): 71-85.
Olson, Joel. *The Abolition of White Democracy*. Minneapolis: University of Minnesota Press, 2004.
Omi, Michael, and Howard Winant. *Racial Formation in the United States*. 3rd ed. New York: Routledge, 2015.
Onuf, Peter. "'To Declare Them a Free and Independent People': Race, Slavery, and National Identity in Jefferson's Thought." *Journal of the Early Republic* 18, no. 1 (1998): 1-46.
Orren, Karen, and Stephen Skowronek. *The Search for American Political Development*. Cambridge: Cambridge University Press, 2004.
Ortega y Gasset, José. *Revolt of the Masses*. New York: Norton, 1960.
Ozawa, Takao. "Naturalization of a Japanese Subject." Japanese American Research Project (Collection 2010, Reel 39). Department of Special Collections, Young Research Library. University of California, Los Angeles.
Ozawa v. United States. 260 U.S. 178 (1922).
Parekh, Serena. *Hannah Arendt and the Challenge of Modernity: A Phenomenology of Human Rights*. New York: Routledge, 2008.
Pateman, Carole. *The Sexual Contract*. Stanford: Stanford University Press, 1988.
Patterson, Orlando. *Slavery and Social Death: A Comparative Study*. Cambridge, MA: Harvard University Press, 1982.
Pierson, Paul. *Politics in Time: History, Institutions, and Social Analysis*. Princeton, NJ: Princeton University Press, 2004.
Pitkin, Hannah. *The Attack of the Blob: Hannah Arendt's Concept of the Social*. Chicago: University of Chicago Press, 1998.
———. *The Concept of Representation*. Berkeley: University of California Press, 1967.
Plato. *The Republic*. Translated by Tom Griffith. Cambridge: Cambridge University Press, 2000.
Plessy v. Ferguson. 163 U.S. 537 (1896).
Prashad, Vijay. *The Karma of Brown Folk*. Minneapolis: University of Minnesota Press, 2000.

Prewitt, Kenneth. "Immigrants and the Changing Categories of Race." In *Transforming Politics, Transforming America*, edited by Taeku Lee, S. Karthick Ramakrishnan, and Ricardo Ramirez, 19–31. Charlottesville: University of Virginia Press, 2006.
Prucha, Francis. *American Indian Treaties: The History of a Political Anomaly*. Berkeley: University of California Press, 1994.
———, ed. *Documents of United States Indian Policy*. 3rd ed. Lincoln: University of Nebraska Press, 2000.
———. *The Great Father: The United States Government and the American Indians*. Vol. I. Lincoln: University of Nebraska Press, 1984.
Public Law 503 of 1942. 56 Stat. 173 (1942).
Public Law 405 of 1944. 58 Stat. 677 (1944).
Pulido, Laura. *Black, Brown, Yellow, and Left: Radical Activism in Los Angeles*. Berkeley: University of California Press, 2006.
Rancière, Jacques. *Disagreement: Politics and Philosophy*. Translated by Julie Rose. Minneapolis: University of Minnesota Press, 1999.
Rasch, William. "Human Rights as Geopolitics: Carl Schmitt and the Legal Form of American Supremacy." *Cultural Critique* 54 (2003): 120–47.
———. *Sovereignty and Its Discontents: On the Primacy of Conflict and the Structure of the Political*. London: Birkbeck Law, 2004.
Renteln, Alison Dundes. "A Psychohistorical Analysis of the Japanese American Internment." *Human Rights Quarterly* 17, no. 4 (1995): 618–48.
Ricoeur, Paul. *Time and Narrative*. Vol. I. Translated by Kathleen McLaughlin and David Pellauer. Chicago: University of Chicago Press, 1984.
Robinson, Donald. *Slavery in the Structure of American Politics, 1765–1820*. New York: Harcourt Brace Jovanovich, 1970.
Robinson, Greg. *By Order of the President: FDR and the Internment of Japanese Americans*. Cambridge, MA: Harvard University Press, 2001.
Rogin, Michael. *Fathers and Children: Andrew Jackson and the Subjugation of the American Indian*. New York: Alfred A. Knopf, 1975.
Rosanvallon, Pierre. *Democracy Past and Future*. Edited by Samuel Moyn. New York: Columbia University Press, 2006.
Rosen, Deborah. *American Indians and State Law: Sovereignty, Race, and Citizenship, 1790–1880*. Lincoln: University of Nebraska Press, 2007.
Rossiter, Clinton. *Constitutional Dictatorship: Crisis Government in the Modern Democracies*. Rev. ed. New York: Harcourt, Brace and World, 1963.
Saito, Leland. *Race and Politics: Asian Americans, Latinos, and Whites in a Los Angeles Suburb*. Urbana: University of Illinois Press, 1998.
Saito, Natsu Taylor. "Symbolism under Siege: Japanese American Redress and the 'Racing' of Arab Americans as 'Terrorists.'" *Asian Law Journal* 8, no. 1 (2001): 1–29.
Saranillio, Dean Itsuji. "Why Asian Settler Colonialism Matters: A Thought Piece on Critiques, Debates, and Indigenous Difference." *Settler Colonial Studies* 3, no. 3–4 (2013): 280–94.
Satz, Ronald. *American Indian Policy in the Jacksonian Era*. Lincoln: University of Nebraska Press, 1975.
Sawyer, Mark. *Racial Politics in Post-Revolutionary Cuba*. Cambridge: Cambridge University Press, 2006.

Schmitt, Carl. "The Age of Neutralizations and Depoliticizations." Translated by Matthias Konzen and John McCormick. In *The Concept of the Political: Expanded Edition*, translated by George Schwab, 80–96. Chicago: University of Chicago Press, 2007.

———. *The Concept of the Political: Expanded Edition*. Translated by George Schwab. Chicago: University of Chicago Press, 2007.

———. *Constitutional Theory*. Translated by Jeffrey Seitzer. Durham, NC: Duke University Press, 2008.

———. *The Crisis of Parliamentary Democracy*. Translated by Ellen Kennedy. Cambridge, MA: MIT Press, 1985.

———. *Dictatorship*. Translated by Michael Hoelzl and Graham Ward. Cambridge: Polity, 2014.

———. *The Leviathan in the State Theory of Thomas Hobbes: Meaning and Failure of a Political Symbol*. Translated by George Schwab and Erna Hilfstein. Westport, CT: Greenwood, 1996.

———. *The Nomos of the Earth in the International Law of the* Jus Publicum Europaeum. Translated by G. L. Ulmen. New York: Telos, 2003.

———. *On the Three Types of Juristic Thought*. Translated by Joseph Bendersky. Westport, CT: Praeger, 2004.

———. *Political Romanticism*. Translated by Guy Oakes. Cambridge, MA: MIT Press, 1986.

———. *Political Theology: Four Chapters on the Concept of Sovereignty*. Translated by George Schwab. Chicago: University of Chicago Press, 2005.

———. *Theory of the Partisan: Intermediate Commentary on the Concept of the Political*. Translated by G. L. Ulmen. New York: Telos, 2007.

———. *The Tyranny of Values*. Translated by Simona Draghici. Washington, DC: Plutarch, 1996.

———. *Writings on War*. Translated by Timothy Nunan. Cambridge: Polity, 2011.

Seth, Vanita. *Europe's Indians: Producing Racial Difference, 1500–1900*. Durham, NC: Duke University Press, 2010.

1798 Georgia Constitution. *GeorgiaInfo*. University of Georgia Libraries. Accessed April 18, 2017. http://georgiainfo.galileo.usg.edu/topics/government/related_article/constitutions/georgia-constitution-of-1798.

Shapiro, Kam. *Carl Schmitt and the Intensification of Politics*. Lanham, MD: Rowman and Littlefield, 2008.

Shelby, Tommie. *We Who Are Dark: The Philosophical Foundations of Black Solidarity*. Cambridge, MA: Harvard University Press, 2005.

Sheth, Falguni. *Toward a Political Philosophy of Race*. Albany: State University of New York Press, 2009.

———. "The War on Terror and Ontopolitics: Concerns with Foucault's Account of Race, Power Sovereignty." *Foucault Studies* 12 (2011): 51–76.

Sieyès, Emmanuel. *What Is the Third Estate?* Translated by M. Blondel. London: Pall Mall, 1963.

Singh, Jakeet. "Religious Agency and the Limits of Intersectionality." *Hypatia* 30, no. 4 (2015): 657–74.

Singh, Nikhil Pal. *Black Is a Country: Race and the Unfinished Struggle for Democracy*. Cambridge, MA: Harvard University Press, 2004.

Skocpol, Theda. *Social Policy in the United States: Future Possibilities in Historical Perspective*. Princeton, NJ: Princeton University Press, 1995.

Skowronek, Stephen. *Building a New American State: The Expansion of National Administrative Capacities, 1877–1920*. Cambridge: Cambridge University Press, 1982.

Smith, Paul Chaat, and Robert Allen Warrior. *Like a Hurricane: The Indian Movement from Alcatraz to Wounded Knee*. New York: New Press, 1996.

Smith, Rogers. *Civic Ideals: Conflicting Visions of Citizenship in U.S. History*. New Haven, CT: Yale University Press, 1997.

Stampp, Kenneth. *The Peculiar Institution: Slavery in the Ante-Bellum South*. New York: Alfred A. Knopf, 1956.

Stannard, David. *American Holocaust: The Conquest of the New World*. Oxford, UK: Oxford University Press, 1992.

Stark, Heidi Kiiwetinepinesiik. "Criminal Empire: The Making of the Savage in a Lawless Land." *Theory & Event* 19, no. 4 (2016). Accessed January 18, 2017. https://muse.jhu.edu/article/633282.

Steinberger, Peter. "Rationalism in Politics." *American Political Science Review* 109, no. 4 (2015): 750–63.

Stevenson, Brenda. *Life in Black and White: Family and Community in the Slave South*. Oxford, UK: Oxford University Press, 1996.

"Success Story of One Minority Group in U.S." *U.S. News & World Report*, December 26, 1966.

Sundstrom, Ronald. *The Browning of America and the Evasion of Social Justice*. Albany: State University of New York Press, 2008.

Takaki, Ronald. *A Different Mirror: A History of Multicultural America*. Rev. ed. New York: Little, Brown, 2008.

———. *Iron Cages: Race and Culture in 19th-Century America*. Rev. ed. Oxford, UK: Oxford University Press, 2000.

———. *Strangers from a Different Shore: A History of Asian Americans*. Rev. ed. Boston: Little, Brown, 1998.

Tateishi, John. *And Justice for All: An Oral History of the Japanese American Detention Camps*. New York: Random House, 1984.

tenBroek, Jacobus, Edward Norton Barnhart, and Floyd Matson. *Prejudice, War, and the Constitution: Causes and Consequences of the Evacuation of the Japanese Americans in World War II*. Berkeley: University of California Press, 1954.

Tesler, Michael. *Post-Racial or Most-Racial? Race and Politics in the Obama Era*. Chicago: University of Chicago Press, 2016.

Tolan, John. *National Defense Migration: Report of the Select Committee Investigating National Defense Migration, House of Representatives, 77th Congress, 2nd Session*. Washington, DC: Government Printing Office, 1942.

Treaty of Dancing Rabbit Creek (Treaty with the Choctaw, 1830). 7 Stat. 333 (1830).

Treaty of Hopewell (Treaty with the Cherokee, 1785). 7 Stat. 18 (1785).

Treaty of Payne's Landing (Treaty with the Seminole, 1832). 7 Stat. 368 (1832).

Treaty of Pontitock Creek (Treaty with the Chickasaw, 1832). 7 Stat. 381 (1832).

Treaty with the Chickasaw, 1830. In *Treaties with American Indians: An Encyclopedia of Rights, Conflict and Sovereignty*, vol. II, edited by Donald Fixico, 464–68. Santa Barbara, CA: ABC-CLIO, 2008.

Tully, James. "Aboriginal Property Rights and Western Theory." In *Theories of Empire, 1450–1800*, edited by David Armitage, 345–72. Aldershot, UK: Ashgate, 1998.
Turner, Frederick Jackson. "The Significance of the Frontier in American History." In *Rereading Frederick Jackson Turner: "The Significance of the Frontier in American History" and Other Essays*, edited by John Mack Faragher, 31–60. New York: Henry Holt, 1994.
Turner, Jack. *Awakening to Race: Individualism and Social Consciousness in America*. Chicago: University of Chicago Press, 2012.
U.C. Regents v. Bakke. 438 U.S. 265 (1978).
Vattel, Emeric de. *The Law of Nations, or, Principles of the Law of Nature, Applied to the Conduct and Affairs of Nations and Sovereigns*. New ed. London: G. G. and J. Robinson, 1797.
Villa, Dana. *Arendt and Heidegger: The Fate of the Political*. Princeton, NJ: Princeton University Press, 1996.
Von Vacano, Diego. *The Color of Citizenship: Race, Modernity and Latin American/Hispanic Political Thought*. Oxford, UK: Oxford University Press, 2012.
Wallace, Anthony. *The Long, Bitter Trail: Andrew Jackson and the Indians*. New York: Hill and Wang, 1993.
War Relocation Authority. *The Evacuated People: A Quantitative Description*. Washington, DC: Government Printing Office, 1946.
Weglyn, Michi Nishiura. *Years of Infamy: The Untold Story of America's Concentration Camps*. Rev. ed. Seattle: University of Washington Press, 1996.
Wei, William. *The Asian American Movement: A Social History*. Philadelphia: Temple University Press, 1993.
Wilkins, David, and Heidi Kiiwetinepinesiik Stark. *American Indian Politics and the American Political System*. 3rd ed. Lanham, MD: Rowman and Littlefield, 2011.
Williams Jr., Robert. *The American Indian in Western Legal Thought: The Discourses of Conquest*. Oxford, UK: Oxford University Press, 1990.
Winant, Howard. *New Politics of Race: Globalism, Difference, Justice*. Minneapolis: University of Minnesota Press, 2004.
———. *Racial Conditions: Politics, Theory, Comparisons*. Minneapolis: University of Minnesota Press, 1994.
———. *The World Is a Ghetto: Race and Democracy since World War II*. New York: Basic, 2001.
Wolfe, Patrick. "Settler Colonialism and the Elimination of the Native." *Journal of Genocide Research* 8, no. 4 (2006): 387–409.
Wolfenstein, Victor. "Race, Racism and Racial Liberation." *Western Political Quarterly* 30, no. 2 (1977): 163–82.
———. *The Victims of Democracy: Malcolm X and the Black Revolution*. Rev. ed. New York: Guilford, 1993.
Wood, Gordon. *Creation of the American Republic, 1776–1787*. Chapel Hill: University of North Carolina Press, 1969.
Woodward, C. Vann. *The Strange Career of Jim Crow*. Commemorative ed. Oxford, UK: Oxford University Press, 2002.
Worcester v. Georgia. 31 U.S. 515 (1832).
Wu, Ellen. *The Color of Success: Asian Americans and the Origins of the Model Minority*. Princeton, NJ: Princeton University Press, 2014.

X, Malcolm. "The Ballot or the Bullet." In *Malcolm X Speaks: Selected Speeches and Statements*, edited by George Breitman, 23–44. New York: Pathfinder, 1989.

X, Malcolm, and Alex Haley. *The Autobiography of Malcolm X*. New York: Grove, 1965.

Yamamoto, Eric, Margaret Chon, Carol Izumi, Jerry Kang, and Frank Wu. *Race, Rights and Reparation: Law and the Japanese American Internment*. Gaithersburg, MD: Aspen Law and Business, 2001.

Yancey, George. *Black Bodies, White Gazes: The Continuing Significance of Race*. Lanham, MD: Rowman and Littlefield, 2008.

Yip, Steve. "Serve the People—Yesterday and Today: The Legacy of the Wei Min She." In *Legacy to Liberation: Politics and Culture of Revolutionary Asian Pacific America*, edited by Fred Ho, Carolyn Antonio, Diane Fujino, and Steve Yip, 15–30. Edinburgh, UK: AK, 2000.

Young, Cynthia. *Soul Power: Culture, Radicalism, and the Making of the U.S. Third World Left*. Durham, NC: Duke University Press, 2006.

Young, Iris. *Justice and the Politics of Difference*. Rev. ed. Princeton, NJ: Princeton University Press, 2011.

Young-Bruehl, Elisabeth. *Hannah Arendt: For Love of the World*. 2nd ed. New Haven, CT: Yale University Press, 2004.

Zerilli, Linda. *Feminism and the Abyss of Freedom*. Chicago: University of Chicago Press, 2005.

Žižek, Slavoj. *Event: A Philosophical Journey through a Concept*. New York: Melville House, 2014.

Index

Page numbers followed by the italic letter *t* refer to tables.

Adams, John, 35
affirmative action cases, 63
African Americans: Black Lives Matter, 55, 188; black power/black nationalist movement, 153–162, 153*t*, 183; Reconstruction and, 60–61, 67, 71; WWII, segregated 92nd Division in, 138n104. *See also* civil rights movement; Civil War; slavery
Agamben, Giorgio, 114, 129, 137, 148
agonism and antagonism: Asian American panethnicity and, 178, 179; in black power/black nationalist movement, 154, 155, 157, 159, 161; in civil rights movement, 38, 39, 48, 49, 51, 53, 57, 62, 65, 66; Indian removals and, 81; Japanese internment and, 119, 138, 144; multiculturalism and, 179, 180, 182–185; racial empowerment movements and, 150–152, 154, 155, 157, 159, 161, 167, 171, 178, 179, 180, 182–185; red power movement and, 167, 171; theory of extraordinary racial politics and, 13, 192, 193*t*, 195, 198–199. *See also* friend/enemy distinction
Alcatraz, Native American occupation of (1969–1971), 153, 162–171, 180, 193
Alcatraz Proclamation, 162, 168–169, 171

Alcoff, Linda Martín, 199
Aleut Indian internment in WWII, 140
Allen, Danielle, 33
Alt-Right, 188, 196, 199
American Indians. *See* Indians
American Revolution: civil rights movement compared, 27–28, 32, 33; class conflict in revolutionary period, 42n42, 45; French Revolution compared, 32, 35, 39, 46, 66; racial enmity in, 35–40; regional division in federal constitution, 40–46
Amerindians. *See* Indians
amity lines, 73
antagonism. *See* agonism and antagonism; friend/enemy distinction
Arendt, Hannah: on black power/black nationalist movement, 158–161; civil rights movement and, 32–36, 39–40, 46–50, 53–59, 64–67, 190, 191, 192; "The Crisis in Education," 57; everyday racial politics in relation to extraordinary racial politics and, 16–18, 20–23, 190; existential nature of extraordinary politics and, 195, 198; Indian removals and, 72, 102–103; Japanese internment and, 122n36, 130; public constitution and,

12–16, 191, 200; on public freedom, 11, 14, 15, 27, 32, 64, 72, 149, 191–194; racial empowerment movements and, 149–152, 158–161, 164–165, 165n67, 167, 170, 173, 176, 185, 190, 192; racial formation and, 5; "Reflections on Little Rock," 55–59; on storytelling and political theory, 24, 189
Arendt, Hannah, works: *The Human Condition*, 11; *Lectures on Kant's Political Philosophy*, 149; *Between Past and Future*, 1, 187; *On Revolution*, 31
Arnold, Benedict, 116
Ashley, General, 109
Asian American panethnicity movement, 153t, 171–180, 181, 183
assimilation: of Indians, 87, 89, 94, 95, 106, 140–141, 163, 167–168; of Japanese Americans, 28, 113, 115, 117–119, 129, 132, 134n90, 138–141, 146–148, 194; Jewish, 14; linguistic, of European immigrants, 57; racial empowerment movements rejecting, 172, 173, 176, 184; "the social" and, 102n120
Azuma, Eiichiro, 142–143

Bacon's Rebellion (1676), 38
Bell, Derrick, 31, 198
Beltrán, Cristina, 22, 149, 198
Benjamin, Walter, 200
Bhabha, Homi, 200
BIA (Bureau of Indian Affairs), 140
black Americans. *See* African Americans
Black Lives Matter, 55, 188
Black Panthers, 158n38, 173
black power/black nationalist movement, 153–162, 153t, 183
black/white binary, 8n21, 187
Boyer, LaNada, 149, 162, 165–170, 192–193
Brown v. Board of Education (1954), 31, 47n66, 58–60, 63
Bruyneel, Kevin, 74n10, 107n135
Bureau of Indian Affairs (BIA), 140

Cabral, Amilcar, 173
Cass, Lewis, 86–87, 99, 104
census, racial identity questions in, 45, 68
Cherokee: *Cherokee Nation v. Georgia* (1831), 80, 83, 84, 98; Confederacy, alliance treaties with, 94n89; confederation into U.S., possibility of, 105; Dancing Rabbit Creek, Choctaw Treaty of (1830), and, 91, 93–95; formalization of government by, 80–81, 106; Hopewell, Treaty of (1785), 93–94, 95; New Echota, Treaty of (1835), 90n76; removal efforts, 71, 79–80; Trail of Tears (late 1830s), 79; Western and Eastern Cherokee, 79–80; *Worcester v. Georgia*, 76, 77, 79–87, 91, 95, 99, 103
Cherokee Nation v. Georgia (1831), 80, 83, 84, 98
Chicano/a and Latino/a movements, 22, 29n106, 150n5, 198
Chickasaw, 71, 93n84, 98, 106
Chinese Americans: Asian American panethnicity movement, 153t, 171–180; assimilation and anti-assimilation, 172, 173; ethnic splitting of Asian Americans during Japanese internment, 180; immigration issues (mid- to late-19th century), 115–116; naturalization extended to, in WWII, 125–126
Chinese Exclusion Act, 1943 repeal of, 125
Chippewa (Ojibwa/Ojibwe), 163
Choctaw, 71, 91–94, 97–99, 105–106
Chuh, Kandice, 141–142
civil disobedience, 33, 47, 50–53, 67
Civilization Fund Act (1819), 85
Civil Rights Act (1964), 54, 60
Civil Rights Congress, 162
civil rights movement, 2, 27–28, 31–69, 191–193; anti-segregation protests, legitimation of racial struggle through, 47–55; Arendt and, 32–36, 39–40, 46–50, 53–59, 64–67; as citizen-driven extraordinary racial politics, 192, 193t; as constitutional re-foundation, 28t, 33–34, 46–47, 53, 56, 62, 64–69, 65t, 68; direct action in, 47, 49–52, 53, 55; European labor movements compared, 54; extraordinary achievements of, 31–32, 54–55; Little Rock crisis and Little Rock Nine, 55–58, 160; nationalization of, 58–64, 146–147; new social movements patterned on, 52n90; political selfhood achieved in, 54; power of extraordinary racial politics to disrupt everyday racial politics and, 19; public constitution in, 28t, 32; racial empowerment movements and, 180–181, 182; racial enmity in slave states and, 35–40, 44, 51; racial formation in, 28t, 32, 34; racial trajectory of, 7; Reconstruction, post-Civil War, 60–61;

regional division in federal constitution, 40–46; reverse discrimination and legalistic color-blindness, 55, 62–64; school desegregation crisis, 55–60

Civil War: civil liberties in, 123; civil rights movement and, 51, 61, 62, 65, 69; "Indian Territory" versus North and South in, 108; Naturalization Law (1790), revision of, 117n19; theory of extraordinary racial politics and, 7, 8, 30

COINTELPRO (FBI, Counter Intelligence Program), 183n145

colonialism: postcolonialism, 171, 187; racial empowerment movements and, 147, 166, 169, 175, 181, 182; slavery in America and, 61; theory of extraordinary racial politics and, 1, 8, 10, 23, 187. *See also* Indian removals

color-blindness, 2, 55, 62–66, 113, 147, 188, 197–198

common/community sense, racial empowerment movements appealing to, 149, 150–152, 153–154, 153*t*, 158–159, 162, 169, 173, 182, 185

comparative ethnic studies, 23–24

consent fictions: Indian removal treaties, 72, 87, 94–95, 141; Japanese internment and allegiance/loyalty declarations, 135–139

constitutional law, racial exceptionality in, 77–78, 82–83, 126–129, 144

Coulthard, Glen, 100, 101

Creek, 71, 94n89, 96n95, 106

creolization, 4, 17, 189–190

dancing, Indian, 164–165

Dancing Rabbit Creek, Choctaw Treaty of (1830), 90–95, 97–99, 106

Daniels, Roger, 121

Declaration of the Rights of Man, 114

Deloria, Vine, Jr., 168

DeWitt, John, 119–120, 124, 133, 134, 137, 145, 194–195

direct action, 47, 49–52, 53, 55

discovery doctrine, 79, 83, 168

Doi, Shig, 136

Dred Scott v. Sanford (1857), 61

Du Bois, W.E.B., 10, 51; *The Souls of Black Folk*, 62

Eaton, John, 107

Eisenhower, Dwight, 56

Elazar, Daniel, 60, 61

Emancipation Proclamation, 196

emergency racial politics: in black power/black nationalist movement, 161; Emancipation Proclamation as, 196; Japanese internment as, 112, 114–115, 129, 142, 144, 148

Emmons, Delos, 120, 124

Endo, Mitsuye, 126, 127–129. *See also Ex Parte Endo*

enemies and friends. *See* friend/enemy distinction

Espiritu, Yen Le, 180

European and U.S. spatial orders, 73–74

everyday racial politics in relation to extraordinary racial politics, 2, 5, 10, 15–23, 25, 190, 191*t*

Executive Order 9066, 111–112, 113, 120, 121

existential nature of extraordinary racial politics, 19–21, 189–195

Ex Parte Endo (1944), 127–129, 138

extraordinary racial politics, 1–30, 187–201; affirmation and revitalization of, 195–201; comparative ethnic studies and, 23–24; defined, 2, 17; disruption, power of, 18–19; everyday racial politics in relation to, 2, 5, 10, 15–23, 25, 190, 191*t*; existential nature of, 19–21, 189–195; gender and class issues, 29; goals of, 23; Great Transformation (1950s-1970s), 7, 9, 26, 34, 185, 188, 201; historical events, power of enacting, 19–21; pendulum of American populism and, 1–2, 187–189, 196; as public constitution, 3–5, 10–16, 17, 20, 21, 24, 26, 27, 28*t*, 29–30, 190 (*See also* public constitution); as racial formation, 5–10, 11, 16, 17, 22, 24–27, 28*t*, 190 (*See also* racial formation); relationship between public constitution and racial formation, 3–4; specific case studies of, 23–29, 28*t*, 189–195 (*See also* civil rights movement; Indian removals; Japanese internment in WWII; racial empowerment movements); tragic and disastrous consequences of, 23

Fanon, Frantz, 17

FBI, Counter Intelligence Program (COINTELPRO), 183n145

Ferguson, Edwin, 138–139

Fisher v. University of Texas (2013), 63

"fish-ins" in Pacific Northwest, 162n55
Fong, Edmund, 113
Fort Gibson, Seminole Treaty of (1833), 90n76
Fort Laramie, Sioux Treaty of (1868), 168
Foucault, Michel, 166, 171
Fourteenth Amendment, 63
Fraser, Nancy, 151
Freedmen's Bureau, 62
freedom, existential, and extraordinary racial politics, 19–21
freedom, public, 11, 14, 15, 27, 32, 64, 72, 149, 191–194
French Revolution, 32, 35, 39, 46, 66, 130
friend/enemy distinction: Asian American panethnicity movement and, 179; black power/black nationalist movement and, 156, 157–158, 159; "Indian Country," transformation of, 107–108; Japanese internment and, 38, 112, 119–122, 129–139, 148; Mao Zedong on, 179n129; OIA (Office of Indian Affairs), moved from War to Interior Department, 107, 140–141; in political and legal theory, 11–12, 13, 15, 18, 22, 27; in racial empowerment movements, 156, 157–158, 159, 166, 179; red power movement and, 166; "savage" excepted from "civilized" rule, in Indian removals, 28, 72, 77–78, 97, 99–100, 102; slave states, racial enmity in, 35–40; treaties of Indian removal, violence provisions in, 92–94

Gallie, W. B., 18
General Indian Citizenship Act (1924), 163n58
Gines, Kathryn, 32, 57n110
Glick, Philip, 138–139
Goldberg, David Theo, 197
Gordon, Jane, 4, 175, 189
Gordon, Lewis, 20, 23, 185
Gramsci, Antonio, and Gramscians, 152, 184, 188
Gratz v. Bollinger (2003), 63
Great Backlash (1970s-1980s), 188
Great Transformation (1950s-1970s), 7, 9, 26, 34, 185, 188, 201
Grutter v. Bollinger (2003), 63
Guantanamo Bay, 114, 144

Habal, Estella, 172, 175–176, 178, 192–193
Hagan, William, 90
Haitian Revolution, 39
Hanchard, Michael, 196
Hawaii and Japanese internment in WWII, 124–125, 134, 135, 136
hegemony and racial empowerment movements, 151–152, 157, 180, 182–183
Hemmings, Sally, 36n12
Herring, Elbert, 107
Hirabayashi, Gordon, 126, 128
Hirabayashi v. United States (1943), 126–129
Ho, Fred, 172–175, 177
Hollinger, David, 184
Holocaust, 114, 147–148
homo economicus, 198
homo sacer, 137
Honig, Bonnie, 114, 136, 144
Hopewell, Cherokee Treaty of (1785), 93–94, 95
humanity, as concept, 20, 23
human rights approach: to Japanese internment, 143–144; in racial empowerment movements, 162
Hayashi, Brian, 120

IHTA (International Hotel Tenants Association), 172, 177–180
Illinois (Indians), 76
imperialism, U.S., 108
Indian removals (1830s-1840s), 2, 28, 71–109, 193–195; assimilation and, 87, 89, 94, 95, 106; authority of U.S. to extinguish native title, 76; *Cherokee Nation v. Georgia* (1831), 80, 83, 84, 98; "civil" demarcated from "wild" space, 88; confederation of Indian states, possibility of, 105–106; consent fictions employed in, 72, 87, 94–95, 141; constitutional law, racial exceptionality in, 77–78, 82–83; Dancing Rabbit Creek, Choctaw Treaty of (1830), 90–95, 97–99, 106; executive re-ordering of, 103–104; federal government as prime actor in, 75; to "Indian Territory" or "Indian Country," 71, 72, 92, 105, 106–108; Japanese internment compared, 107–108, 112, 134, 139–141; *Johnson v. McIntosh* (1823), 76–79, 82, 83, 84, 85, 86, 105, 168; land appropriation, as vehicle of, 88–90, 100–102, 108;

Marxist accounts of, 100–101; *nomos,* situated within, 72–73, 90, 94, 103, 105–109; OIA (Office of Indian Affairs), 86, 97n103, 99, 107–108, 140–141; paternalism and, 97–103, 104; Pontitock Creek, Chickasaw Treaty of (1832), 98; public constitution in, 3, 28*t,* 72; public order and, 27, 193–195, 195*t*; racial and spatial reordering effected by, 72–75, 87–88, 97, 100–102, 105–109; racial formation in, 3, 28*t,* 72; Removal Act (1830), 90–91, 100n110, 104; "savage" excepted from "civilized" rule, 28, 72, 97, 99–100, 102; Seminole War resisting, 95–97; settler contracts and, 88–89; treaties of removal, 23, 87–104; treaty federalism and, 74, 82, 95; treaty system, as site for both Indian agency and dispossession, 23, 89–90; violence provisions in treaties, 92–94; *Worcester v. Georgia* (1832), 76, 77, 79–87, 91, 95, 99, 103. *See also specific Indian polities, e.g.* Cherokee

Indians: Aleut Indian internment in WWII, 140; assimilation of, 87, 89, 94, 95, 106, 140–141, 163, 167–168; dancing by, 164–165; "fish-ins" in Pacific Northwest, 162n55; Fort Laramie, Sioux Treaty of (1868), 168; General Indian Citizenship Act (1924), 163n58; pan-Indianism, 153*t,* 162–163, 168, 169; post-WWII "termination" of, 140, 163, 166; powwows, 163–164; red power movement and Alcatraz occupation, 153*t,* 162–171, 193; terminology for, 71n1

International Hotel anti-eviction campaign (1968–1977), 153, 171–180, 183

International Hotel Tenants Association (IHTA), 172, 177–180

Issei (first-generation Japanese Americans), 112, 117, 118, 132, 135, 142, 193

IWK (I Wor Kuen), 172–174, 177

I Wor Kuen (IWK), 172–174, 177

Jackson, Andrew, 71, 74, 80, 85, 96n95, 98, 100–101, 103–105, 109, 111, 194–195; "Farewell Address," 71, 104

Japanese American Citizens League (JACL), 118, 136–137

Japanese internment in WWII, 2, 28–29, 111–148, 193–195; allegiance/loyalty declarations, 135–139; alternative framings of, 142–144; armed services, Japanese Americans serving in, 135–138; assimilation and, 28, 113, 115, 117–119, 129, 132, 134n90, 138–141, 146–148, 194; constitutional law, racial exceptionality in, 126–129, 144; as "emergency politics," 112, 114–115, 129, 142, 144, 148; ethnic splitting of Asian Americans in, 180; evacuation and interment, 115–129; from exclusion to internment, 122–126; Executive Order 9066, 111–112, 113, 120, 121, 126; *Ex Parte Endo* (1944), 127–128; friend/enemy distinction and, 38, 112, 119–122, 129–139, 148; German "Final Solution" compared, 147–148; in Hawaii, 124–125, 134, 135, 136; *Hirabayashi v. United States* (1943), 126, 127; human rights approach to, 143–144; Indian removals compared, 107–108, 112, 134, 139–141; internment camps, 112, 122–123, 128, 137–138, 147; Issei (first-generation Japanese Americans), treatment of, 112, 117, 118, 132, 135, 142, 193; Kibei (Nisei educated in Japan), treatment of, 112, 132; *Korematsu v. United States* (1944), 127; leave policies, 112, 128, 129–133, 135, 137, 138–139; liberal democratic paradoxes of, 145–148; Nisei (second-generation Japanese Americans), treatment of, 112, 117–118, 126, 132–137, 139, 193, 195; Pacific Coast, exclusion of all Japanese from, as "military necessity," 119–122; public constitution in, 3, 28*t,* 112, 120n27, 146; public order and, 193–195, 195*t*; racial formation in, 28*t,* 112, 126, 146; racial states of exception and, 112–115, 145–148; release and resettlement, 129–144; sovereignty, role of concept of, 112–113, 115, 120, 131, 142, 144, 145; transnationalism of Japanese Americans and, 142–143; treatment of European enemy nationals and descendants versus, 111–112, 122, 125; Tule Lake maximum security camp, 137–138; WCCA, 122, 140; WDC, 119, 122, 123, 126, 130, 133, 134; WRA, 123, 127, 129–135, 137, 140, 141, 143

Jefferson, Thomas, 35–37, 41, 52, 67, 157, 192–193; *Notes on the State of Virginia,* 36

Johnson, Thomas, 76, 77n20
Johnson v. McIntosh (1823), 76–79, 82, 83, 84, 85, 86, 105, 168
judgment and racial empowerment movements, 150–153, 153t, 165, 167, 185

Kalyvas, Andreas, 2, 19, 20–21
Kant, Immanuel, 56n104, 150–151, 155
Katipunan ng mga Demokratikong Pilipino (KDP), 172, 175, 177–180
Kawaguchi, Tom, 136
KDP (Katipunan ng mga Demokratikong Pilipino), 172, 175, 177–180
Kennedy, John F., 50n77, 54–55
Kibei (Nisei educated in Japan), 112, 132
King, Martin Luther, Jr., 47–53, 157, 192–193; "Letter from Birmingham Jail," 47–50, 51–53; *Why We Can't Wait,* 31
Korean War, 161
Korematsu, Fred, 114, 126–128, 144
Korematsu v. United States (1944), 127–129, 136

Laclau, Ernesto, 174
land appropriations: Alcatraz Proclamation and, 169; Indian removals (1830s-1840s) as vehicle of, 88–90, 100–102, 108
Latino/a and Chicano/a movements, 22, 29n106, 150n5, 198
Lea, Homer, 116, 119
Lefort, Claude, 22, 55, 147
liberal democratic paradoxes of Japanese internment, 145–148
liberalism and liberal democracy: civil rights movement and, 31, 41, 46, 54–56, 63, 65–68; Indian removals and, 79, 84, 89, 108; Japanese internment and, 112–115, 136, 141, 144, 145–148; on pendulum of American populism, 187, 188; racial empowerment movements and, 184, 186; theory of extraordinary racial politics and, 1, 4, 7, 13, 15, 16, 22n81, 26, 196–200
Lincoln, Abraham, 52, 196
Little Rock crisis and Little Rock Nine, 55–58, 160
Lowe, Lisa, 1

Machiavelli, Niccolò, 11n34, 41
Madison, James, 39, 40–43, 45, 46, 49, 59, 60, 66, 200n47

Malcolm X, 153–162, 165, 172, 180; *Autobiography,* 153; "The Ballot or the Bullet," 154, 156, 159
Manifest Destiny, 108
manong (immigrant Filipinos), 176
Mao Zedong and Maoism, 173–174, 179
Marable, Manning, 67–68
Marshall, John, and Marshall Court, 75, 77–79, 82–87, 93, 103, 105, 134, 194–195
Marx, Anthony, 60–61
Marx, Karl, 63n137, 101, 174
Marxism: Indian removals and, 100–101; racial empowerment movements and, 158n38, 172–174, 177–178, 181; theory of extraordinary racial politics and, 4, 16, 17n61, 26n103, 28
McClure, Kirstie, 46, 156, 165
McDonald, Behonor, 198
McIntosh, William, 76
Mills, Charles: everyday racial politics and extraordinary racial politics, relationship between, 16, 18, 23, 190; Indian removals and, 88–89, 98; *The Racial Contract,* 6, 8; racial formation and, 5, 28
Mohawk, 168
Monroe, James, 75nn13–14, 79, 105, 109
Monroe Doctrine (1823), 73, 74, 79, 84, 108–109
Mouffe, Chantal, 21–22, 51, 146, 151–152, 174, 199
Muhammad, Elijah, 154
multiculturalism: pendulum of American populism and, 187–188; race, problematization of, 197; racial empowerment movements and, 150, 180–186
Myer, Dillon, 132, 133–134, 140–141, 145, 194–195

NAACP (National Association for the Advancement of Colored People), 31, 47n66, 59
National Association for the Advancement of Colored People (NAACP), 31, 47n66, 59
nationalization of civil rights movement, 58–64, 146–147
National Japanese American Student Relocation Council (NJASRC), 132
Nation of Islam (NOI), 154–156, 158, 162, 172, 173, 175
Native Americans. *See* Indians

Naturalization Law (1790), 117n19
New Echota, Treaty of (1835), 90n76
Nisei (second-generation Japanese Americans), 112, 117–118, 126, 132–137, 139, 193, 195
Nixon, Richard, 183
NJASRC (National Japanese American Student Relocation Council), 132
No Dakota Access Pipeline (NoDAPL), 188, 199
NOI (Nation of Islam), 154–156, 158, 162, 172, 173, 175
nomos, Indian removals situated within, 72–73, 90, 94, 103, 105–109
nonwhite/white binary, 8–9, 13n45, 15, 18, 22, 150, 162, 172, 173–175, 179n131, 187
Nordwall, Adam, 162–165, 167, 169, 170n84, 172
Nyugen, Viet Thanh, 187

Oakes, Richard, 168, 169, 170n84
Obama, Barack, 187, 188
Office of Indian Affairs (OIA), 86, 97n103, 99, 107–108, 140–141
Ohlone, 169
OIA (Office of Indian Affairs), 86, 97n103, 99, 107–108, 140–141
Ojibwa/Ojibwe (Chippewa), 163
Okihiro, Gary, 143–144
Olson, Joel, 67
Omi, Michael, and Howard Winant, *Racial Formation in the United States,* 18; on extraordinary racial politics, 3, 5–10, 16, 18, 19, 25–26, 34, 190, 197; Japanese internment and, 129–130; racial empowerment movements and, 149, 152
Osceola (Seminole chief), 97
Ozawa, Takao, 116–117. *See also Takao Ozawa v. United States*

panethnic Asian American movement, 153t, 171–180, 181, 183
pan-Indianism, 153t, 162–163, 168
Pateman, Carole, 8n22, 88, 89
paternalism and Indian removals, 97–103, 104
Patterson, Orlando, 44
Patterson, William, 42
Payne's Landing, Seminole Treaty of (1832), 96

Pearl Harbor, 111, 115, 117, 123, 124
Piankeshaw, 76
Pitkin, Hannah, 19n68, 170
Plessy v. Ferguson (1896), 59
Pontitock Creek, Chickasaw Treaty of (1832), 98
postcolonialism, 171, 187
powwows, 163–164
Prucha, Francis, 99
public constitution: Arendt and, 12–16, 191, 200; civil rights movement and, 28t, 32; defined, 10–11; extraordinary racial politics as, 3–5, 10–16, 17, 20, 21, 24, 26, 27, 28t, 29–30, 190; human faculties and, 20; Indian removals and, 3, 28t, 72; Japanese internment and, 3, 28t, 112, 120n27, 146; racial empowerment movements and, 28t, 150, 162, 182; racial formation, relationship to, 3–5; reaffirmation of extraordinary racial politics and, 188, 190, 197, 200; Schmitt and, 11–16
public freedom, 11, 14, 15, 27, 32, 64, 72, 149, 191–194
public order, 12–13, 15, 26, 193–194, 195t

racial contracts: concept of, 8–10, 23, 25; Indian removal treaties as, 87–90; settler contracts compared, 88–89; sexual contracts compared, 8n22, 88, 89
racial empowerment movements (1960s-1970s), 2, 29, 149–186, 192–193; anti-assimilationism and, 172, 173, 176, 184; Asian American panethnicity and International Hotel anti-eviction campaign, 153t, 171–180, 181, 183; black power/black nationalism of Malcolm X, 153–162, 153t, 183; Chicano/a and Latino/a movements, 22, 29n106, 150n5, 198; as citizen-driven extraordinary racial politics, 192, 193t; civil rights movement and, 180–181, 182; common/community sense, appeals to, 149, 150–152, 153–154, 153t, 158–159, 162, 169, 173, 182, 185; criteria for success/failure of, 149–153; existential freedom and, 21; friend/enemy distinction in, 156, 157–158, 159, 166, 179; hegemony and, 151–152, 157, 180, 182–183; human rights approach in, 162; judgment and, 150–153, 153t, 165, 167, 185; multiculturalism and,

150, 180–186; official responses to, 183; the political and the social in, 22, 149, 150, 152, 164, 182–183; public constitution in, 28*t*, 150, 162, 182; public order and public freedom in, 27; racial formation and, 28*t*, 150, 182n39; red power and Alcatraz occupation, 153*t*, 162–171, 193; segregation and, 157, 186; sovereign power and, 150, 159; Third World solidarity and, 158, 165, 172–175, 182; white/nonwhite binary in, 150, 162, 172, 173–175, 179n13

racial formation: civil rights movement and, 28*t*, 32, 34; defined, 6; extraordinary politics as, 5–10, 11, 16, 17, 22, 24–27, 28*t*, 190; Indian removals and, 3, 28*t*, 72; Japanese internment and, 28*t*, 112, 126, 146; public constitution, relationship to, 3–5; racial empowerment movements and, 28*t*, 150, 182n39; reaffirmation of extraordinary racial politics and, 189, 190, 196, 197, 200

racial trajectories, 6–7

radical democrats: affirmation and revitalization of extraordinary racial politics and, 189, 192, 196, 199; civil rights movement and, 54, 55, 63, 65, 66, 68; racial empowerment movements and, 150, 151, 152, 184

Reconstruction, 60–61, 67, 71

red power movement, 153*t*, 162–171, 183

Removal Act (1830), 90–91, 100n110, 104

reverse discrimination claims, 55, 62–64

Revolutionary War. *See* American Revolution

Rezal, Carl, 176

Ricaree, 109

"rise of the social," 13–14, 19n68, 34, 36, 102

Rogin, Michael, 100–101, 108

Roosevelt, Franklin D., 111, 119, 124n45, 128

Ross, John, 80

Rossiter, Clinton, 123, 148

Rutledge, John, 42

Sanders, Bernie, 199, 200

Sawyer, Mark, 6n16

Schmitt, Carl: civil rights movement and, 36–39, 62n129; *The Concept of the Political*, 11; everyday racial politics in relation to extraordinary racial politics and, 16–18, 20–23, 190; existential nature of extraordinary politics and, 195; Indian removals and, 72–73, 76, 78, 93, 96, 100, 101, 103, 106, 190, 193–195; Japanese internment and, 111–115, 119, 120n27, 123, 124, 127n63, 130–131, 133, 143–148, 190, 193–195; liberal democracy and, 197; *The* Nomos *of the Earth*, 71; *Political Theology*, 111; public constitution and, 11–16; on public order, 12–13, 15, 26, 193–194, 195*t*; racial empowerment movements and, 149, 167, 192; racial formation and, 5

segregation: civil rights movement, anti-segregation protests in, 47–55; of Japanese American 442nd Combat Team, 136; racial empowerment movements and, 157, 186; school desegregation crisis, 55–60

Seminole, 71, 90n76, 95–97, 101, 193, 195

Seminole Wars (1816–18, 1835–42), 95–97

settler colonialism. *See* colonialism

settler contracts, 88–89

sexual contracts, 8n22, 88, 89

Sheth, Falguni, 22, 128

Shoshone-Bannock, 165, 192

Sioux, 168

slavery: anti-Abolitionist riots, 196; Cherokee slavery, 81; Emancipation Proclamation, 196; political versus ethical-humanitarian objections to, 43; racial enmity and, 35–40, 44, 51; as racial institution, 44; regional division in federal constitution and, 40–46; slave revolts, 51; three-fifths compromise, 42–45

the social and the political: American Revolution and slavery, 33, 34, 36, 39, 44–46; civil rights movement and, 33, 34, 36, 39, 44–46, 53–59, 62; Indian removals and, 100, 102, 104; racial empowerment movements and, 22, 149, 150, 152, 164, 182–183; theory of extraordinary racial politics and, 12–16, 19n68, 22, 196–197

Socrates, 159

Southeastern Amerindians. *See* Indian removal

Southern Christian Leadership Conference, 48

sovereign power: Japanese internment in WWII and, 112–113, 115, 120, 131, 142,

144, 145; racial empowerment movements and, 150, 159
Stark, Heidi Kiiwetinepinesiik, 95
states' rights, 19, 58, 60
Supreme Court, U.S.: on antebellum status of slaves/African Americans, 61; civil rights movement and, 31, 47n66, 58–60, 63; Indian removals and racialized exceptional norms created by, 75–87; on Japanese American naturalization before WWII, 116–117, 118; Japanese internment in WWII and, 126–129, 144. *See also specific cases and justices*

Takaki, Ronald, 10
Takao Ozawa v. United States (1922), 116–117, 118, 119
Taney, Roger, and Taney Supreme Court, 61
Tea Party, 188
tenBroek, Jacobus, 123n42, 139
Third World and third worldism, 158, 165, 172–175, 182
three-fifths compromise, 42–45
Trail of Tears (late 1830s), 79
treaties, Indian. *See* Indian removals; Indians; *specific treaties by name*
treaty federalism, 74, 82, 95
Trump, Donald, and Trumpism, 1–2, 55, 69, 187, 189, 196, 198, 199, 200
Tully, James, 82, 95
Turner, Frederick Jackson, 73

U.C. Regents v. Bakke (1978), 63, 127n64
United Bay Area Council of American Indian Affairs, 165
United Filipino Association, 177
U.S. and European spatial orders, 73–74

Vattel, Emeric de, 82, 83
Vietnam War, 175
Voting Rights Act (1965), 54

War Relocation Authority (WRA), 123, 127, 129–135, 137, 140, 141, 143
Warren, Earl, and Warren Supreme Court, 58, 60
Wartime Civil Control Administration (WCCA), 122, 140
WDC (Western Defense Command), WWII, 119, 122, 123, 126, 130, 133, 134
Weglyn, Michi Nishiura, 121
Wei, William, 181, 185
Wei Min She (WMS), 174, 177–178
Western Defense Command (WDC), WWII, 119, 122, 123, 126, 130, 133, 134
white/black binary, 8n21, 187
white devilry, Malcolm X on, 153–155, 157–158
white identity politics, 150n5, 198
white/nonwhite binary, 8–9, 13n45, 15, 18, 22, 150, 162, 172, 173–175, 179n131, 187
Williams, Cy, 163–164
Williams, Robert, 76
Winant, Howard. *See* Omi, Michael, and Howard Winant, *Racial Formation in the United States*
WMS (Wei Min She), 174, 177–178
Woodward, C. Vann, 181
Worcester, Samuel, 81
Worcester v. Georgia (1832), 76, 77, 79–87, 91, 95, 99, 103
World War II: Aleut Indian internment in, 140; armed services, Japanese Americans serving in, 135–138; Chinese Americans, naturalization extended to, 125–126; German "Final Solution" compared to Japanese internment, 147–148; Holocaust, 114, 148; Pearl Harbor, 111, 115, 117, 123, 124; segregated 92nd Division, 138n104; U.S. treatment of European enemy nationals and descendants in, 111–112, 122, 125. *See also* Japanese internment in WWII
WRA (War Relocation Authority), 123, 127, 129–135, 137, 140, 141, 143

"yellow peril," 115–118
Yip, Steve, 177
Young, Iris, 198

Fred Lee is an Assistant Professor of Political Science and Asian/Asian American Studies at the University of Connecticut, Storrs.